The Lay of the Land

THE LAY OF THE LAND

Metaphor as Experience and History in American Life and Letters

by Annette Kolodny

The University of North Carolina Press • Chapel Hill

First printing, May 1975
Second printing, February 1984

Manufactured in the United States of America
Library of Congress Catalog Card Number 74-23950
ISBN 0-8078-1241-2

Library of Congress Cataloging in Publication Data

Kolodny, Annette, 1941–
The lay of the land.

Bibliography: p.
Includes index.
1. American Literature–History and criticism. 2. United States–History–Philosophy.
3. Nature in literature. I. Title.
PS88.K65 810'.9'36 74-23950
ISBN 0-8078-1241-2
ISBN 0-8078-4118-8

For my mother, Esther Rivkind Kolodny, in appreciation of her love and unceasing encouragement; and for my friend and teacher, Norman Grabo, from whom I will never stop learning. Both, in their way, made this book possible.

Contents

Preface

The original impetus for the following investigation was my growing distress at what we have done to our continent; its final shape was determined by the need to isolate, for the purposes of examination, an area of interconnection that had not previously been given the kind of attention I believed it deserved. The richness, the potency, the continued repetition of the land-as-woman symbolization in American life and letters, all suggested a pervasive and dynamic psychohistorical import that demanded examination in and for itself.

That that symbolization appears to have had important consequences for both our history and our literature should not suggest, however, that it accounts for everything, or that to it, alone, we must attribute all our current ecological and environmental ills. No such simplistically reductive thesis is intended. At best, I am examining here only a link in a much larger and much more complex whole; but it is a vital and, in some cases, a structuring link—and one that has been for too long ignored.

In pursuing this study, I crossed a number of discipline boundaries, and employed elements from widely varying methodologies. For many, such an approach will raise more questions than it answers; but then my primary aim is to generate discussion.

The six years that I spent on this study have served to convince me that fundamental change can occur only within the mind. If we seriously contemplate any meaningful reordering of our relations with our landscape, then we need—in addition to improved environmental protection laws and more recycling facilities—a better grasp of the ways in which language provides clues to the underlying motivations behind action; provides clues, if you will, to our deepest dreams and fantasies.

The omission of women's materials, in light of the study's subject matter, may strike some readers as curious—but it *was* intentional: insofar as the masculine appears to have taken power in the New World, it seemed necessary to understand its relationship to the landscape first. That women's writings and linguistic usages have all along been offering us alternate means of expression and perception is a possibility I am even now beginning to explore, and one that I hope others will want to explore with me.

Finally, if these pages leave the reader with any single conviction, I hope it is this: our future (if we have one) need not continue the errors of our past nor continue betraying its pastoral promise.

It is customary, I know, to thank by name those who have been of particular help in putting together a work such as this, and then give a more general acknowledgment of gratitude to others, too numerous to name. But such is not the case here: there are not too many people to thank, just too much to thank them for.

At every stage of composition, this book benefited from the comments and criticisms of friends and colleagues. Earlier versions of the manuscript were progressively rethought and revised in response to the suggestions of David Leverenz, Henry Mayer, Jim MacIntosh, and, most importantly, the brilliant insights of Joanna Wilcove. The present form of the Audubon section, moreover, bears the mark of Fred Crews's keen Freudian observations and Ruth Schorer's exquisite editing. But, for my mentors and advisers at The University of California, Berkeley, who aided and encouraged me to pursue this project, even as it grew from a doctoral thesis into a book, I can summon no adequate expressions of gratitude. The unstinting kindness and generosity of Norman Grabo, Mark Schorer, Henry Nash Smith, and Charles Sellers are by now axiomatic among their students.

The final manuscript shows the care of my research assistant at The University of British Columbia, Christina Parkin, whose intelligence and patience made it possible to check and recheck hundreds of quotations and notes. The whole was then made readable through the diligent efforts of my typist in Vancouver, Doreen Todhunter.

Research for the book was completed under the auspices of a generous and timely grant from Canadian philanthropist and itinerant scholar, Paddy Stewart; and the final stages of composition and editing were made possible by a grant from The Canada Council.

I am grateful for permission to reprint material that has appeared previously, in somewhat different form, in the *Southern Literary Journal* (1972) and *Women's Studies* (1973). I am similarly indebted to the authors and to Random House for allowing me to quote extensively from Robert Penn Warren's beautiful poem, *Audubon: A Vision* (New York, 1969), and from Dr. Joel Kovel's provocative study, *White Racism: A Psychohistory* (New York: Pantheon Books,

1970). I am also grateful to be able to quote from Lew Welch's "Chicago Poem" from *Ring of Bone* by Lew Welch, Copyright 1973, by permission of Donald Allen, Literary Executor of the Estate of Lew Welch.

Last, but far from least, I wish to thank my husband, Dan Peters, for *not* trying to check notes or help me with proofreading; instead, to give me ample time to prepare this book for publication, he repeatedly put off work on his own long-awaited biography of Zelmo Beaty and took over all household chores for prolonged periods. Greater love hath no man.

Abbreviations

B	"The Bear"
D	*The Deerslayer*
DA	"Delta Autumn"
DAS	*Delineations of American Scenery and Character*
ET	*Crevecoeur's Eighteenth-Century Travels in Pennsylvania and New York*
F	*The Forayers*
GG	*The Great Gatsby*
H	*The History of the Dividing Line Betwixt Virginia and North Carolina*
HRK	*Henderson the Rain King*
KW	*Katharine Walton*
LAF	*Letters from an American Farmer*
LM	*The Last of the Mohicans*
M	*Mellichampe*
P	*The Pathfinder*
Par	*The Partisan*
Pi	*The Pioneers*
PPF	*The Poems of Philip Freneau*
Pr	*The Prairie*
S	*The Scout*
SEA	*Sketches of Eighteenth-Century America*
SH	*The Secret History of the Dividing Line Betwixt Virginia and North Carolina*
W	*Woodcraft*

The Lay of the Land

1.
Unearthing Herstory
An Introduction

You don't know what you've got 'til it's gone,
They paved Paradise and put up a parking lot.
—JONI MITCHELL, *"Big Yellow Taxi"*

For the brief space of perhaps two weeks at the end of May 1969, a small plot of deserted ground just south of the University of California campus at Berkeley dominated headlines and news broadcasts across the country. That such an apparently local incident as the "Battle for People's Park" could so quickly and so effectively capture a nation's attention suggests that it had touched off a resonant chord in the American imagination. If the various legal, political, moral, and ecological issues involved in the controversy are as confused and confusing today as they were in 1969, they do at least all seem to cohere around a single unifying verbal image that appeared in almost all of the leaflets, handbills, and speeches printed during the uproar:

The earth is our Mother
the land
The University put a fence around
the land—our Mother. [1]

In what has since been partially paved over and designated a parking lot, the advocates of People's Park dared fantasize a natural maternal realm, in which human children happily working together in the spontaneous and unalienated labor of planting and tilling might all be "sod brothers."[2] So powerful was the fantasy, in fact, that many seriously believed that, armed "with sod, lots of flowers, and spirit," those evicted from the park might return and "ask our brothers in the [National] Guard to let us into our park."[3]

If the wished-for fraternity with the National Guard was at least erratically realized, the return to "the land—our Mother," the place, they insisted, "where our souls belong,"[4] was thwarted completely. The disposition of the land through "proper channels"—including city council and university officials—was characterized variously as "the rape of People's Park" or, more graphically, as a case of "The University . . . / fucking with our land."[5] For many, hurt and angered at the massive repression their fantasy had engendered, People's Park became "a mirror in which our society may see itself," a summing up of American history: "We have constituted ourselves socially and politically to conquer and transform nature."[6]

In fact, the advocates of People's Park had asserted another version of what is probably America's oldest and most cherished fantasy: a daily reality of harmony between man and nature based on an experience of the land as essentially feminine—that is, not simply the land as mother, but the land as woman, the total female principle of gratification—enclosing the individual in an environment of receptivity, repose, and painless and integral satisfaction.[7] Such imagery is archetypal wherever we find it; the soul's home, as the People's Park Committee leaflet and three hundred years of American writing before it had asserted, is that place where the conditions of exile—from Eden or from some primal harmony with the Mother—do not obtain; it is a realm of nurture, abundance, and unalienated labor within which all men are truly brothers. In short, the place America had long promised to be, ever since the first explorers declared themselves virtually "ravisht with the . . . pleasant land" and described the new continent as a "*Paradise* with all her Virgin Beauties."[8] The human, and decidedly feminine, impact of the landscape became a staple of the early promotional tracts, inviting prospective settlers to inhabit "valleyes and plaines streaming with sweete Springs, like veynes in a naturall bodie," and to explore "hills and mountaines making a sensible proffer of hidden treasure, neuer yet searched."[9]

As a result, along with their explicit hopes for commercial, religious, and political gains, the earliest explorers and settlers in the New World can be said to have carried with them a "yearning for paradise." When they ran across people living in what seemed to them "the manner of the golden age," and found lands where "nature and liberty affords vs that freely, which in *England* we want, or it costeth vs dearely," dormant dreams found substantial root.[10] When, for instance, Arthur Barlowe's account of his "First Voyage Made to the Coasts of America . . . Anno 1584," described the Indian women who greeted him and his men as uniformly beautiful, gracious, cheerful, and friendly, with the wife of the king's brother taking "great pains to see all things ordered in the best manner she could, making great haste to dress some meat for us to eat," he initiated a habit of mind that came to see the Indian woman as a kind of emblem for a land that was similarly entertaining the Europeans "with all love and kindness and . . . as much bounty." Not until the end of the seventeenth century, when the tragic contradictions inherent in such experience could no longer be ignored, were the Indian women depicted more usually as hag-like, ugly, and immoral. The excitement that greeted John Rolfe's marriage to Pocahontas, in April of 1614, may have been due to the fact that it served, in some symbolic sense, as a kind of objective correlative for the possibility of Europeans' actually possessing the charms inherent in the virgin continent. Similarly, the repeated evocation of the new continent as "some delicate garden abounding with all kinds of odoriferous flowers," and the sometimes strident insistence that early explorers had "made a Garden vpon the top of a Rockie Ile . . . that grew so well,"[11] tantalizes with the suggestion that the garden may in fact be "an abstraction of the essential femininity of the terrain." Paul Shepard undoubtedly has a point when he claims that "we have yet to recognize the full implication of the mother as a primary landscape,"[12] especially since, as psychiatrist Joel Kovel has argued, "the life of the body and the experiences of infancy, . . . are the reference points of human knowledge and the bedrock of the structures of culture."[13]

If the initial impulse to experience the New World landscape, not merely as an object of domination and exploitation, but as a maternal "garden," receiving and nurturing human children, was a reactivation of what we now recognize as universal mythic wishes, it had one radically different facet: *this* paradise really existed, "Whole" and "True," its many published descriptions boasting "the *proofe* of the present benefit this Countrey affoords"[14] (italics mine). All the descriptions of wonderful beasts and strangely contoured humans notwithstanding, the published documents from explorers assured the reader of the author's accuracy and unimpeachable reliability. No mere literary convention this; an irrefutable fact of history (the European discovery of America) touched every word written about the New World with the possibility that the ideally beautiful and bountiful terrain might be lifted forever out of the canon of pastoral convention and invested with the reality of daily experience. In some sense, the process had already begun, as explorer after explorer claimed to have "personally . . . wth diligence searched and viewed these contries" before concluding them to be "the fairest, frutefullest, and pleasauntest of all the worlde."[15] Eden, Paradise, the Golden Age, and the idyllic garden, in short, all the backdrops for European literary pastoral, were subsumed in the image of an America promising material ease without labor or hardship, as opposed to the grinding poverty of previous European existence; a frank, free affectional life in which all might share in a primal and noncompetitive fraternity; a resurrection of the lost state of innocence that the adult abandons when he joins the world of competitive self-assertion; and all this possible because, at the deepest psychological level, the move to America was experienced as the daily reality of what has become its single dominating metaphor: regression from the cares of adult life and a return to the primal warmth of womb or breast in a feminine landscape. And when America finally produced a pastoral literature of her own, that literature hailed the essential femininity of the terrain in a way European pastoral never had, explored the historical consequences of its central metaphor in a way European pastoral had never dared, and, from the first, took its metaphors as literal truths. The traditional mode had embraced its last and possibly its most uniquely revitalizing permutation.

As Joel Kovel points out, of course, "It is one thing to daydream and conjure up wishful images of the way things ought to be in order that one's instinctually-based fantasies may come true;" at the time of America's discovery, this had become the province of European pastoral. "It is quite another matter, and a more important one in cultural terms,"[16] he continues, to begin experiencing those fantasies as the pattern of one's daily activity—as was the case in sixteenth- and seventeenth-century America. For only if we acknowledge the power of the pastoral impulse to shape and structure experience can we reconcile the images of abundance in the early texts with the historical evidence of starvation, poor harvests, and inclement weather.[17] To label such an impulse as "mere fantasy" in order to dismiss it ignores the fact that fantasy is a particular way of relating to the world, even, as R. D. Laing suggests, "part of, sometimes the essential part of, the meaning or sense . . . implicit in action."[18] In 1630 Francis Higginson, "one of the ministers of Salem," claimed that "Experience doth manifest that there is hardly a more healthfull place to be found in the World" and boasted that "since I came hither . . . I thanke God I haue had perfect health, and . . . whereas beforetime I cloathed my self with double cloathes and thicke Wastcoats to keepe me warme, euen in the Summer time, I doe now goe as thin clad as any, onely wearing a light Stuffe Cassocke vpon my Shirt and Stuffe Breeches and one thickness without Linings."[19] The fact that he died the next year of pneumonia, or, as Governor Dudley phrased it, "of a feaver," in no way negates what the good minister claimed his "Experience doth manifest." American pastoral, unlike European, holds at its very core the promise of fantasy as daily reality. Implicit in the call to emigrate, then, was the tantalizing proximity to a happiness that had heretofore been the repressed promise of a better future, a call to act out what was at once a psychological and political revolt against a culture based on toil, domination, and self-denial.

But not many who emigrated yearning for pastoral gratifications shared Higginson's "Experience." Colonization brought with it an inevitable paradox: the success of settlement depended on the ability to master the land, transforming the virgin territories into something else—a farm, a village, a road, a canal, a railway, a mine, a factory, a city, and finally, an urban nation. As a result, those who had initially responded to the promise inherent in a feminine landscape were now faced with the consequences of that response: either they recoiled in horror from the meaning of their manipulation of a naturally generous world, accusing one another, as did John Hammond in 1656, of raping and deflowering the "naturall fertility and comelinesse," or, like those whom Robert Beverley and William Byrd accused of "slothful Indolence," they succumbed to a life of easeful regression, "spung[ing] upon the Blessings of a warm Sun, and a fruitful Soil" and "approach[ing] nearer to the Description of Lubberland than any other."[20] Neither response, however, obviated the fact that the despoliation of the land appeared more and more an inevitable consequence of human habitation—any more than it terminated the pastoral impulse itself. The instinctual drive embedded in the fantasy, which had first impelled men to emigrate, now impelled them both to continue pursuing the fantasy in daily life, and, when that failed, to codify it as part of the culture's shared dream life, through art—there for all to see in the paintings of Cole and Audubon, in the fictional "letters" of Crevecoeur, the fallacious "local color" of Irving's Sleepy Hollow, and finally, the northern and southern contours clearly distinguished, in the Leatherstocking novels of James Fenimore Cooper and in the Revolutionary War romances of William Gilmore Simms. "Thus," as Joel Kovel argues, "the decisive symbolic elements [of a culture's history] will be those that represent not only repressed content, but ego activity as well."[21]

Other civilizations have undoubtedly gone through a similar history, but at a pace too slow or in a time too ancient to be remembered. Only in America has the entire process remained within historical memory, giving Americans the unique ability to see themselves as the wilful exploiters of the very land that had once promised an escape from such necessities. With the pastoral impulse neither terminated nor yet wholly repressed, the entire process—the dream and its betrayal, and the consequent guilt and anger—in short, the knowledge of what we have done to our continent, continues even in this century, as Gary Snyder put it, "eating at the American heart like acid."[22] How much better might things have turned out had we heeded the advice of an earlier American poet, Charles Hansford, who probably wrote the following lines about the middle of the eighteenth century:

To strive with Nature little it avails.
Her favors to improve and nicely scan
Is all that is within the reach of Man.
Nature is to be follow'd, and not forc'd,
For, otherwise, our labor will be lost.[23]

From accounts of the earliest explorers onward, then, a uniquely American pastoral vocabulary began to show itself, releasing and emphasizing some facets of the traditional European mode and all but ignoring others. At its core lay a yearning to know and to respond to the landscape as feminine, a yearning that I have labeled as the uniquely American "pastoral impulse." Obviously, such an impulse must at some very basic level stem from desires and tensions that arise when patterns from within the human mind confront an external reality of physical phenomena. But the precise psychological and linguistic processes by which the mind imposes order or even meaning onto the phenomena—these have yet to be understood. Let us remember, however, that gendering the land as feminine was nothing new in the sixteenth century; Indo-European languages, among others, have long maintained the habit of gendering the physical world and imbuing it with human capacities. What happened with the discovery of America was the revival of that linguistic habit on the level of personal experience; that is, what had by then degenerated into the dead conventions of self-consciously "literary" language, hardly attended to, let alone explored, suddenly, with the discovery of America, became the vocabulary of everyday reality. Perhaps, after all, the world *is* really gendered, in some subtle way we have not yet quite understood. Certainly, for William Byrd, topography and anatomy were at least analogous, with "a Single Mountain [in the Blue Ridge range], very much resembling a Woman's breast" and a "Ledge that stretch't away to the N.E. . . . [rising] in the Shape of a Maiden's Breast."[24]

Or, perhaps, the connections are more subtle still: was there perhaps a *need* to experience the land as a nurturing, giving maternal breast because of the threatening, alien, and potentially emasculating terror of the unknown? Beautiful, indeed, that wilderness appeared—but also dark, uncharted, and prowled by howling beasts. In a sense, to make the new continent Woman was already to civilize it a bit, casting the stamp of human relations upon what was otherwise unknown and untamed. But, more precisely still, just as the impulse for emigration was an impulse to begin again (whether politically, economically, or religiously), so, too, the place of that new beginning was, in a sense, the new Mother, her adopted children having cast off the bonds of Europe, "where mother-country acts the step-dame's part."[25] If the American continent was to become the birthplace of a new culture and, with it, new and improved human possibilities, then it was, in fact as well as in metaphor, a womb of generation and a provider of sustenance. Hence, the heart of American pastoral—the only pastoral in which metaphor and the patterns of daily activity refuse to be separated.

2.

Surveying the Virgin Land

The Documents of Exploration and Colonization, 1500–1740

The land was ours before we were the land's.
She was our land more than a hundred years
Before we were her people. She was ours
In Massachusetts, in Virginia,
But we were England's, still colonials.
—ROBERT FROST, *"The Gift Outright"*

On the second of July, 1584, two English captains, Philip Amadas and Arthur Barlowe, entered the coastal waters off what is now North Carolina and enjoyed "so sweet and so strong a smell as if we had been in the midst of some delicate garden abounding with all kinds of odoriferous flowers"; from this they determined "that the land could not be far distant." Some days later, landing on a beach "very sandy and low toward the water's side, but . . . full of grapes," they took possession of the land "in the right of the Queen's most excellent majesty" and, "according to her majesty's grant and letters patent," turned it over to the use of "Walter Raleigh, Knight, at whose charge and direction the said voyage was set forth." These ceremonies completed, the two captains proceeded to explore the newly discovered territory and, in their later letter to Raleigh, declared it to be a realm of "wonderful plenty," its rich soil supporting an abundance of game and growing crops "plentiful, sweet, fruitful and wholesome," with "divers other wholesome and medicinable herbs and trees." When the Indians on Roanoke Island greeted the weary explorers "with all love and kindness and with as much bounty (after their manner) as they could possibly devise," the good captains declared them to be "such as live after the manner of the golden age," and left them, after a brief stay, convinced that "a more kind and loving people there cannot be found in the world."[1]

Less than two years later, Master Ralph Lane, the first governor of Raleigh's colonial enterprise in Virginia, averred that his own personal experience in the new colony proved it to have "the goodliest soil under the cope of heaven," with a "climate so wholesome, that we had not one sick since we touched the land here." "So abounding with sweet trees," "so many sorts of apothecary drugs, such several kinds of flax," wheat, corn, and sugar cane, was it, in fact, that he "dar[d] assure [himself], being inhabited with English, no realm in Christendom were comparable to it." "Besides that, it is the goodliest and most pleasing territory of the world; for the continent is of a huge and unknown greatness."[2] Through documents like these, published and circulated widely, England first came to know America. Typical of the "big sell" approach were the enormous Hakluyt collections, comprised of accounts of voyages to the New World—some planned, some already executed, some wholly imaginary, and some a confusing combination of the three; but all cohered to justify John Ribault's assertion that the New World was "the fairest, frutefullest, and pleasauntest of all the worlde, aboundinge" in everything needful and desired by man. Quoting from Ribault in his own 1584 "Discourse of Western Planting," the elder Hakluyt delighted in repeating descriptions of "a place wonderfull fertile and of strong scituation, the grounde fatt, so that it is like that it woulde bringe forthe wheate and all other corne twise a yere"[3] because they implied that here, at last, men might prosper with only minimum effort—an implication designed to spur the kinds of ventures Hakluyt was himself investing in. By the end of the century, private individuals and joint stock companies alike were busy printing, for an avid reading public, the adventures of those who, like Columbus, declared the New World "a land to be desired, and, seen, it is never to be left."[4] Unintentionally, perhaps, their language also reinforced a particular mode of English response, articulated most explicitly by Raleigh himself in 1595 when he described Guiana as "a countrey that hath yet her maydenhead, never sackt, turned, nor wrought."[5] It was an invitation utilized by Robert Johnson in his "Nova Britannia" (1609), when he described not only Virginia's "Valleyes and plaines streaming with sweete Springs, like veynes in a naturall bodie," but also that territory's "hills and mountaines making a sensible proffer of hidden treasure, neuer yet searched"; and again by John Smith, in 1616, when he praised even the rough New England seacoast as a kind of virginal garden, "her treasures hauing yet neuer beene opened, nor her originalls wasted, consumed, nor abused."[6] Later documents suggest that these intentionally suggestive invitations had their effect.

If the new American "*Paradise* with all her Virgin Beauties" was, in fact, supposed to provide material ease "from the *spontaneous* Wealth, which overruns the Country," and, by implication, an escape from human labor and grinding poverty, then, declared Thomas Morton in 1632, New England had suffered rude neglect on the part of colonists who had left her

Like a faire virgin, longing to be sped,
And meete her lover in a Nuptiall bed.[7]

His "New English Canaan" countered the harsher reports of a cold, barren, and inhospitable New England coast by insisting that any lack of abundance in those colonies was the unfortunate result of the present inhabitants' own reticence. By ignoring "the bewty of the Country with her naturall indowements," the colonists were forcing their potentially fertile Canaan to remain a fruitless "wombe," which

Not being enjoy'd, is like a glorious tombe,
Admired things producing which there dye,
And ly fast bound in darck obscurity.

Cataloging "the temperature of the Climent, sweetnesse of the aire, fertility of the Soile, and small number of the Salvages," he concludes that the land is "not to be paraleld in all Christendome." Its physical layout, promising ease and repose, includes "many goodly groues of trees; dainty fine round rising hillucks: delicate faire large plaines, sweete cristall fountaines, and cleare running streames, that twine in fine meanders through the meads, making so sweete a murmering noise to heare, as would even lull the sences with delight a sleepe." In short, he tells us, "The more I looked, the more I liked it."[8]

But if Morton complained that the land's implicit sexuality had not been explored, John Hammond, in 1656, complained because it had. In a treatise titled "Leah and Rachel; or, The Two Fruitfull Sisters Virginia and Mary-land," he detailed his personal love affair with the two colonies in hopes of removing "such Imputations as are scandalously cast on those Countries, . . . wherein is plenty of all things necessary for Humane subsistance." The headnote chosen to preface the text (a quote from *Ecclesiastes)*, however, suggests also a filial relationship:

> *If children live honestly and have wherewith, they shall put away the shame of their Parents.*

The stance of the son defending his mother's honor does not structure the succeeding narrative but, in its stead, the lover fondly remembering two mistress's delights; utilizing a biblical parallel to justify his apparent fickleness, he explains, "Having for 19 yeare served Virginia the elder sister, I casting my eye on Mary-land the younger, grew in amoured on her beauty, resolving like Jacob when he had first served for Leah, to begin a fresh service for Rachell." Repeating several times throughout the narrative that his only purpose is to relate "their present condition impartially," he is scrupulous not to "over extoll the places, as if they were rather Paradices than earthly habitations." Nevertheless, the landscape he depicts is, in fact, one of "fertility and natural gratefulnesse," "not only plentifull but pleasant and profitable, pleasant in regard of the brightnesse of the weather, the many delightfull rivers, . . . [and] the abundance of game." In spite of this, "odiums and cruell slanders [have been] cast on those two famous Countries of Virginia and Mary-land," which, Hammond insists, are in no way the fault of the lands themselves, but, as with Maryland, attributable to "those Vipers she hath received and harboured with much kindnesse and hospitalitie." In other words, the human inhabitants have proven themselves ingrates. In Virginia, the prey of "an indigent and sottish people," "the general neglect and licensiousnesses there" had gotten so out of hand that laws finally had to be passed "compelling them not to neglect (upon strickt punishments) planting and tending . . . quantities of Corn." The point emphasized in Hammond's pages, then, is the unwillingness of the people to engage in labor—a situation that he himself seems to realize stems from the original Paradisal image of the place, an image by which many had been lured and by which many were still living, hoping to make a daily reality of what Hammond calls "the Fiction of the land of Ease."

His subsequent experiences in Maryland only seemed to repeat the pattern of Virginia. "In amoured on her beauty," as he explains, he had barely "enjoyed her company with delight and profit" for two years before he "was enforced by reason of her unnatural disturbances to leave her weeping for her children and would not be comforted, because they were not." Repeated religious and political wranglings, most notably, Ingle's rebellion of 1645, and the imposition of onerous taxes and trade restrictions by commissioners of Parliament in 1651—in short, the total mismanagement of land and government—results, for Hammond, in the spectre of a generous mother raped and violated by her own children: "Twice hath she been deflowred by her own Inhabitants, stript, shorne and made deformed; yet such a naturall fertility and comelinesse doth she retain that she cannot but be loved, but be pittied." But there was something more sinister behind the violation than mere religious differences and political power struggles. Although incapable of defining what precisely constituted the difficulty in the colonists' relationship to the land, he nevertheless intuited an odd intentionality in their activities: "But it was not religion, it was not punctilios they stood upon, it was that sweete, that rich, that large Country they aimed at." Its very ambiguity makes the statement stand out oddly in a treatise that is otherwise entirely clear, with reasons supplied for every action. Several pages earlier, in fact, Hammond had suggested that Maryland's subsequent difficulties were in some way inevitable, owing to the fact "that its extraordinary goodnes hath made it rather desired than envied, which hath been fatall to her (as beauty is often times to those that are endued with it)." Still, in diligently informing his readers of "how she hath suffered," he leaves them with the image of a land once "courted . . . as a refuge," now "deflowred by her own Inhabitants," her maternal aspect now become that of "a widdow," "weeping for her children."[9] The real dangers of the pastoral impulse, Hammond's treatise seems almost to be warning its readers, is not the "*Fiction* of the land of Ease," but its reality—with the confusion of filial and erotic responses terminating in the horrors of incest.

Whether because Hammond's implicit warning had been heeded, or because the warm and fertile landscape itself seemed to invite the refinement, the blatantly sexual allusions were more and more deleted from writings about the South, so that, within about ten years after Hammond's account, the language of George Alsop's "Character of the Province of Maryland" (1666) appears more typical. Sticking fairly consistently to the mothering, nurturing elements in the landscape, Alsop describes a region that is "Pleasant, in respect of the multitude of Navigable Rivers and Creeks that conveniently and most profitably lodge within the armes of her green, spreading, and delightful Woods"; and he depicts a place where Nature's "natural womb (by her plenty) maintains and preserves the several diversities of Animals that rangingly inhabit her Woods; as she doth otherwise generously fructifie this piece of Earth with almost all sorts of Vegetables, as well Flowers with their varieties of colours and smells." Pleased though he is to "view Mary-Land drest in her green and fragrant Mantle of the Spring," he is careful to emphasize the maternal aspect of that femininity, its "fertile womb" supplying her children "a super-abounding plenty."[10]

But, as we might expect, the maternal image, however often invoked, was not comfortably sustained. Appropriate to the land as the place to begin again, the birthplace and nurse of both man and colony, the image could also lead to an experience of incestuous violation, as in Hammond, or, as in Robert Beverley's 1705 edition of *The History and Present State of Virginia*, to an experience of what Alsop hailed a "super-abounding plenty" as virtually suffocating, a paralyzing superfluity. Beverley claimed to "be asham'd to publish this slothful Indolence of my Countrymen," but felt compelled to expose the dangers inherent in "liv[ing] in so happy a Climate, and hav[ing] so fertile a Soil, that no body is poor enough to beg, or want Food, though they have abundance of People that are lazy enough to deserve it." The only thing the English seem to have done to the land "since their going thither," he sadly admits, "has been only to make some of these Native Pleasures more scarce, by an inordinate and unseasonable Use of them; hardly making Improvements equivalent to that Damage"—and all this both in spite of and because of "the extream fruitfulness of that Country."[11] For, as Leo Marx has pointed out, "having begun with Nature's garden as his controlling metaphor, Beverley discovers in mid-career that he cannot accept what it implies. He does not like what has happened to the British in Virginia. He denounces them for their soft, slack ways. Yet the apparent source of this evil condition is the lush green land itself, the landscape on which his high hopes had rested at the outset."[12] The problem clearly is one of appropriate response: the apparently undemanding generosity of Virginia inevitably invites her human children to "spunge upon the Blessings of a warm Sun, and a fruitful Soil, and almost grutch [begrudge] the Pains of gathering in the Bounties of the Earth."[13] Or, to put it another way, the instinctual drives inherent in the pastoral impulse having been so completely gratified, there was no further reason for action; the dreams that attended emigration had all come true. Not that Beverley wanted in any way to deny those dreams; on the contrary, as Marx points out, "he was looking for a conception of life which would combine (to use the language of Freud) the Indians' high level of instinctual gratification with those refinements of civilization based on performance—work—hence a degree of repression."[14]

What Marx, and perhaps Beverley himself, never quite understood was that from the very beginning, and in spite of its less appealing ramifications, pastoral in America was not only a habit of mind, but also, a habit of action.

With the eighteenth century, in fact, the pattern of indolent engulfment takes over in the South, submerging Hammond's experience of despoliation and violation in assurances that newcomers "shall confine our first Endeavours to such easy Benefits, as will (without the smallest waiting for the Growth of Plants) be offer'd to our Industry from the *spontaneous* Wealth, which overruns the Country." And so, in urging "the design'd Establishment of a New Colony to the South of Carolina," in 1717, Robert Mountgomry assured prospective investors and colonists that "*Carolina*, and especially its *Southern* Bounds, is the most amiable Country of the Universe." The judicious opinion "extracted from our *English Writers*, who are very numerous, and universally agree" was "that Nature has not bless'd the World with any Tract, which can be preferable to it, that *Paradise* with all her Virgin Beauties."[15]

It was an image with which John Peter Purry wholly concurred when, "in September, 1731," he drew up an alleged on-the-spot "Description of the Province of South Carolina," declaring it to be "an excellent Country," in which "a Man who shall have a little Land . . . and who is not willing to work above 2 or 3 Hours a Day, may very easily live." Or, to put it more succinctly, as he does later on, "Persons may grow rich in *Carolina* without being at much Expence or Labour." The less appealing characteristics of the area, briefly alluded to, include "several sorts of Insects, and especially . . . great Rattle-Snakes," which, like the snake in a previous garden, leave one "in Danger of your Life every Moment."[16] Similar references to snakes echo throughout the eighteenth-century evocations of the southern garden, finally to become, in the nineteenth-century, with the landscape set-pieces of William Gilmore Simms, the fictive representation of the psychological dangers inherent in pastoral. The eighteenth-century, however, is content to regard them as only an inconvenient annoyance in what is otherwise at best "the Land of Eden" or, at worst, "Lubberland."

Both terms were used by William Byrd of Westover, who perceived the South as at once a land of "great Plenty, and consequently great content" and simultaneously a temptation to "Idlenesse." His celebrated attack on backwoods North Carolina as approaching "nearer to the Description of Lubberland than any other, by the great felicity of the Climate, the easiness of raising Provisions, and the Slothfulness of the People," is repeated throughout *The History of the Dividing Line Betwixt Virginia and North Carolina, Run in the Year of Our Lord 1728* and focuses particularly upon those who, despite their apparent poverty and "Indolence," appear "perfectly contented." Viewing with displeasure the lack of cultivated land and the inadequate development of useful trades among the settlers along the Virginia-North Carolina border, he is forced to admit that "Idleness is the general character of the men in the Southern Parts of this Colony as well as in North Carolina." And, just as had his brother-in-law Robert Beverley, before him, so too does Byrd attribute the situation to the "Advantages" of the landscape itself: "The Air is so mild, and the Soil so fruitful, that very little Labour is requir'd to fill their Bellies, especially where the Woods afford such Plenty of Game." In short, all conspire to "discharge the Men from the Necessity of killing themselves with Work."[17]

In 1733 Byrd described "a Journey to the Land of Eden," that is, twenty thousand acres that he had purchased along the recently surveyed border. Here again he complained "that people live worst upon good land, and the more they are befriended by the soil and the climate the less they will do for themselves." Clearly, where the land is most overpoweringly maternal, "its waters, as sweet as milk,"[18] regression will be most complete. Byrd himself is caught up in an overwhelming orality, as, in describing his two surveying ventures, he never tires of detailing the variety of foods he enjoyed, the ample supply of succulent game which his party shot and cooked, and the delighted discoveries of wild nuts and fruits. The narratives really sound more like descriptions of one long feast than journals of surveying activities.

The only trouble with paradise, according to Beverley and Byrd, then, was its ability to overwhelm and gratify; for others in the South, paradise had somehow eluded their daily reality. Colonists in Georgia, in 1741, angrily railed against the fact that "such fatal Artifice was used, . . . such specious Pretences were made use of, and such real Falsities advanced, and the smallest Foundations of Truth magnify'd to Hyperbole; that we, who had no Opportunity of knowing otherways, or means of learning the real Truth, and being void of all Suspicion of Artifice or Design, easily believed all these, and fell into the Decoy." A group of documents that the disappointed colonists claimed to be "A True and Historical Narrative of the Colony" were prefaced with the kinds of claims they said had lured them hither; characteristic of these were claims for " 'All sorts of Corn yield[ing] an amazing Increase; One Hundred fold is the common Estimate' ";—and this in spite of the fact that early settlers practiced a " 'Husbandry . . . so slight, that they can only be said to scratch the Earth, and meerly to cover the Seed: All the best sort of Cattle and Fowls are multiplied without number.' " In their "Geographical and Historical Account of [the colony's] present State," the disillusioned Georgians further complained of poor weather, disappointing soil, various kinds of governmental mismanagement, and the paucity of land actually available. As a result, they complained, "the County [that] was laid out as an *Earthly Paradise*" had actually turned out to be a place of "Hardships and Oppressions," her settled areas another of the raped and ravaged maternal landscapes, "her Plantations a Wild, her Towns a Desert; her Villages in Rubbish; her Improvements a By-Word, and her Liberties a Jest: An Object of Pity to Friends, and of Insult, Contempt, and Ridicule to Enemies."

But these documents do more than emphasize the fact that, for many, the full and painless gratification of pastoral longings was not possible on the American continent; they also make clear how powerful those longings were—and how difficult to abandon. For, in summing up "the REAL Causes of the Ruin and Desolation of the Colony," the colonists first listed "the Representing the Climate, Soil, &c. of Georgia in false and too flattering Colours; at least, the not contradicting those Accounts when publickly printed and dispers'd, and satisfying the World in a true and genuine Description thereof." All of which again points to the emigrants' own willing credulity, "being void," as they themselves admitted, "of all Suspicion of Artifice or Design."[19] But even in the face of the physical hardships and political corruptions that these pages document, some in Georgia still clung to their dreams of an earthly paradise and blamed any thwarting of that dream not on the inadequate landscape, but upon "the Sins of the Inhabitants." In a letter dated 23 July 1741, the Reverend Mr. Boltzius, at Ebenezer, was still insisting that in Georgia, "Wheat, Rice, and other Grain, must be sowed very thin, because each Grain brings forth fifty, an hundred, or more Stalks and Ears. The Land," he insisted, "is really very fruitful, if the Sins of the Inhabitants, and the Curse of God for such Sins, doth not eat it up, which was formerly the unhappy Case of the blessed Land of *Canaan*."[20]

In New England, and despite such glowing accounts as Francis

Higginson's and Thomas Morton's, a number of individuals had taken great pains to prevent their Canaan from being similarly despoiled; their method was carefully to limit the scope of pastoral possibilities there. The sensuously abundant ambience of the South was to be avoided at all costs since, as John White argued, "the overflowing of riches [is known] to be enemie to labour, sobriety, justice, love and magnanimity: and the nurse of pride, wantonnesse, and contention." His "Planters Plea," published in London in 1630, was probably directed at countering in the North the kinds of indolence John Smith had complained of in his "Notes on Virginia," published in 1624. Unable (perhaps as a result of Smith's picture of Virginia) to conceive of "a riche soile, that brings in much with little labour," as anything other than an invitation to corruption, White stridently attempted to suppress the pastoral impulse altogether by asserting that men have "therefore laboured by all meanes to keepe out the love and desire of [overflowing riches] from their well-ordered States, and observed and professed the comming in and admiration of them to have beene the foundation of their ruine." "The truth is," he concludes, "there is more cause to feare wealth then poverty in that soyle." At best, White will acknowledge "the fitnesse of the countrey for our health and maintenance," but, in studiously avoiding the garden image, he forces the reader to realize that "a Countrey such as this is . . . may yeeld sufficiency"—but only "with hard labour and industry." We hear here, then, that aspect of the Puritan mind that, in its "desire that Piety and godliness should prosper," self-consciously turned away from the seductions of a feminine landscape.[21]

A year later, Governor Dudley, only nine months after landing at the Massachusetts Bay Colony, wrote his friend and former employer, the Countess of Lincoln, that "if any come hether to plant for worldly ends that canne live well at home hee comits an errour of which hee will soon repent him." For, as others were later to protest in Georgia, the pastoral impulse that had in fact been one of the spurs to emigration—even in Puritan New England—now proved itself only a lovely illusion. The good governor's "open and plaine dealeinge" was intended to nip the impulse in the bud, "least other men should fall short of their expactacons when they come hether as wee to our great prejudice did, by means of letters sent vs from hence into England, wherein honest men out of a desire to draw over others to them wrote somewhat hyperbolically of many things here." Still, even in its stance of denial, Dudley's letter gives proof of the initial power of the impulse.

Like the "Planters Plea" before it, this letter to England, dated March 1631, is studiously restrained in its description of a land that supplies "materialls to build, fewell to burn, ground to plant, seas and rivers to ffish in, a pure ayer to breath in, good water to drinke till wine or beare canne be made, which togeather with the cowes, hoggs and goates brought hether allready may suffice for food, for as for foule and venison, they are dainties here as well as in England."[22] Attractive, perhaps, but hardly paradisal—hardly, in fact, that same "Countrie of the *Massachusets*" that John Smith had called "the Paradise of all those parts: for, heere are many Iles all planted with corne; groues, mulberries, saluage gardens, and good harbors." And yet, for all their apparent differences in vocabulary, John White and Governor Dudley shared with Smith the same goals that had originally prompted the captain to publish his "Description of New England" in 1616: all were concerned that the easeful, self-indulgent capitulation before an overwhelming abundance, and the consequent outcries against such idleness, which had become the dominant pattern of southern life and writing, not be repeated in the North. It was, in fact, Smith's gradual disillusionment at what the southern pastoral entailed, as described originally in his "A True Relation of . . . Virginia," published in London in 1608 (under the running title, "Newes from Virginia"), which subsequently turned his attention to the cold, rocky New England coast where, with sufficient human labor, he hoped that the *true* garden of the New World might be cultivated. To effect this, Smith tempered his image of "a Garden vpon the top of a Rockie Ile" with what became a dominant feature of New England promotional tracts: an emphasis on the need for human labor. Very cleverly Smith followed all his catalogs of New England riches with the human activity required to make use of those potentially "good fruites for mans vse." For instance, "where there is victuall to feede vs; wood of all sorts, to build Boats, Ships, or Barks; the fish at our doores, pitch, tarre, masts, yards, and most of other necessaries onely for making," he immediately sees the place as one in which "euery man may be master and owne labour and land." The appeal, however, unlike that of the later Puritans, is to the certainty that by means of such "industrie," a man may "quickly grow rich." But, again giving voice to the longing for pastoral experience, Smith emphasizes the pleasure aspect, rather than the toil, of activity in the northern garden, until, finally, the two are all but synonymous. "What pleasure," he asks, "can be more then . . . in planting Vines, Fruits, or Hearbs, in contriuing their owne Grounds," or in "recreat[ing] themselues before their owne doores, in their own boates vpon the Sea, where man, woman and childe, with a small hooke and line, by angling, may take diuerse sorts of excellent fish, at their pleasures?"[23]

Still, we cannot ignore the peculiar quality of ambivalence that informs so many of the texts written in the northern colonies. For, however more emphatic or more strident their tone might have been, their ambivalence had been shared, from the very first, even by those who had praised "bare nature [for being] so amiable in its naked kind."[24] During the years that Robert Johnson's pamphlet "Nova Britannia" (1609) was circulated in England, it enjoyed not only official sanction but, also, as Howard Mumford Jones terms it, the added flavor of "personal tang."[25] After wholly accepting and repeating early explorers' tales of being "ravisht with the . . . pleasant land," Johnson very subtly injects the suggestion that where "the ayre and clymate [are] most sweete and wholsome" and "the soile is strong and lustie of its owne nature," men are in danger of "beeing in a golden dreame." Ostensibly what he is worried about is the withdrawal of funds for further exploration and colonization, should these ventures not prove immediately profitable; that is, "if it fall not out presently to our expactation, we slinke away with discontent, and draw our purses from the charge."[26] But as his solution to the problem is the encouragement of more and more settlement and more and more active cultivation of the land, he also hints that the threat presented by the "golden dreame" is not one so much of disappointed petulance but of indolent passivity. By the end of the pamphlet, in fact, he virtually ignores the Edenic image he had utilized at the outset and insists on the need to *make* Virginia a beautiful and prosperous garden. The woman who had "so ravisht" the early explorers, he seems to be saying, ought not to be trusted too completely.

Finally, of course, that early quality of ambivalence took several different forms. By the eighteenth century, as we have seen, both the New England and the southern colonies were pouring out what R. W. B. Lewis has noted as the characteristic American literary response to the natural world—that is, "repeated efforts to revert to a lost childhood and vanished Eden"; but the outcries in these texts are not only, as he would have it, "at the freshly discovered capacity of the world to injure," but at the recognition of our human capacity to injure the world.[27] For, even if the North had managed to suppress the "golden dreame" more effectively than had the South, the two finally shared the same spectre of human violation of the landscape. If Thomas Morton could bewail New England's "fruitful wombe / Not being enjoy'd," later writers deplored the eroticism that ended in images of incestuous impregnation and rape, or like the author of the "Planters Plea," stridently warned against the attractions of a landscape that might, by its very abundance, prove the nurse of human discord rather than human blessings. The emotional force of these documents, with their often brutal details and expressions of personal anger, suggests that behind the public or communal response was another, deeply profound, personal response. Certainly none of these men had intended to reveal the psychological substratum their vocabulary suggests; if anything, each attempted to avoid confronting his own personal and potentially guilt-ridden involvement: John Hammond blames others for having proven ungrateful children to Virginia and Maryland; the authors of the Georgia narratives lay the blame for that lady's ruin at the feet of governmental mismanagement and false advertising; and Thomas Morton blamed the rest of New England for its sexual reticence—but never suggested that he himself might alter the situation. We can understand their attempted withdrawal from involvement only if we realize that a full recognition of their chosen verbal images would have demanded conscious complicity in what is finally a bold exercise of masculine power over the feminine—a feminine, moreover, that was being experienced as at once Mother and Virgin, with all the confusions possible between the two. In short, as these early documents amply demonstrate, the new American continent had become the focus for both personalized and transpersonalized (or culturally shared) expressions of filial homage and erotic desire.

But, possibly as a direct result of these uneasy images of violation, so precarious appeared the maintenance of pastoral possibilities that, barely a hundred years after colonization first began, its frailty had entered the nation's dream life—as it was, a century later, to structure its fiction. In a journal published in 1774, two years after his death, John Woolman recorded a dream he had had "about the ninth year of my age":

> I saw the Moon rise near the West, and run a regular course Eastward, so swift that in about a quarter of an hour, she reached our Meridian, when there descended from her a small Cloud on a Direct line to the Earth, which lighted on a pleasant Green about twenty yards from the Door of my Father's House (in which I thought I stood) and was immediately turned into

a Beautiful green Tree. The Moon appeared to run on with Equal swiftness, and soon set in the East, at which time the Sun arose at the place where it commonly doth in the Sumer, and Shineing with full Radiance in a Serene air, it appeared as pleasant a morning as ever I saw.

All this time I stood still in the door, in an Awfull frame of mind, and I observed that as the heat increased by the Riseing Sun, it wrought so powerfully on the little green Tree, that the leaves gradually withered, and before Noon it appear'd dry and dead. There then appeared a Being, Small of Size, moving Swift from the North Southward, called a "Sun Worm."

Simply enough, a feminine moon had engendered "a Beautiful green Tree" that is at once attractive and vulnerable; for a moment all is in harmony—or apparently so. Then, with the paragraph break, there also comes a radical break in mood. The heat of the sun, traditionally a masculine generative force, its phallic implications emphasized here by its *rising* and by the appearance of the "Sun Worm," soon withers and destroys the tree—in short, another exercise of masculine power over a frail and vulnerable feminine—and agitates the mind of the dreamer. Though Woolman never examines the meaning of the dream, he makes clear that he considered it an important experience—not only because it stands as one of the few dreams recorded in the journal but also because his own note, just following it, reads, "Tho' I was A Child, this dream was instructive to me." Just what it taught him, he never says, but a pattern becomes clear if we read on to the very next item in the journal—this one a reminiscence:

Another thing remarkable in my childhood was, that once, as I went to a neighbor's house, I saw, on the way, a Robbin sitting on her nest, and as I came near she went off, but having young ones, flew about, and with many cries expressed her Concern for them. I stood and threw stones at her, till one striking her, she fell down dead. At first I was pleas'd with the Exploit, but after a few minutes was seized with Horror, as haveing in a sportive way kild an Innocent Creature while she was carefull for her young. I beheld her lying dead, and thought those young ones for which she was so carefull must now perish for want of their dam to nourish them; and after some painfull considerations on the subject, I climbed up the Tree, took all the young birds, and killed them supposing that better than to leave them to pine away and die miserably: and believ'd in this case, that scripture proverb was fulfilled, "The tender mercies of the wicked are Cruel." I then went on my errand, but, for some hours, could think of little else but [the Cruelties I had committed, and was much troubled.][28]

Again, the narrative involves an exercise of destructive masculine power over a vulnerable feminine; but here it is not only the offspring that is destroyed, but the engendering mother as well. She is, in fact, his first victim. There is also a moment of stasis, with the boy "pleas'd with the Exploit." But then, horrified at the implications of what he has done, he finds himself forced to complete the carnage—as earlier, a rising sun had continued pouring forth its heat until it finally withered the little tree. No wonder he is "troubled."

If we understand that the nine-year old Woolman was just reaching that stage where it becomes necessary to throw off the maternal yoke and begin to assert early manhood and independence, then we can see in the destruction of the mother bird and her young the destruction of an objective correlative for any of Woolman's own lingering and boyish dependence on the maternal ambience. But the cost of such brutal assertions, he quickly realizes, far outweighs their initial pleasure. The boy leaving the nest in order to become a man is in grave danger of destroying not only the nest itself but the mother who provided its nurture. And yet to remain in the nest also involves dangers. What both the dream and the incident with the robin have forced into at least symbolic consciousness is the inevitable conflict locked into the heart of American pastoral: that which is contained within the matrix of the feminine, however attractive as "a Beautiful green Tree," or as nurturing as a mother robin, must inevitably fall helpless victim to masculine activity. Little wonder the dream left the "Sun Worm" as the final image to be imprinted on the dreamer's mind. The pastoral stasis, the moment of "full radiance in a serene air" or of pleasure at an exploit, cannot be maintained; its components are apparently too volatile. How much of this Woolman was able to articulate as an adult, when he spent most of his days as an itinerant minister for the Society of Friends, traveling up and down the colonies, one can only guess at. Perhaps it is enough that this Quaker from New Jersey, sometime tailor, shopkeeper, and schoolmaster, left us the journal.

All of which attests to the success of collections such as the Hakluyts' and demonstrates the consequences of a pattern of exploration and colonization the early promotional tracts had only dimly hinted at. Certainly Hakluyt never *intended* to renew the ancient dream of pastoral possibility; on the contrary, "the greate necessitie and manifolde comodyties" to be gained from further exploration were, as far as he was concerned, circumscribed by the desire for personal wealth; glory and fame, both for oneself and for

England; and, finally, by the opportunity to extend both Christianity and the British Empire at one and the same time.[29] Hard-headed businessman and prospective investor as he was, Hakluyt took great pains to paint as inviting a picture as he could but also reminded his readers, as in his "Notes on Colonisation," that the New World benefits were not only to be enjoyed, but also employed:

> If you finde great plenty of tymber on the shore side or upon any portable river, you were best to cut downe of the same the first wynter, to be seasoned for shippes, barkes, botes and houses.
>
> And if neere such wood there be any river or brooke upon the which a sawing mill may be placed, it would doe great service, and therefore consideration woulde bee had of suche place.

Anxious as he was to establish England's economic self-sufficiency, he encouraged prospective settlements virtually to exploit and, if necessary, alter the new continent. "If . . . places be found marshie and boggie," he advises, "then men skilful in draining are to be caried thither."[30] It is a doctrine of use and labor that conflicts with sentiments expressed in other places in Hakluyt's own collection and, more importantly, with the "*Joyfull Newes out of the newfounde worlde*" everywhere circulated that there, in a landscape "plesaunte and delectable to beholde as ys possible to ymagine," men could finally enjoy "suche frutefulnes that any seede beinge sowen therein will bringe furthe moste excellente frute."[31]

In fact, the fruit commonly left "a bitter Tang in the stomach."[32]

3.

Laying Waste Her Fields of Plenty

The Eighteenth Century

Thou Mother with thy equal brood,
Thou varied chain of different States . . .
—WALT WHITMAN, Leaves of Grass

The agrarianism of the new nation was, in its way, an expression of continuing pastoral impulses, with the individual fantasies of an emigrant population becoming organized into a cultural whole.[1] As Hector St. John de Crevecoeur had explained, in his *Letters from an American Farmer*, the newcomer "becomes an American by being received in the broad lap of our great *Alma Mater*. Here individuals of all nations are melted into a new race of men."[2] It was a definition that had at its base the literal acceptance of a return to primal harmony within the bosom of a maternal landscape and, as a consequence of that return, a rebirth. Moreover, because the Mother was reputed to be so generous in America, the old European vulgar, striving, acquisitional self could die, to be replaced by the yeoman farmer, loyal at once to the soil that had made this new reality possible and to the republic that promised to codify the new order of things. By the time the new nation declared its independence, the image of a feminine landscape threatened by invading British had become a rallying cry for patriotism, with Philip Freneau complaining that when "warlike hosts on every plain appear,"

War damps the beauties of the rising year:
In vain the groves their bloomy sweets display.[3]

If England or Ireland, acting "the step-dame's part," had "Hatch[ed] sad wars to make her brood the thinner," America, he declared, had opened her generous arms and now "blushes with its children's gore."[4]

If for Sidney and Spenser, "the pastoral ideal and the singing shepherds [stood] apart from any conceivable social organization," the new republic, through poets like Freneau, struggled to convert Europe's archaic pastoral diction into a vocabulary for real-world possibilities. Social castes once "too basically opposed to be reconciled,"[5] as in European pastoral, were now to reconstitute the harmonious primal family, with all men able to begin again in a land experienced as wholly beneficent and maternally abundant. Little wonder, then, that Thomas Jefferson and his contemporaries were "primarily interested in the political implications of the agrarian ideal." As Henry Nash Smith points out, Jefferson "saw the cultivator of the earth, the husbandman who tilled his own acres, as the rock upon which the American republic must stand."[6] Intent on preserving what he called "rural virtue," Jefferson denied the importance of economic profit for evaluating social structures and, instead, committed himself to an agricultural economy. In spite of the demonstrated superiority of large-scale farming, in fact, he continued to advocate the small, independent family-size farm,[7] claiming that "those who labour in the earth" are, as a consequence, gifted with "substantial and genuine virtue." "Corruption of morals in the mass of cultivators is a phaenomenon of which no age nor nation has furnished an example," he argued in his *Notes on Virginia*, and even suggested, by his choice of vocabulary, an almost erotic intimacy in the bond of man and soil: artisans are merely "*occupied* at a work-bench," while, for the farmer, a more appealing relatedness is promised by that "immensity of land *courting* the industry of the husbandman"[8] (italics mine).

Finally, agriculture came to be seen as the primary and indispensable foundation both of national prosperity[9] and of political democracy; as Henry Nash Smith notes, "the idealized figure of the farmer himself, called variously 'husbandman,' 'cultivator,' 'freeman,' or—perhaps most characteristically—'yeoman,' " became a kind of emblematic self-image for the new nation as a whole.[10] The only possible flaw in the image was the inevitable tension it suggested between the initial urge to return to, and join passively with, a maternal landscape and the consequent impulse to master and act upon that same femininity. The range of pastoral expression, therefore, could extend from a healthy sense of intimacy and reciprocity to the most unbridled and seemingly gratuitous destruction.[11] Even President Washington had expressed his dislike for what he called the "slovenly" farmers of America, "who think (generally) of nothing else, but to work a field as long as it will bear anything, and until it is run to gullies and ruined; then at another; without affording either any aid."[12] Jefferson's solution, in "Subjects of Commerce," was to make an impassioned plea for "the cultivation of wheat," not only because of its usefulness, but more important, because it "cloath[es] the earth with herbage, . . . preserving its fertility," in contrast with tobacco which leaves "the earth . . .rapidly impoverished."[13]

In a sense, Jefferson's *Notes on Virginia* continually hints at, but steadfastly refuses to make explicit, the essence of the pastoral paradox: man might, indeed, win mastery over the landscape, but only at the cost of emotional and psychological separation from it.[14] Moreover, the freehold concept flatly contradicted and, in some ways demanded an end to, what Howard Mumford Jones has called "the emotional appeal of the uncharted forest, the unfenced range, the trackless mountains, and the open sky."[15] These wilder, decidedly erotic faces of the landscape offered attractions that Jefferson himself had praised in those two famous set pieces so often quoted, the first describing the Natural Bridge, and the second the confluence of the Shenandoah and Potomac rivers. In the second, he had excitedly guided the eye through a landscape of contrasts, moving the reader from the rushing rhythm of "the Shenandoah, having ranged along the foot of the mountain an hundred miles to seek a vent," to the climactic "moment of. . . junction, . . . [the two rivers] rush[ing] together against the mountain, rend[ing] it asunder, and pass[ing] off to the sea." In the wildness of that congress, the traveler is himself suggestively reborn: "For the mountain being cloven asunder, she presents to your eye, through the cleft, a small catch of smooth blue horizon, at an infinite distance in the plain country, inviting you, as it were, from the riot and tumult roaring around, to pass through the breach and participate of the calm below." The "calm" promised by the glimpse "at an infinite distance [of] the plain country" turns out to be the cultivated landscape of "Frederic town, and the fine country around that."[16] For Jefferson, then, the eroticism of the landscape was as compatible with its maternal image, as the wild forests were with the cultivated tracts, and nowhere does he acknowledge the possibility that the response to one may finally destroy the possibility of experiencing the other. As the century wore on, however, the two became dangerously confused, until, in 1796, Morgan J. Rhees could inform "persons Emigrating From Foreign Countries" that "this wide extended empire, [with its] uncultivated forests and fertile plains, invite[s] the uplifted *ax* and the furrowing *plough*."[17]

To his credit, Jefferson did fear, and in some sense foretell, the destruction of the land that promised so much bounty; significantly, however, he detailed the threat only once, and not in relation to agricultural pursuits, but in relation to the mining of Virginia's mineral deposits. In the caves of the limestone country, "the earthy floors of which are impregnated with nitre," miners perform what comes across as a single but devastating assault "to extract the nitre,"—"never trying a second time the earth they have once exhausted, to see how far or soon it receives another impregnation."[18] The suggestion of guilt on the part of those who enter and are then reluctant to return to the "exhausted" earth is muted, but repeated, in subsequent chapters, attaching itself, in one case, to those who deplete the land with the single-minded cultivation of tobacco and then move westward in search of more fertile lands, never to return. But it is not an issue Jefferson wished to confront directly; instead, he concentrated on describing the wonderful possibilities of the fertile landscape and, whatever his private doubts, remained publicly committed to the maternal image of a "confederacy [that] must be viewed as the nest from which all America, North and South is to be peopled."[19] It was Philip Freneau, poet, political journalist, and Jefferson's own clerk for foreign languages, who first explored the contradictions Jefferson had only hinted at; and, at the same time, Hector St. John de Crevecoeur actually lived them through, projecting both his dream of pastoral realities and its inevitable thwarting into the voice of Farmer James, his idealized American farmer.

The Visionary Line: The Poetry of Philip Freneau

> *Beautiful world of new superber birth that rises to my eyes,*
> *Like a limitless golden cloud filling the western sky,*
> *Emblem of general maternity lifted above all,*
> *Sacred shape of the bearer of daughters and sons,*
> *Out of thy teeming womb thy giant babes in ceaseless*
> *procession issuing . . .*
>
> —WALT WHITMAN, *"Thou Mother with Thy Equal Brood,"* Leaves of Grass

One of his more enthusiastic biographers tells us that "from Concord to Yorktown, during the bleak winter at Valley Forge, and round the campfires on Temple Hill, [Freneau's] verses encouraged the desponding soldiers. The newspapers widely published them, and they were written on slips of paper and distributed throughout the army, or posted in some conspicuous place to be memorized."[20] His appeal was to the heroism of protecting an injured woman from invading British; in "America Independent," written in 1778, he told the partisans, "Your injured country groans while yet [the British] stay," and encouraged them to "Attend her groans, and force their hosts away." Only then, the poem concluded, would "the streams of plenty" again flow "through our soil."[21] In 1782, in a rather weak political allegory employing figures from the Greek pantheon (called "The Political Balance"), he again depicted America as a weak woman, raped and assaulted, requiring succour:

And the demons of murder her honours defaced.
With the blood of the worthy her mantle was stained,
And hardly a trace of her beauty remained.

Her genius, a female, reclined in the shade,
And, sick of oppression, so mournfully played.

[*PPF*, 2:134]

As late as 1795, in a poem "On the Approaching Dissolution of Transatlantic Jurisdiction in America," he hailed the signing of the Jay Treaty as the final freeing of vulnerable femininity from tyrant toils:

From Britain's grasp forever freed,
COLUMBIA *glories in the deed:*
From her rich soil, each tyrant flown,
She finds this fair estate her own.[22]

The personification of the new nation as feminine was hardly original with Freneau and, in fact, followed the contemporary habit of picturing Liberty, Justice, indeed all the republican virtues, as latter-day Greek goddesses. What Freneau consistently and insistently infused into that image, however, was its inextricable connection to the larger femininity of soil and landscape, so that, whatever the ostensible object of the poem, the image of the nation as woman became one and the same with the image of the landscape; the stanza quoted above, motivated by an impending treaty with England, which was supposed to protect American shipping rights on the high seas, is a case in point.[23] Freneau the political activist had made effective journalistic and propagandistic use of the pastoral impulse, while Freneau the poet was to confront over and over again, through the years, the problems that would inevitably trouble "the happy people" who hoped to "find secure repose" in the New World garden (*PPF*, 1:83, ll. 458-59).

Born in New York, in 1752, Freneau spent a good part of his youth in rather comfortable circumstances on a family estate in New Jersey; at the age of sixteen he entered Princeton and came in contact both with literary and with "radical" political enthusiasts. His first major attempt at poetry, written during his last year at Princeton and recited at the 1771 class commencement by its sometime collaborator, H. H. Brackenridge, does in fact give quiet voice to the "Whiggish" tendencies then echoing on that campus. What "The Rising Glory of America" also reveals, however, is the pastoral substructure that governed both Freneau's patriotism and his aesthetic.

Encumbered as it is by an unnecessary dialogue structure and by anachronistic English pastoral diction, the poem nevertheless displays a conscious attempt to experience on the new continent the "sylvan settlements" that, if they were ever to become a daily reality, had only this one last opportunity, here on the world's last frontier, in "the last, the best / Of countries" (*PPF*, 1:61, l. 159; 1:74, ll. 322-23). American history, as Eugenio depicts it, begins with a movement away from an ungiving, unprotective and unloving mother, Britain, to a more genial feminine ambience, America. Britain is cast in the role of the mother abandoning her children—

> *She will not listen to our humble prayers,*
> *Though offered with submission:*
> . . . .
> *She casts us off from her protection,*
>
> [*PPF*, 1:78, ll. 380-81, 384]

—while America, although an "injured country," nevertheless promises to be "A new Jerusalem," a "land, / Whose ample bosom shall receive" her children in peace and plenty, so that, finally, "Paradise anew / Shall flourish" (*PPF*, 1:78, l. 379; 1:82, ll. 438-44). That paradise, of course, is essentially agricultural, with conventional pastoral virtues imputed to

> . . . *the industrious swain,*
> *Who tills the fertile vale, or mountain's brow,*
> *Content to lead a safe, a humble life.*
>
> [*PPF*, 1:67-68, ll. 236-38]

In utilizing pseudohistorical and mythical materials to precedent his vision, however, Freneau makes no attempt to distinguish between the pastoral as a literary convention and the pastoral as a possible real-world experience:

Long has the rural life been justly fam'd,
And bards of old their pleasing pictures drew
Of flowery meads, and groves, and gliding streams:
Hence, old Arcadia–wood-nymphs, satyrs, fauns;
And hence Elysium, fancied heaven below!–
Fair agriculture.

[*PPF*, 1:68, ll. 243–48]

In short, by citing "old Arcadia" and "Elysium" as models for a future agrarian America, he compounds real and ideal in his "visions of the rustic reign" (*PPF*, 1:71, l. 283). Countering this romantic history and its implicit insistence on agrarian economy are alternate attitudes, including Acasto's argument for the importance of commerce (*PPF*, 1:71–72, ll. 283–94) and Eugenio's praise of "fair Science!" (*PPF*, 1:73, l. 307); but the overall impact of the poem is clearly an argument that "these northern realms demand our song" because they were "Designed by nature for the rural reign, / For agriculture's toil" (*PPF*, 1:50, ll. 19–21). What the pastoral vision promises Freneau is escape from aggression, politics, ambition, greed, and all the forms of self-assertion that "prompts mankind to shed their kindred blood" (*PPF*, 1:51, l. 24). And whether we read a young man's claim to seek escape "from the noisy Forum" and "from busy camps, and sycophants, and crowns" (*PPF*, 1:69, ll. 262–63) as no more than an accepted literary pose, as suggested a few lines later by Acasto ("But this alone, . . . / Would scarce employ the varying mind of man" [*PPF*, 1:71, ll. 284–85]), it is nevertheless true that the poem's most attractive scenes are those " 'Midst woods and fields," where only, Leander claims, may one experience "full enjoyment" (*PPF*, 1:70, ll. 264–65).

And yet there is an unexplored contradiction in the poem; the picture of pleasurable toil, which constitutes the initial vision of a pastoral America, is finally superseded by Acasto's vision of a future America in which

The happy people, free from toils and death,
Shall find secure repose.

[*PPF*, 1:83, ll. 458–59]

It is, admittedly, a scriptural millennial vision he hopes

. . . America at last shall have
When ages, yet to come, have run their round,
And future years of bliss alone remain.

[*PPF*, 1:84, ll. 470–73]

And it is, furthermore, a millennium supported not only by nature's "fair fruits" and health-giving climate, but by a new and different mankind also:

The fiercer passions of the human breast
Shall kindle up to deeds of death no more,
But all subside in universal peace.–

[*PPF*, 1:83, ll. 466-68]

"The Rising Glory of America" predicted, in short, beyond the "rural reign" of an America compounded of Arcadia and Elysium, still another "Paradise anew," this one compounded of Canaan and Jerusalem, creating another, unfallen Eden, without thorn or briar:

. . . the lion and the lamb
In mutual friendship linked, shall browse the shrub,
And timorous deer with softened tygers stray
O'er mead, or lofty hill, or grassy plain;
Another Jordan's stream shall glide along,
And Siloah's brook in circling eddies flow:
Groves shall adorn their verdant banks, on which
The happy people, free from toils and death,
Shall find secure repose.

[*PPF*, 1:83, ll. 451-59]

It is not a millennium restricted to American shores, but somehow, the poem suggests, it is only made possible by the purifying influences of a prior "rural reign" in "the last, the best / Of countries" (*PPF*, 1:74, ll. 322-23). America thereby becomes at once the appropriate religious ground and the proper political context for realizing the rebirth image—the political and religious so inextricably intertwined as to be almost indistinguishable. All of which merely repeats the contemporary attitude that America, as a matter of course, would prove the hope of the human race.[24] But if Freneau intended to take this possibility seriously, then he was in some way bound to present a more coherent picture of that landscape in which "secure repose" might eventually be experienced; and this he attempted in 1772, with "The American Village," a work that, as he wrote to his old college friend, James Madison, was being "damned by all good and judicious judges."[25]

What damned it was Freneau's own inability to choose between the poem's two competing pastoral landscapes—the first, a conventional cultivated landscape, "Made fertile by the labours of the swain," and the second, a primitive island paradise of free-roaming hunters and herdsmen, with only limited agriculture. Ostensibly replying to Goldsmith's lament for "Deserted Auburn and forsaken plains" by laying claim to the American continent as the rightful heir to Europe's own imaginative, and now diminished, pastoral landscape, Freneau finds himself first peopling "this western land" with "woodland nymphs" and "Dryads fair," and then altering its wild landscape completely in order to sustain his claim to an American Auburn (*PPF*, 3:381-82).

The soil which lay for many thousand years
O'er run by woods, by thickets and by bears;
Now reft of trees, admits the chearful light,
And leaves long prospects to the piercing sight;
Where once the lynx nocturnal sallies made,
And the tall chestnut cast a dreadful shade:
No more the panther stalks his bloody rounds,
Nor bird of night her hateful note resounds;
Nor howling wolves roar to the rising moon,
As pale arose she o'er yon eastern down.
Some prune their trees, a larger load to bear
Of fruits nectarine blooming once a year:
See groaning waggons to the village come
Fill'd with apple, apricot or plumb;
. . . .
Or see the plough torn through the new made field,
Ordain'd a harvest, yet unknown to yield.

[*PPF*, 3:382-83]

Had the poem ended with the third stanza, from which these lines are quoted, "The American Village" would have stood simply as another in a long line of American replies to Goldsmith,[26] and only later generations would have read with unease of the silencing of the "bird of night" and the wide woods "Now reft of trees." It was not until 1823, after all, that Cooper's Natty Bumppo first declared himself "weary of living in clearings, . . . where the hammer is sounding in my ears from sunrise to sundown."

But Freneau seems to have anticipated that later attitude here, as evidenced by his abrupt departure from the scenes of forced cultivation in favor of his imagined "LOVELY island [that] once adorn'd the sea, / Between New-Albion and the Mexic' Bay" (*PPF*, 3:383). The very lack of widespread cultivation leaves the island almost virginally attractive: "ev'ry wind, conspir'd to shade a brook," while "Wild plumb trees flourish'd on the shaded soil." Happily contented "In the dark bosom of this sacred wood," are natives who know only "agriculture's first fair service."

Small fields had then suffic'd, and grateful they,
The annual labours of his hands to pay;
And free his right to search the briny flood
For fish, or slay the creatures of the wood.

[*PPF*, 3:384-85]

But this, too, Freneau was determined to fit under the umbrella of conventional pastoral, and so he labels its hero "the homely shepherd swain." Unfortunately for all its idyllic beauty, the island never "such souls sublime contain'd" and never could, for

. . . envious time conspiring with the sea,
Wash'd all it's landscapes, and it's groves away.

[*PPF*, 3:385]

Of course, history, with its implications of progress, cultivation and urbanization, would have served equally well; but it was precisely these aspects of contemporary America that he had tried to ignore earlier, turning instead to this imagined primitive landscape. When, finally, he tells the reader—

THUS, *tho' my fav'rite isle to ruin gone,*
Inspires my sorrow and demands my moan;
Yet this wide land it's place can well supply
With landscapes, hills and grassy mountains high.–

[*PPF*, 3:386]

—he effectively leaves us uncertain as to which "isle" it is he refers: England or that which "once adorn'd the sea, / Between New-Albion and the Mexic' Bay." America is supposed to supply its restoration, but just *which* pastoral he wants to see restored here, the cultivated Auburn or the primitive wild, he never makes clear. Probably, he wanted at least a little of each. If, on the one hand, he was committed to answering Goldsmith, he was also aware that the success of Auburn only slightly preceded that age when "dread commerce stretch'd the nimble sail, / And sent her wealth with ev'ry foreign gale" (*PPF*, 3:386). In short, Auburn seemed just a bit too far removed from "the golden season" of primitive pastoral that also had its appeals and that, in some sense, seemed more appropriate to the new, untamed continent. At the same time, he was clearly unable (or perhaps unwilling?) to project what would happen to America when all the forests had been cleared and all the soil cultivated; that is, what would happen when America caught up to

Europe. Should this occur, as his own choice of grammar implies it must, then there will be a millennium—but not the lovely Jerusalem predicted in the earlier poem; should America follow in Europe's path, "The American Village" asserts, it will prove not mankind's salvation, but his ultimate destruction:

When [America] has seen her empires, cities, kings,
Time must begin to flap his weary wings;
The earth itself to brighter days aspire,
And wish to feel the purifying fire.

[*PPF*, 3:387]

And yet, even with this apocalyptic prediction, he could not abandon his emotional commitment to a pastoral America; turning to a 150-line mini-epic of love and heroism, he attempted once again to validate its possibility. Briefly, he retells the story of Colma and her husband, Caffraro, who, with their child, are thrown into Arctic seas during a fierce storm. A small boat approaches to rescue them, but has room only for two; the heroic Colma sacrifices herself that her beloved husband and child might live, asking only that Caffraro embrace "no future bride," but always "Remember Colma, and her beauteous face" (*PPF*, 3:390). It is not a particularly interesting tale, nor does Freneau's poetry do much to improve it. And only if we realize how Freneau intends it to sustain his confused pastoral vision can we begin to understand how it relates to the rest of the poem. What Freneau has done is to once again go backward in time, into the primitive, linking America (in sentiment, at least) to the noble and "Renowned SACHEMS" who once ruled the continent—before, that is, "rav'nous nations with industrious toil, / Conspir'd to rob them of their native soil" (*PPF*, 3:387). The implication, clearly, is that anyone affected by this Indian tale is then empathically linked to the innocence of the primitive "northern shepherd," and, hence, to the harmonious intimacy inherent in the primitive pastoral he represents.

If Freneau learned anything from struggling with this poem it was not, as he had assumed at the outset, a knowledge of how American history would fulfill the dreams of European pastoral; instead, he confronted—perhaps for the first time—the inevitable clash between his own pastoral images and the demands of history. If America in 1772 appeared comparatively wild and untamed, a fact that coincided with Freneau's theories of primitive simplicity and innocence, he nevertheless found himself describing shepherd swains in the process of destroying the "primæval majesty" (*PPF*,

3:386). To preserve both competing landscapes and also, perhaps, his political commitment to Jeffersonian theories of agrarian democracy, he imposed the identical pastoral labels on pioneers, farmers, and Indians alike—but the tensions attendant on such arbitrary labelings were never resolved.

At the end of the poem, the best Freneau can do is to invoke the classic pastoral moment, the moment of stasis, committing himself at once to poetry and to fantasy:

Long, long ago with [*Poetry*] *I could have stray'd,*
To woods, to thickets or the mountain shade;
Unfit for cities and the noisy throng,
The drunken revel and the midnight song;

. . . .

Here then shall center ev'ry wish, and all
The tempting beauties of this spacious ball:
No thought ambitious, and no bold design,
But heaven born contemplation shall be mine.
In yonder village shall my fancy stray,
Nor rove beyond the confines of to-day.

[*PPF*, 3:392-93]

In order to achieve this kind of contentment, however, he had both to sacrifice the reality of the untamed American landscape and to ignore the inevitability of historical processes; as a result, the idealized American village becomes insubstantial and unlocated, existing, if at all, in poetic diction and imagination. With the final lines, this too is denied, as the youthful poet, apparently tired of the rather uneventful scene he had created, or perhaps, simply tired of maintaining his impossible dream, seeks other realms and different subjects:

Now cease, O muse, thy tender tale to chaunt,
The smiling village, or the rural haunt;
New scenes invite me, and no more I rove,
To tell of shepherds, or the vernal grove.

[*PPF*, 3:394]

That same year, 1772, also saw the publication of "Discovery," a poem in which Freneau clearly pitted the wild American landscape against its human destroyers. Here, the projective, expansive activities of a mankind "Fond of exerting power untimely shewn," in order "to conquer what remains unknown" (*PPF*, 1:86), results in the rape of a decidedly and alluringly feminine island:

Some gay Ta-ia *on the watery waste,*
Though Nature clothes in all her bright array,

Some proud tormentor steals her charms away:
Howe'er she smiles beneath those milder skies,
Though men decay the monarch never dies!
Howe'er the groves, how'er the gardens bloom,
A monarch and a priest is still their doom!

[*PPF*, 1:88]

The confrontation reveals, in miniature, both the inescapable threat to pastoral possibilities and the resulting quiet despair that echoes throughout so much of the later poetry. Monarch and priest, for Freneau, are repeatedly symbols of the aggressively destructive masculine orientation of history, before which anything suggestively feminine must fall victim. As a virtually archetypal confrontation, it was, he admitted in "Pictures of Columbus," one in which the lady had been doomed from the first.

The various poems that comprise the "Pictures of Columbus" (written and published just two years after "The American Village" and "Discovery"), show us another dreamer who, like the poet, had pursued "Imaginary worlds through boundless seas." When finally given a promise of their substantial reality in the Inchantress's mirror, Columbus sees, before he ever sets out, "Fine islands,"

Cover'd with trees, and beasts, and yellow men;
Eternal summer through the vallies smiles
And fragrant gales o'er golden meadows play!–

[*PPF*,1:96, Picture III, "The Mirror"]

Recapitulating a previous century's experience, Freneau's Columbus moves too quickly from the reactivation of universal, but often suppressed, human longings to a guilt-ridden outcry against the violation he had thereby unwittingly made possible. His arrival "In these green groves . . . / Where guardian nature holds her quiet reign" (*PPF*,1:115-16) results in only a momentary sojourn amid "Sweet sylvan scenes of innocence and ease, . . . / Their works unsullied by the hands of men" (*PPF*, 1:117, Picture XIV, "Columbus at Cat Island"). For almost immediately he is confronted by that from which he had so happily thought himself escaped. At his feet lies the body of a native, murdered by one of his own crew, for the gold trinkets adorning his body. Crying out, "Is this the fruit of my discovery!," the anguished captain predicts all the devastations to follow—

If the first scene is murder, what shall follow
But havock, slaughter, chains and devastation

In every dress and form of cruelty!

[*PPF*, 1:117]

By having his character experience his crewman's crime as a stab at the bounteous landscape itself, Freneau creates a Columbus who, in attempting to flee the sight of "injur'd Nature," prophecies the migrations that were to become the hallmark of American history:

. . . away, away!
And southward, pilots, seek another isle,
Fertile they say, and of immense extent:
There we may fortune find without a crime.

[*PPF*,1:118, Picture XIV]

With fortune from the first confused with pastoral impulses, Freneau seems to be saying here, Columbus's pursuit, like that of later Americans, would never find a resting place.

But, like his protagonist, Freneau himself could never abandon the search nor, once he had found them, the islands that promised pastoral realities. Even during the difficult years of revolution, Freneau described his repeated residences in the West Indies, on Santa Cruz, Jamaica, and Bermuda, as "all too pleasing."[27] Turning from the woman who was then being raped and pillaged by invading British, he sought that tiny landscape in the ocean where "Fair Santa Cruz, arising, laves her waist" (*PPF*, 1:251, st. 8). What he finds so appealing about "The Beauties of Santa Cruz," which he praised in 1776, was obviously its invitation to totally passive, but luxurious, repose.

Sweet orange grove, the fairest of the isle,
In thy soft shade luxuriously reclin'd,
Where, round my fragrant bed, the flowrets smile,
In sweet delusions I deceive my mind.

[*PPF*, 1:249]

The nature of those "sweet delusions" is never made explicit, but one can ascertain from the quality of the descriptions that the poet is thoroughly enjoying a kind of passive and infantile orality, available in a landscape so abundantly generous that it appears to demand no human labor whatever. "Pomegranates . . . / Ready to fall," "the papaw or mamee" (*PPF*, 1:259, st. 53), offer a maternal Eden of exotic nurture:

Those shaddocks juicy shall thy taste delight,
And yon' high fruits, the richest of the wood,
That cling in clusters to the mother tree,

The cocoa-nut; rich, milky, healthful food.

[*PPF*, 1:259, st. 54]

What the feminine embrace also provided, especially in 1776, was a refuge from the world of "tyrants," and political strife; here "bloody plains, and iron glooms," might be forgotten in a "land of love."[28] The appeal, then, goes beyond the merely physical sating of hunger and corresponds to the universal urge to return, tantalizing us with its dim reminders of a totality of gratifications, experienced only once, in the dim past of infancy. Then, only, were we innocent of "Absence and death, and heart-corroding care, / . . . [which] cloud the sun-shine of the mind" (*PPF*, 1:267, st. 98). Sadly, inevitably, of course, that sunshine *is* clouded, and even here, as in childhood, an ugly reality intrudes itself upon the primal harmony: a "slave that slowly bends this way" leaves the poet's "heart distrest" (*PPF*, 1:262, st. 72). And, like Columbus, he too seeks another, still innocent paradise:

Give me some clime, the favorite of the sky,
Where cruel slavery never sought to reign–

[*PPF*, 1:264, st. 79]

But, having written Columbus's story, Freneau knows that no such paradises remain; and so he "shun[s] the theme" (st. 79), and turns instead to scenes of a hurricane's devastation:

These isles, lest Nature should have prov'd too kind,
Or man have sought his happiest heaven below,
Are torn with mighty winds, fierce hurricanes,
Nature convuls'd in every shape of woe.

[*PPF*, 1:264, st. 80]

The suggestion, clearly, is that Nature herself has conspired to defeat the realization of pastoral impulses. But it is a suggestion the poet neither explores nor continues; instead, he turns to his more usual villain, proud princes—in this case, England—and hopes that even if they "o'er the globe . . . extend [their] reign," they spare "one grotto" in Santa Cruz as a haven for the poet:

Here–though thy conquest vex–in spite of pain,
I quaff the enlivening glass, in spite of care.

[*PPF*, 1:266, st. 96]

The end of the poem, apparently encouraging the patriots at home while the speaker remains happily embraced by his island paradise, could appear supercilious or even hypocritical—but only if we ignore the powerfully seductive and embracing qualities attributed to the landscape in the earlier stanzas and fail to acknowledge how their imagery suggests the processes by which the mind reasserts infantile configurations and the claim of infantile gratifications even amid adult experience:

> *Still there* [*i.e., in the colonies*] *remain–thy native air enjoy,*
> *Repell the tyrant who thy peace invades,*
> *While, pleas'd, I trace the vales of Santa Cruz,*
> *And sing with rapture her inspiring shades.*
>
> [*PPF*,1:268, st. 108]

Given the fact that Freneau did return to his native shore and engage actively in the politics of founding the new republic, we must see these lines as an expression of his continuing commitment to pastoral pleasures, a fit habitation for which he was hard-pressed to discover on the mainland. His subsequent incarceration on a British prison-ship, of course, fanned the patriotic fires and, without further delay, Freneau once more actively defended the woman assaulted, "her honours defaced" (*PPF*, 2:134).

By 1782, however, we can see him struggling to maintain his initial revolutionary zeal. Wearied, or even angry, that the "war still rages and the battle burns," he questions the possibility of ever seeing happiness reign. In "A Picture of the Times, With Occasional Reflections," published that year, he admits that "Discord" is no longer specific to European shores; it now "flies" "round the world triumphant" (*PPF*, 2:165). In "every breast" Passion and Reason wage battle. Once, however, he maintains, all men lived harmoniously in an "age of innocence and ease," an innocence made possible by the very primitiveness of its setting. Then, "The hoary sage beneath his sylvan shade" governed, like a good son of Thomas Paine, with the consent of the governed. He "Impos'd no laws but those which reason made; . . . He judg'd his brethren by their own consent; . . . In virtue firm, and obstinately just." But this primitive preagricultural communal pastoral "Of some small tribe" is finally destroyed by Freneau's all-purpose enemy, "Ambition," which, in this poem, takes the particular form of "regal pride" denying "equal right to equal men" (*PPF*, 2:166, 167, 165). More anger is directed at those "servile souls" who "basely own'd a brother for a lord," however, than at the monarchs themselves (*PPF*, 2:165). Nevertheless, the result of breaking up the original fraternal community, for Freneau, is a heritage of "wrath, and blood, and feuds and wars," "And man turned monster to his fellow man" (*PPF*, 2:165). If Freneau's summary history of mankind strikes us as hopelessly naive, it nevertheless points up that communal aspect of golden-age mythology that still held its grip on the American imagination.

At the writing of this poem, however, Freneau saw no such happy possibility around him; instead, after a brief diatribe against George III, "the tyrant," he closes on a note of hopelessness. "Ambition!," both for power and for wealth, everywhere "Tempts the weak mind, and leads the heart astray!" As a result, happiness is relegated to the realm of fond illusion,

. . . still sought but never found,
We, in a circle, chase thy shadow round;
Meant all mankind in different forms to bless,
Which yet possessing, we no more possess:–

[*PPF*, 2:167]

Happiness becomes, in the last lines, a kind of visionary dream, like pastoral itself, the impulse for which, firmly possessed by the mind or imagination, is yet sought vainly in everyday reality:

Thus far remov'd and painted on the eye
Smooth verdant fields seem blended with the sky,
But where they both in fancied contact join
In vain we trace the visionary line;
Still as we chase, the empty circle flies,
Emerge new mountains or new oceans rise.

[*PPF*, 2:167]

What arrests the attention in the final line (if the wording is intentional, that is, and not merely the accident of hurried composition) is the suggestion that the landscape itself presents a physical barrier, separating the poet from "the visionary line." If we see in the blending of "Smooth verdant fields" with sky a visual emblem for the meeting of real and ideal, analogous perhaps to the kinds of happiness the poem had earlier praised, then we see another instance of what pastoral has always been for Freneau—reluctant though he was to admit it; but here the landscape itself hinders access to that union of reality and ideality, much as the Mother must finally reject the erotic claims of a loving son. If such a reading is permitted, then we have one of the few early examples of Freneau's intuition that Nature herself might throw up barriers to men's fondest dreams. It was a proposition he had quickly abandoned in the earlier "Beauties of Santa Cruz," and which, even here, he only vaguely suggests. In later years, of course, he refined it into a philosophical principle. In 1782, however, he contented himself by relegating his visions of happiness and ideal landscapes to the world to come, a stance with its heritage in Christian as well as Stoic writing:

Then seek no more for bliss below,
Where real bliss can ne'er be found,
Aspire where sweeter blossoms blow
And fairer flowers bedeck the ground.

[*PPF*, 2:107]

What these lines "To an Old Man"[29] predicted was the general trend of Freneau's nature poetry after the war. His intense awareness of the transitory, fleeting quality of the world may be seen in this light, then, not only as an aesthetic comment on "The Vanity of Existence,"[30] as one title suggests, but also as a generalized and regretful emotional response to the very real and inescapable destruction of pastoral possibilities that he saw going on all about him.

As though to partially compensate for that loss, Freneau seems to have invented for himself a primitivist *persona*, "The Pilgrim," a lover of wild nature and a biting critic of civilization. In a series of nineteen essays that appeared from 21 November 1781 through 14 August 1782 in the *Freeman's Journal*, Freneau addressed his countrymen through the voice of a man who claimed to live in a forest north of Philadelphia, happily sequestered in a cavern or grotto near a stream, and chary of his solitude; if anyone attempts to find him, he warns, he will leave the country. In the first essay of the series, as Philip Marsh summarizes it, the Pilgrim "describes himself as a lover of all men and animals and an enemy to kings, ambitious men, all war and bloodshed, even the eating of flesh": "I subsist wholly upon roots and vegetables . . . I have not had an hour's sickness these forty years past, am altogether devoid of ambition, and have never experienced the least inclination to shed the blood of any man, or injure him in the slightest degree." He is, in short, a European version of the happy island primitives earlier pictured in "The American Village." But, even as that island was washed away by the sea, so too, this primitive idyll is gradually diluted, until, as Marsh points out, "the pilgrim becomes less a primitivist and more a man-about-town," his subjects turning from the forest to "the manners, morals, and politics of Philadelphia."[31] Clearly, the politics of the new nation now commanded Freneau's attention and, with the 1780's, the promising poet became a full-time essayist.

The events of the years to follow, including the signing of the Treaty of Paris in 1783, his brief appointment as clerk for foreign languages to Jefferson (then secretary of state) from 1791 to 1793, his various editing activities and repeated involvements in political causes, and the War of 1812—all promoted the oscillations of renewed hopes and enthusiasms, followed by the inevitable disillusionments and renunciations, until finally, in 1815, he attempted a kind of tentative truce with his warring impulses. A few poems will suffice to outline the process. With the new nation finally, if precariously, on its feet, he optimistically hailed "the EMIGRATION TO AMERICA and Peopling the Western Country." Published in 1785, the ten short stanzas of the poem by that title easily accept the need "to tame the soil, and plant the arts" amid the "western woods, and lonely plains" (*PPF*, 2:280). Unlike the mood of misgiving that was given expression in the earlier "American Village," here there is only calm acceptance of the alteration of nature for human use and the advent of commerce. "No longer," he declares, "shall [the waters of the Mississippi] useless prove, / Nor idly through the forests rove." Now, at last, they shall be put to use, as "commerce plans new freights for them]." But, recalling his own suspicions of "dread commerce," he immediately qualifies the line by claiming for America the moral protections of "virtue," generosity, and "heaven-born freedom." The new nation, he insists, will be innocent of "the voice of war" and "Europe's all-inspiring pride," a place where "Reason shall new laws devise." How this political and moral paradise is to be maintained he never explains more than to applaud the colonies for having forsaken "kings and regal stage." The only blight on the landscape that he will admit is the African who "still . . . complains, / And mourns his yet unbroken chains." When his contemporary, Crevecoeur, described the caged and dying black in Charlestown, it forced his readers to reassess and finally abandon the paradisal picture that had preceded; for Freneau, however, the slave stands only as an unpleasant fact of present life that, he optimistically assumes, "a future age" will improve. The poem ends, in fact, with his muse predicting for America "happier systems . . . / Than all the eastern sages knew" (*PPF*, 2:281-82).

What remnant of pastoral gratification he is able to protect amid the necessities of political upheaval and economic progress is consigned now to the rural, semicultivated landscape of sparse population, "that Nature for her happiest children made" (*PPF*, 3:46). First published in 1790, "The Bergen Planter" pictures a humble "rustic," happily watching "the seasons come and go, / His autumn's toils returned in summer's crops" (*PPF*, 3:45). Comparing the simplicities of the planter's life to the vanities and indignities of "distant forms and modes," the poem makes an effective political statement for the Jeffersonian agrarian democracy that Freneau had always espoused:

> *In humble hopes his little fields were sown,*
> *A trifle, in your eye—but all his own.*
>
> [*PPF*, 3:46]

Typical of the type is Freneau's address "To Crispin O'Conner, A Back-Woodsman," written two years later. Having left Ireland, "Where mother-country acts the step-dame's part, . . . / Hatch[ing] sad wars to make her brood the thinner," Crispin had sought happier scenes "Far in the west." There, "a paltry spot of land" becomes, through Crispin's unremitting labor, a prosperous garden, until, finally, the proud owner "Bids harvests rise where briars and bushes grew" (*PPF*, 3:74, 75). Both the poet's address to Crispin and "Crispin's Answer," also published in 1792, approve the need for Crispin to alter the wilderness in order to make it bountiful. In fact, claims Crispin, he came not only in search of "Equal Rights" but in search of a place "my axe to ply" (*PPF*, 3:75).

Taken as a group, then, the poems written approximately between 1785 and 1795 reveal a quiet, if growing, discomfort at the consequences of human mastery and cultivation. If, in 1785, he could still look with equanimity at the progress of "Emigration to America and Peopling the Western Country," seeing "Where Nature's wildest genius reigns" the acceptable necessity "To tame the soil, and plant the arts" (*PPF*, 2:280), by 1790, in "LINES, Occasioned by a Law passed by the Corporation of New York, . . . for cutting down the trees in the streets of that City," he bewails the fact that human civilization inevitably destroys the desired union with the land. Written as a "Citizen's Soliloquy," the lines nostalgically regret the abandoned pastoral vision—

> *"Thrice happy age, when all was new,*
> *And trees untouched, unenvied grew,"*
>
> [*PPF*, 3:53]

—and see, in the trees' imminent destruction, a negation of many years' intimacy and friendship:

> *"The fatal Day, dear trees, draws nigh,*
> *When you must, like your betters, die,*
> *Must die!—and every leaf will fade*
> *That many a season lent its shade,*
> *To drive from hence the summer heat,*

And made my porch a favorite seat."

[*PPF*, 3:53]

The loss is at once personal and political, suggesting (if not explicitly) the guilt that was to emerge at the beginning of the next century as so much a part of the American fictional self-image.

"And you, my trees, in all your bloom,
Who never injured small or great,
Be murdered at so short a date!"

[*PPF*, 3:55]

In the course of civilizing the landscape, the poem implies, man makes of it his helpless victim and inevitably betrays an earlier or hoped-for intimacy.

Once more, therefore, he tried to grasp the illusive primitive pastoral, projecting himself, in 1795, into the mind and experiences of "TOMO CHEEKI, the CREEK INDIAN in Philadelphia." Beginning with the 23 May 1795 issue of the *Jersey Chronicle*, Freneau published a series of fourteen essays that purported to be "translations" from a manuscript by Tomo Cheeki, a Creek Indian who had previously visited the city "to settle a treaty of amity," and then departed, leaving in his hotel room "a large bundle of papers." As Philip Marsh points out, the device of the discovered Indian manuscript was not original with Freneau and probably owed its conception to an earlier attempt of Addison's. The use Freneau made of the device, however, is important because it succinctly foreshadows what were to become the major themes of American pastoral fiction. The note of nostalgia for an irrevocably lost pastoral landscape, which was to echo through Cooper, is here in the second number, as the Indian emerges from "many pathless woods" into the city and exclaims, "But what is all this I behold!—how changed is the country of my fathers!" The romantic depictions of a landscape nurturing and protecting human children, with which Cooper was to surround Natty Bumppo and Simms his Revolutionary War partisans, is also here in what Philip Marsh describes as "a fine utopia of Indian natural living": "Wherever we run it is amidst the luxuriant vegetation of Nature, the delectable regale of flowers and blossoms, and beneath trees bending with plump and joyous fruits." Anticipating Natty Bumppo's quarrel with Judge Temple, Tomo Cheeki insists, "in the forests, we acknowledge no distinction of property. The woods are as free as the waters." More interesting still is the anticipation of Faulkner's vision of an earth that abides and takes back its own, despite the human illusion of mastery and possession: in contemplating the many changes of inhabitants the land has already known, the Indian predicts that yet another time will come, after the whites have gone, "when the ancient chaos of woods will in its turn, take [the] place of all this fantastic finery; when the wild genius of the forest will reassume his empire." For Freneau, the Indian *persona* provided a way of expressing what later became the religious and philosophical mediator between the world he had hoped for and the one he knew: "CHANGE," says Tomo Cheeki, "seems to be the system of Nature in this world."[32]

Having imaginatively participated, through the Indian, in the history of the continent itself, then, Freneau was finally able to put aside the conflicting millennial visions of his early poetry and compose, in 1797, still another "millennium," this one giving evidence of a single unifying and pervasive "system" behind all the confusion and "apparent discord" that "still prevails" in both man and nature (*PPF*, 3:176).[33] Possibly following the model of the Indian's perceptions, Freneau now espouses a "system" that, in its wake, effectively dooms the pastoral possibility altogether—

The forest yields to active flame,
The ocean swells with stormy gales.

[*PPF*, 3:176]

And man himself, as part of that same "system," cannot escape its inherent disharmonies:

And do you think that human kind
Can shun the all-pervading law–
That passion's slave we ever find–
Who discord from their nature draw:–
Ere discord can from man depart
He must assume a different heart.

[*PPF*, 3:177]

Nothing that he wrote after this, however, suggests that he saw either a "different heart," or any withdrawal of "passion's" claims upon the human or the natural.

What remained as a real-world fit habitation for his pastoral impulses by the end of the century were, essentially, those same few landscapes—in the South or West Indies—that he had praised twenty years earlier; and to one of these he traveled in 1798, ostensibly to visit relatives, but, perhaps, as his poem commemorating the occasion claimed, also in hopes of finding there "a happier home, / Retirement for the days to come" (*PPF*, 3:200). In recalling his joy "On Arriving in South Carolina, 1798," he sounds once again like the young man who could not bear to leave the seductive embrace of Santa Cruz:

The fairest, loveliest, scenes disclose–
All nature charms us here.

[*PPF*, 3:201]

Its fertile fields boast the traditional southern plenty and temperate climate; and echoing the sentiments of the first English explorers to the region, Freneau declares the land "a paradise restored" (*PPF*, 3:201). Its pastoral implications are made clear by the invocation of the conventional diction, with "rural love . . . bless[ing] the swains," but what strikes him as more attractive still is not the cultivated "paradise," but the "lofty hills" of "sweet nature's wilderness." There, only, the poem suggests, does he feel really secure "from wars and commerce far away." The suggestively erotic waters of undammed rivers roam "the prospect to the western glade," and fructify "the ancient forest, undecay'd." And it is "these the wildest scenes" he claims, which "awed the sight" (*PPF*, 3:201-2). The poem ends with a wish for possession—but precisely which he wished to possess, the cultivated "paradise" or "the wildest scenes . . . / That ever awed the sight," he does not say. Perhaps we are to hear some impossible combination of the two in the acres "where all nature's fancies join":

But, where all nature's fancies join,
Were but a single acre mine,
Blest with the cypress and the pine,
I would request no more;
And leaving all that once could please,
The northern groves and stormy seas–
I would not change such scenes as these
For all that men adore.

[*PPF*, 3:202]

If we want, we can say the poem is hypocritical for refusing to explain what precisely has made "the northern groves" less attractive. His own earlier poetry and essays would suggest that commerce had damaged the possibility of pastoral for him in the fast-growing urban centers of the Northeast, while the South, with its continued agrarian economy, could still claim the mythic and poetic associations of "rural haunts" and "fragrant woods" (*PPF*, 3:200). That this was made possible by an economy dependent on slave labor this poem ignores. As it also ignores the inevitable consequences of the possession he so ardently desires; clearly, increased possession of the land would lead to more cultivation until, finally, the cultivated acres would edge out "sweet nature's wilderness" (*PPF*, 3:202). But Freneau refuses to abandon either landscape or to see beyond his own stubbornly maintained commitment to a pastoral "retirement for the days to come." It was a stubbornness supported perhaps by the vagaries of a life that had led him not to the farm, but to the city. As more than one biographer has noted, Freneau was essentially a wanderer and, unlike Crevecoeur, "he was not even a true farmer, only a resident on a farm."[34]

Still, the kinds of contentment and the life of contemplation that pastoral had always seemed to offer remained, throughout his work, at least an imaginative conception to which he could turn. And, as the poems of his last, active years, collected and published in two tiny volumes in 1815, attest, he had, in fact, turned to the kinds of contemplation he had predicted for himself as early as 1772, in "The American Village." While poems of war, politics, and patriotism dominate the second volume, the first is devoted to questions of belief and faith, with such titles as "On the Uniformity and Perfection of Nature" and "On the Universality and Other Attributes of the God of Nature" indicating the general areas of concern. And here, as Philip M. Marsh has pointed out, was "where the author's real interest lay."[35] What they also reveal, amid the more optimistic Deist sentiments, was a final admission that pastoral impulses could never be realized in the real world, doomed as they were both by the nature of man and by the larger order of things. The War of 1812 had prompted him to complain,

The world has wrangled half an age,
And we again in war engage.

[*PPF*, 3:376]

In "The Brook of the Valley," from which these lines are quoted, he sought some refuge near a "sweet , sequester'd rill [that] / Murmurs through the valley still" (*PPF*, 3:376). But even untamed nature now offers no escape, having become instead an emblem for "the human passions" (*PPF*, 3:377). Like the restless and changing activities of human civilization, so, too, he realizes, the brook is at one time "flowing, peaceful," at another, "angry" or "overflow'd" (*PPF*, 3:376, 377).

Emblem, thou, of restless man;
What a sketch of nature's plan!
Now at peace, and now at war,
Now you murmur, now you roar;

Muddy now, and limpid next,
Now with icy shackles vext–
What a likeness here we find!
What a picture of mankind!

[*PPF*, 3:377]

If the intimate harmony between man and the landscape still evaded him, at least he could contemplate their analogies; to see this as either a reconciliation between his pastoral impulse and the pressures of history or as a repression of that impulse altogether, however, is inadequate. To the last, Freneau struggled to proclaim the pastoral possibility of America, his verses marked, as one contemporary critic noted, "with a certain rusticity" that had long been out of date.[36] His last known poem, a manuscript fragment dated 28 November 1827, still invoked "Nymphs and Swains on Hudson's quiet shore," and asked, "Blest in your *Village*, who would wish for more?" But the absolute-ness of the happiness is subtly qualified by the following suggestion:

Compare your state with thousands of our kind;
How happy are you in the lot you find!–

That Crispin O'Conner or the Bergen planter were called upon to compare their state with the starving poor of Europe made good polemical sense during the years of revolution and early federalist struggles. But why did he feel it necessary to bolster his pastoral assertion with comparisons now, when democracy had apparently triumphed and the republic stood on firm foundations? The first lines of the poem provide a kind of answer: it is a poem of winter, the winter of the year, the winter of an old man's life, the dormancy of dreams.

The sun hangs low!–so much the worse, we say,
For those *whose pleasure is a Summer's day;*
Few are the Joys which stormy Nature yields
From blasting winds and desolated fields;
Their *only pleasure in that season found*
When orchards bloom and flowers bedeck the ground.

"For *those* whose pleasure is a Summer's day" and the feminine ambience of fertile orchards, whose ideal retreat had from the first been "Some gay *Ta-ia* on the watery waste, . . . clothe[d] in all her bright array" (*PPF*, 1:88), the "blasting winds and desolated fields" of a wintery New York landscape could only have proved a disappointment. And so, to make it all just a little less disappointing, he turned to comparisons, a device he had used with great success at an earlier date, and finally broke off the fragment when the task became hopeless:

> *Contrast the Scene with Greenland's wastes of Snow*
> *Where darkness rules and oceans cease to flow.*[37]

Still, for all its limitations, its awkwardnesses, its archaic diction, its proclivities for grandiose, overgeneralized statement, Freneau's poetry exposed that single tension that was to structure so much American literature to follow: the growing disillusionment with the pastoral possibility in conflict with a commitment to maintain that possibility—almost at any cost. And were we to look for a compendium of what constituted the threats to a pastoral America, we would not have to go beyond Freneau; from the first he struggled not only to describe a pastoral landscape appropriate to the New World experience, but, more important still, to delineate what one could or would actually do in the garden. Over and over again, he pitted his own delight in the passivity to be enjoyed within the luxuriously feminine ambiences of tropical islands against the various human urges toward mastery and progress, both political and agricultural, which he saw all around him—conflicts that Simms and Cooper would later convert to the uses of fiction. And finally, if reluctantly, he gave the lie to the myth that mankind had been reborn in the New World paradise; not so, declared Freneau, he had simply brought his European corruptions with him and, slowly but surely, was laying waste the garden.

Freneau, of course, was only the first of many who failed to locate an appropriate and enduring pastoral landscape in the New World; but while later dreamers came up against the brick walls of politics or industrial progress, Freneau, in the eighteenth century, was also forced to joust with language. Like so many of his contemporaries, he wanted to perceive America as the realization of a European pastoral mythology. In trying to visualize an American Auburn, however, he saw that the price of such a pastoral was the destruction of what made "this wide land" so appealing in the first place, "with [its] landscapes, hills and grassy mountains high" (*PPF*, 3:386). He therefore tried to use the diction to describe *both* the primitive and untamed continent *and* the contemporary eagerness to clear the forests and cultivate the soil; but it would not work. The imported Arcadia tended to constrict and stylize the kinds of possibilities that an American landscape might really offer, and, too, an archaic literary convention was simply not adequate to the task of exploring the various, and sometimes conflicting, configurations of filial and erotic responses. What was truly the subject matter of his poetry—the tension between the primitive, passive pastoral and the active, cultivated Arcadia—existed in a psychological landscape he could never quite render.

He did, however, make excellent political and propagandistic use of a diction that, as Harold Toliver points out, had always had a tendency to level "all social elements to an Arcadian democracy and [bring] into question the value of honor and fame when the simple pleasures of shepherdom are so readily available."[38] What strikes us as out of place and even absurd, as when Freneau calls the Indian "The Shepherd of the Forest" or the country inn a rural temple, becomes, in this light, an aesthetic appeal to that quality of fraternal and communal democracy that has always been an element of pastoral, both European and American. The Bergen planter or Crispin O'Conner may indeed have been the political heirs of knights masquerading as shepherd swains, but Freneau's adoption of conventional pastoral vocabulary repeatedly proved inadequate to the complexities of American experience. Struggling to depict some kind of real-world landscape in which to experience the pastoral impulse and thus forge a pastoral "vision" for the new nation, he succeeded only in tracing a "visionary line," flying in "the empty circle" of language that had no clear external reference. Obviously, Freneau had neither the talent nor the insight to forge a new, specifically American pastoral diction and a new, appropriately indigenous, "shepherd swain." That remained a task for the nineteenth century.

The Dubious Pleasures of an American Farmer: Crevecoeur's Letters and Sketches

> *A world primal again, vistas of glory incessant*
> *and branching,*
> *A new race dominating previous ones and grander far,*
> *with new contests,*
> *New politics, new literatures and religions,*
> *new inventions and arts.*
>
> —WALT WHITMAN, *"Starting from Paumanok,"* Leaves of Grass

Born in France and educated for a time in England, Michel-Guillaume St. Jean de Crevecoeur arrived in the New World saturated with the Enlightenment's faith that here, in an uncontaminated environment, Europe might produce the kind of society it had only dreamt of on the old continent. Assigned a cadetship in a French regiment in the St. Lawrence Valley, he arrived in Canada about 1754 and quickly earned his commission as a lieutenant for his abilities as an engineer and cartographer. He enthusiastically mapped the landscape of New France, joined in the assault on Fort Henry, at Lake George, in 1757, and was wounded at the Battle of Quebec in 1759. Resigning his commission, he headed into what were then the English colonies and traveled their extent, earning his way as a salesman and surveyor. In 1765 he took out New York citizenship and adopted the anglicized name, John Hector St. John. Four years later he married the daughter of a wealthy merchant and purchased an estate in Orange County, settling down to become what he later described to the Duke de la Rochefoucauld as only "a simple surveyor of lands, a cultivator of my own grounds, [and] a wanderer through the forests of the country."[40] It was no more self-conscious a pose than was the pride he took in "the sweet and pleasant days" that followed one another at his farm, Pine Hill, or the letters he began composing in the voice of Farmer James—all of it underscoring what Leo Marx has noted as "the literalness of the pastoral ideal in a New World setting." "Here the writer is no mere observor or dreamer; he *is* the American husbandman."[41]

Joining himself both literally and literarily to that "new race of men"[42] who, by cultivating the new American landscape, had "in some measure regained the ancient dignity of our species" (*LAF*, I, 12), Crevecoeur watched his family grow and prosper on the fertile acreage of Pine Hill and attempted to give his pastoral experiences conscious and coherent form through the voice of Farmer James. The framework for the narrative is set up in Letter I, as Farmer James, with his wife and a neighbor, contemplate corresponding with "Mr. F. B.," a cultured and much-traveled European who has lately visited and requested such a correspondence. Disclaiming any pretense to superior education or culture, Farmer James admits that he could "describe our American modes of farming, our manners, and peculiar customs, with some degree of propriety, because I have ever attentively studied them," but cautions, "my knowledge extends no farther" (*LAF*, 7-8). (Although this assertion is belied by subsequent allusions to classical learning and sophisticated rhetorical circumlocutions, the initial pose of having only limited learning is retained by the speaker.)

Insisting that he will write about "nothing . . . but what lies within the reach of my experience and knowledge" (*LAF*, I, 9), James proceeds to forge a new language for the new and different American pastoral vision. "In the *Letters from an American Farmer*," as Leo Marx points out, "there is no mention of Arcadia, no good shepherd, no stock of poeticisms derived from Virgil. . . . Instead of Arcadia, we have the wild yet potentially bucolic terrain of the North American continent; instead of the shepherd, the independent, democratic husbandman with his plausible 'rural scheme'; instead of the language of a decadent pastoral poetry, the exuberant idiom, verging toward the colloquial, of the farmer."[43] But most important, and what Marx has failed to note, is that James also explores the central metaphor of American pastoral experience, the metaphor of the land as woman. The landscape experienced as feminine allowed, indeed invited, the newly arrived immigrant to feel himself reborn, transformed into something that had never been possible in the bosom of a cruel "step-dame." "Here," James insists, "individuals of all nations are melted into a new race of men" (*LAF*, III, 43). In Letter III alone, which attempts to answer F. B.'s query, "What is an American?," the word "new" appears seventeen times, often, as Russel Nye points out, "in company with such words as 'metamorphosis,' 'regeneration,' and 'resurrection.'" He further notes: "The change from European to American, as Crevecoeur describes it, rests on . . . the opportunity to begin again."[44]

It is an opportunity made possible by intimacy with the soil, a fact underscored by James's comparison of "the poor of Europe" to "so many useless plants, wanting vegetative mould and refreshing showers. . . . They withered, and were mowed down by want, hunger and war; but now, by the power of transplantation, like all other plants they have taken root and flourished!" (*LAF*, III, 41–42). This same health-giving, nurturing quality is also invoked quite literally, as Farmer James boasts of placing "my little boy on a chair which screws to the beam of a plough—its motion and that of the horses please him, he is perfectly happy and begins to chat. . . . the odoriferous furrow exhilarates his spirits, and seems to do the child a great deal of good, for he looks more blooming since I have adopted that practice" (*LAF*, II, 25).

Psychologically, the image of return and rebirth in a place where "every thing is prosperous and flourishing" (*LAF*, I, 12) promised not only renewed harmony between man and nature, but also between man and man. A kind of primal fraternity might be reconstituted then, predicated on a continually generous and giving maternal ambience that obviated the necessity for competition. If only the new emigrant "behaves with propriety, and is faithful, he is caressed, and becomes as it were a member of the family" (*LAF*, III, 59). Translated into political terms, this hailed a reign of peaceful and prosperous fraternity, the power lusts and aggressions of a decaying Europe no longer necessary nor possible. "I envy no man's prosperity" (*LAF*, II, 38), boasts Farmer James. As far as he is concerned, the continent is "boundless," promising "fields of future cultivation" for all those willing to claim them (*LAF*, I, 12). That the future does, indeed, hold the promise of a communal fraternal pastoral is assured, for Farmer James at least, by the precedent of the past: "This formerly rude soil has been converted by my father into a pleasant farm, and in return it has established all our rights; on it is founded our rank, our freedom, our power as citizens, our importance as inhabitants of such a district. These images I must confess I always behold with pleasure, and extend them as far as my imagination can reach: for this is what may be called the true and the only philosophy of an American farmer" (*LAF*, II, 25). The appeal of such images, of course, contributed a great deal to the development of agrarian democratic theories during the War for Independence and remained, for Crevecoeur, an appeal he could never quite dismiss—even after the harsh realities of history had burned and sacked his beloved Pine Hill and driven his *persona*, Farmer James, "far . . . from the accursed neighborhood of Europeans" and into "the bosom of the woods" (*LAF*, XII, 211, 223).

Probably as late as 1778, in his sketch of "The American Belisarius," Crevecoeur was still depicting the kind of fraternal agrarian community that always remained, for him, "truly pleasing, [and] pastoral" (*SEA*, 231-32).[45] One of several family histories that make up *The Sketches of Eighteenth-Century America*, this one tells the story of S. K., "the son of a Dutch father and of an English mother" who "quitted the paternal estate he enjoyed, and prepared to begin the world anew in the bosom of this huge wilderness" (*SEA*, 230). "Struck with the singular beauty and luxuriance of one" particular piece of land, he settles there, and so cultivates it that, "in a few years this part of the wilderness assumed a new face and wore a smiling aspect" (*SEA*, 230-31). He then purchases "two valuable pieces of land," adjacent to his own, and invites "his two brothers-in-law to remove there; generously making them an offer of the land, of his teams, and every other necessary assistance." The result is an idealized social community, at once harmonious and noncompetitive; once having purchased and removed to "this sequestered situation," the brothers-in-law "became to S. K. two valuable neighbours and friends. Their prosperity, which was his work, raised no jealousy in him" (*SEA*, 231). Implicitly, the success of the venture is tied to Crevecoeur's exploration of the image of a landscape totally feminine, gratifying both in its maternal and in its virginal aspects: for, if the experience of beginning "anew in the bosom of this huge wilderness" (*SEA*, 230) makes the primal fraternal harmony once again possible, the economic success of cultivation is similarly dependent on a very literal understanding of the title "husbandman." "They all grew rich very fast," Crevecoeur tells us, because "the virgin earth abundantly repaid them for their labours and advances" (*SEA*, 231). It is the same title, with all its positive implications, which Farmer James cherishes, using it interchangeably with "farmer" and "cultivator." To be called one of these, he declares, is to carry "an appellation which will be the most fortune one a man of my class can possess, so long as our civil government continues to shed blessings on our husbandry" (*LAF*, II, 38).

That this will not prove the case is, of course, the subject of the final letter in the series. The tendency of a number of critics to ignore the tensions and warning signals that disrupt the otherwise idyllic early narratives, however, leads them to read the final letters as sudden and angry responses to the Revolution, rather than as inevitable consequences of problems that had been given expression with Letter II. For what Farmer James is describing is no version of Edward Hicks's "Peaceable Kingdom"; here the lion does not lie down with the lamb.[46] On the contrary, James declares himself "astonished to see that nothing exists but what has its enemy, one species pursue and live upon the other" (*LAF*, II, 26). And possibly the most vicious pursuers, because their acts are wanton and unnecessary, are his own neighbors. Anticipating Cooper's description of the pigeons shot in flocks and Natty's angry outburst in *The Pioneers*—"This comes of settling a country! . . . here have I known the pigeons to fly for forty long years, and, till you made your clearings, there was nobody to skear or to hurt them"—Farmer James expresses real dismay at "the singular barbarity of man . . . so strongly delineated . . . in the catching and murthering" of quail during the harsh winter months. Only one man, it seems, "one of the most famous and extraordinary farmers that has ever done honour to the province of Connecticut," has assisted the birds and "saved this species from being entirely destroyed." For the rest, "they perished all over the country, none of their delightful whistlings were heard the next spring, but upon this gentleman's farm; and to his humanity we owe the continuation of their music" (*LAF*, II, 28). Nevertheless, the tone of the first eight letters is determinedly optimistic, and to this the critics have responded, hearing, through Farmer James's voice, Crevecoeur's own ardent desire to experience himself as one of the "new race of men," helping to create "the most perfect society now existing in the world" (*LAF*, III, 43, 41).

What disrupts the vision, as early as Letter III, is Crevecoeur's unhappy discovery of quite another type of son clambering for a place at the maternal board. Beyond the seacoast and urban societies of fishermen and merchants, whom James contentedly acknowledges as necessary to his "people of cultivators" (*LAF*, III, 40), and beyond the rural settlements of the "independent freeholders" such as James himself, are the ever-increasing frontier areas, inhabited by the "back settlers," "near the great woods, near the last inhabited districts," living in "discord, want of unity and friendship" (*LAF*, III, 45-46). That third and most quoted letter, which attempts in its rambling way to tell F. B. just "what is an American," finally acknowledges that that same landscape that offers a "plenty of provisions" (*LAF*, III, 58), and whose "simple cultivation" apparently "purifies" the husbandman (*LAF*, III, 45), may also, as the 1630 "Planters Plea" had insisted, prove "the nurse of pride, wantonnesse, and contention."[47] For these backwoods settlers, too, have undergone a kind of rebirth process, their "new mode of life bring[ing] along with it a new set of manners," but the process here has resulted only in "a strange sort of lawless profligacy" (*LAF*, III, 52). According to Farmer James, it seems to result both from "the proximity of the woods" and from their tendency to trust a little too much in "the natural fecundity of the earth." "In a little time their success in the woods makes them neglect their tillage," and, as James explains it, "in order therefore to make up the deficiency, they go oftener to the woods." The result is not only the breakdown of family relations, "their wives and children liv[ing] in sloth and inactivity," but also, the denial of the communal and fraternal pastoral community itself: "The chase renders them ferocious, gloomy, and unsociable; a hunter wants no neighbour, he rather hates them, because he dreads the competition" (*LAF*, III, 51–52).

What Farmer James has explicated here is the other side of his controlling image: the total female matrix of attraction and satisfaction offers not only protection and nurture, but also arouses sexuality and the desire for exclusive possession. Moreover, the urge to return in order to begin again carries with it the danger of too complete a regression, here resulting in "a mongrel breed, half civilized, half savage" (*LAF*, III, 52). The words Crevecoeur chooses for James's conclusion on the subject are, psychologically, very revealing: "Thus our bad people are those who are half cultivators and half hunters; and the worst of them are those who have degenerated altogether into the hunting state" (*LAF*, III, 53). Of course, Crevecoeur could have no way of knowing that it was precisely such a figure, stylized in the figure of Natty Bumppo, who would come closest, at least in fiction, to living out the pastoral impulse. For Crevecoeur, child of the Enlightenment as he was, the isolated hunter, living wholly satisfied and without toil in the heart of the forest, threatened the human community and civilization itself: "If manners are not refined, at least they are rendered simple and inoffensive by tilling the earth; all our wants are supplied by it, our time is divided between labour and rest, and leaves none for the commission of great misdeeds. As hunters it is divided between the toil of the chase, the idleness of repose, or the indulgence of inebriation. Hunting is but a licentious idle life" (*LAF*, III, 53).

What appears so dangerous, then, in "the unlimited freedom of the woods" (*LAF*, III, 52), is the potential for losing that which sets men apart, self-conscious and civilized, from the mindless cycles of nature. The embrace may turn to engulfment, as Beverley and Byrd had so bitterly deplored in the warm and fertile South. Significantly, Crevecoeur, too, particularly singles out "the back-settlers of both the Carolinas, [and] Virginia" as having "been long a set of lawless people" (*LAF*, III, 54). His confident assumption that "time will efface those stains: in proportion as the great body of population approaches them they will reform, and become polished and subordinate" (*LAF*, III, 54-55) was to prove true, in part; but, as William Gilmore Simms's novels were to reveal, the price paid for maintaining the southern pastoral was a heavy one. Crevecoeur himself recoiled at part of the price in Letter IX—but that is to get ahead of ourselves.

Letter III also anticipates Cooper's treatment of the Bush family in *The Prairie* by noting, somewhat ironically, "thus are our first trees felled, in general, by the most vicious of our people" (*LAF*, III,

55). The guilt of the initial assault is thus foisted upon those who, in fact, make possible "the arrival of a second and better class, the true American freeholders" (*LAF*, III, 55), a "more industrious people, who will finish their improvements, convert the loghouse into a convenient habitation, and . . . change in a few years that hitherto barbarous country into a fine fertile, well-regulated district" (*LAF*, III, 47). In effect, the entire process of creating a pastoral reality in America seems threatened from the outset; the cultivators "who inhabit the middle settlements, by far the most numerous" and, according to James, the most praiseworthy Americans, exist only as the end of a process that begins with foresters, hunters, traders, and that whole class of frontier society he accuses of "shocking violations" (*LAF*, III, 45, 55). At this point, the dream rests on very shaky foundations indeed.

And it does not last much longer. After Letters VI, VII, and VIII, which detail life and manners in the fishing communities off Nantucket and nearby Martha's Vineyard, the locale shifts to Charles-Town, where the opening description of a luxurious, self-indulgent, litigious and commercialized society immediately leads to "Thoughts on Slavery" and, thence, to a consideration of the evil, tyrannical and power-hungry aspects of human society. Something about the physical environment itself seems to have led to "excesses of all kinds" (*LAF*, IX, 159). "The rays of their sun seem to urge them irresistibly to dissipation and pleasure," while, the narrator notes with dismay, "the poison of slavery, the fury of despotism, and the rage of superstition" all continue, "even under those mild climates which seem to breathe peace and happiness" (*LAF*, IX, 159, 170). "There human nature appears more debased," he concludes, "than in the less favoured climates" (*LAF*, IX, 170). If Freneau could ignore the "slave that slowly bends this way" and continue happily painting "with rapture" "the vales of SANTA CRUZ," Crevecoeur can not. The "melancholy scene" of what he himself subtitles the "Horrid Treatment of a Negro Slave" abruptly cuts short the ninth letter, as the narrator encounters a man caged and suspended from a tree, left to die of thirst and hunger while "large birds of prey" and "swarms of insects" hover about, "eager to feed on his mangled flesh and to drink his blood" (*LAF*, IX, 171, 172). The explanation given—"I heard that the reason for this slave being thus punished, was on account of his having killed the overseer of the plantation. They told me that the laws of self-preservation rendered such executions necessary" (*LAF*, IX, 173)—rings hollow, in no way justifying the enormity of the horror; the narrator's closing phrases are skeptical in the extreme. Nothing now could ameliorate the guilt of those who, in abusing their fellow man, defeat the generosity "of an indulgent nature, a kind parent, who for the benefit of mankind has taken singular pains to vary the genera of plants, fruits, grain, and the different productions of the earth; and has spread peculiar blessings in each climate" (*LAF*, IX, 168).

From this point on, then, any possibility of realizing a lasting communal pastoral in America is denied completely, and Letters X through XII must be understood as completing the disintegration dimly foretold in Letter II. Critics who claim that Letters X and XI "bear little relation to . . . major themes,"[48] ignore the fact that, taken as a whole, all twelve letters dramatically duplicate the process of pastoral itself: the dream about to be fulfilled, the momentary grasping of its reality, and its inevitable disruption and destruction. Letter X, "On Snakes; and on the Humming Bird," details the "dreadful" sufferings of men bitten by copperheads and rattlesnakes, a squirrel devoured by the black snake, and ends with a mortal battle between a black snake and a water snake, the two "biting each other with utmost rage; . . . their bodies . . . entwined, . . . convulsed with strong undulations" (*LAF*, X, 174–75, 177–78, 180–81); the emphasis on snakes is hardly coincidental. The pastoral garden has indeed been invaded, not merely by men, but by elements that are part of nature itself. Retrospectively, the kingbirds that had been wantonly slaughtered by humans, in Letter II, evoke less of our sympathy now when we read about hummingbirds that "will tear and lacerate flowers into a hundred pieces" and fight among themselves "until one of the combatants falls a sacrifice and, dies" (*LAF*, X, 179).

With this preceding it, the interpolated letter from the Russian visitor strikes us at once hopelessly naive and yet, wholly understandable. What the visitor thinks he perceives, during the course of his stay with "Mr. John Bertram, the celebrated Pennsylvania botanist" (*LAF*, XI, 182), is that same vision of pastoral harmony and noncompetitive social community that Farmer James had himself earlier invoked as the imminent, if not yet actualized, reality of America. And the Russian, too, concludes that " 'tyranny never can take a strong hold in this country, the land is too widely distributed: it is poverty in Europe that makes slaves' " (*LAF*, XI, 190). The visit to the Quaker meetinghouse, which concludes the letter, similarly tantalizes with its golden age allusions to "the fraternity" of the group, and its vocabulary suggestive of the peaceable kingdom (*LAF*, XI, 196-97).

By following immediately upon the Russian's " 'two months among these good people,' " which he has claimed as "the golden days of my riper years" (*LAF*, XI, 196-97), the opening words of Letter XII wrench at the reader's heart with all the anguished force of disillusionment and dashed dreams: "the hour is come at last that I must fly from my house and abandon my farm!" (*LAF*, XII, 198). The same Revolution that had forced Crevecoeur himself into temporary exile, now forces Farmer James into choosing between two mutually opposed but compelling 'familial' obligations. Asserting again the need to "belong to some community bound by some ties" (*LAF*, XII, 199), James finds it impossible to choose between Mother England and the newly constituted American family. "If I attach myself to the Mother Country, which is 3000 miles from me, I become what is called an enemy to my own region" (*LAF*, XII, 202), he explains; and he could never arm himself "against that country where I first drew breath, against the playmates of my youth, my bosom friends, my acquaintance" (*LAF*, XII, 202, 203). As with Freneau's immigrant rustics, Crevecoeur also has James experience England as a cruel and unloving mother, responsible for sowing discord among her American children: "Alas, she herself, that once indulgent parent, forces me to take up arms against her. She herself, first inspired the most unhappy citizens of our remote districts, with the thoughts of shedding the blood of those whom they used to call by the name of friends and brethren" (*LAF*, XII, 209). For James, then, the true horror of the war lies in the spectre of familial dissolution, and George III, renowned for having "the most numerous, as well as the fairest, progeny of children, of any potentate now in the world," is unfathomable to him because he does not "put a stop to that long destruction of parents and children" (*LAF*, XII, 206). Finally, of course, the war threatens not only James's immediate family, but more broadly, the validity of his most cherished image; a fraternal pastoral community no longer appears to identify his American "brethren."

But if the snake has invaded the garden, it has not defeated the impulse to experience the garden. Determined still "to keep ourselves busy in tilling the earth" (*LAF*, XII, 222), James removes his family "far . . . from the accursed neighbourhood of Europeans" and "into a state approaching nearer to that of nature" (*LAF*, XII, 211), seeking security among those who "are her immediate children" (*LAF*, XII,

216), the Indians: "They know nothing of the nature of our disputes, they have no ideas of such revolutions as this; a civil division of a village or tribe, are events which have never been recorded in their traditions" (*LAF*, XII, 219). The fact that James's perception is not entirely accurate (the Indian nations had long been engaged in internecine warfare) does not diminish the faith with which he trusts that "my wife, my children, and myself may be adopted soon after our arrival" (*LAF*, XII, 221) into "the bosom of that peace" (*LAF*, XII, 229) that the Indian village now represents to him. That the Indians have achieved "so many necessary qualifications for happiness" he attributes to the fact that they "most certainly are much more closely connected with nature than we are; . . . the inhabitants of the woods are her undefiled offspring" (*LAF*, XII, 216).

The fear he had expressed, in Letter III, of the wild and uncultivated landscape, he now counters by his determination to keep himself and his children employed "in the labour of the fields, as much as I can; I am even resolved to make their daily subsistence depend altogether on it." This, he assures his correspondent, will prevent "any of us becoming wild; it is the chase and the food it procures, that have this strange effect" (*LAF*, XII, 221-22). What he is trying to sustain, obviously, is the integrity of the human social community—nurtured by the landscape, but not, like the backwoodsmen or the indolent southerners, so totally dependent upon it as to become regressively "mongrel" or infantile, engulfed by its plenitude. "This removal from a cultivated country, into the bosom of the woods" (*LAF*, XII, 223), will not threaten engulfment because James intends to take his cultivation with him. For the moment, the more threatening implications of the pastoral image appear under control. The Mother, after all, must be impregnated in order to be bountiful. And insofar as the husbandman aids, but does not force, her willing bounty, he at once maintains his separate masculine and consciously human identity while reaping the benefits of an acceptable and guiltless intimacy. The movement onto the frontier, in this case, then, has been a desperate attempt both to preserve the real-world possibility of pastoral and to maintain some balance between the attractive and frightening implications of that impulse. Farmer James's closing prayer, therefore, attempts to see as compatible the conflicting claims of a paternal deity, who encourages the activities of civilization, and a receptive maternal ambience, which offers nurture in exchange for passivity: ". . . and if the *labour*, the *industry*, the frugality, the union of man, can be an agreeable offering to him, we shall not fail to receive his paternal blessings. There I shall *contemplate* nature in her most wild and ample extent" (*LAF*, XII, 229 [italics mine]).

Crevecoeur's hurried sale of the *Letters* to a London publisher in 1780 does, in a sense, establish the essential unity of author and *persona*: both had fled their farms in the wake of the Revolution. Like James, Crevecoeur could not take sides during the conflict and, as a result, he was forced to leave farm and family behind him and remove to Europe. The *Letters* were finally brought out in 1782, by which time Crevecoeur had made his way back to France. They made of him a minor celebrity on the continent,[49] where he remained, until the French government sent him to New York, in 1783, to act as consul general to the new republic. There he found his farm destroyed, his wife dead and his children in the care of a stranger; and, although Jefferson's secretary praised his diplomatic abilities, Crevecoeur himself confided to La Rochefoucauld, "If I had but 200 pounds income, I would return to cultivating my land and my friends, and he who wanted it could become the consul."[50] His heart was still with Farmer James, and, in fact, he brought out an expanded version of the *Letters*, in French, in 1787. (A previous translation had appeared in 1784.) Still, much of the original manuscript remained unpublished, until, that is, the materials were collected in a full American edition and published in 1925, under the title, *Sketches of Eighteenth-Century America*.

One of these *Sketches*, "The History of Mrs. B.," recapitulates and summarizes the movement that had been so haltingly worked out, letter by letter, in the first volume. Initially, Mrs. B. related her family's removal to the Wyoming Valley in northwestern Pennsylvania, a place "so long talked of, and so long promised, on which we were sure to meet plenty, ease, and happiness." There, she and her family reveled in those "extensive plats of admirable grounds . . . [that] seemed to be the seat of fertility" (*SEA*, 208); but human strife, the wrangling of neighbors, litigation over land claims and, finally, war, all upset the pastoral possibility "along these delightful banks" (*SEA*, 209). Attempting to escape the evils of human contention or, as she herself phrases it, because "we loved peace and [owing] to the strong desire of acquiring it, we resolved to remove . . . sixty miles up the river; to abandon the labour of three years and to submit ourselves once more to the toils of first settlement." Here, she says, "we thought ourselves far happier" (*SEA*, 211). "We found the inhabitants satisfied with their lands, with their lots. They spent their time in useful labours and sought to disturb nobody. . . . Here we soon lived in affluence. The beautiful grass of this country, the uninterrupted repose we enjoyed made us soon forget our pristine calamities" (*SEA*, 211-12).

The communal pastoral seems once again restored as she declares the place "a little paradise," where "not a wrangle or dispute ever tarnished our tranquillity in the space of three years or more" (*SEA*, 212). But that is the sum total of its life span. "The great national dispute caused great divisions in the opinions of the people," and soon the communal family, as well as her immediate family, are torn apart by "the cruel necessities of the times" (*SEA*, 212, 214). As with the narrator of Letter XII, the idyll has been interrupted—in this case irrevocably: "We bade, without knowing it, an eternal adieu to our house; to those fertile fields which were ploughed with so much ease, and which yielded us such plentiful crops. Thus by the fatality of the times were cut off the reasonable hopes we had conceived of living tolerably easy in our old age and providing amply for each of our children" (*SEA*, 214). For Mrs. B., as this sketch ends, there is no hope of return.

The travel narratives that he composed in old age offer no more optimistic a picture either, really, and, in fact, emphasize Crevecoeur's growing ambivalence at the prospect of continued and unlimited cultivation.[51] Creeping into their paragraphs, even when he is not apparently trying to make such a statement, is the bitter awareness that the same "brotherly harmony" that converts "the most dismal forests, [and] the driest deserts" into areas "covered with flowers, with fruits, with harvests," is also guilty of "the distressing habit of looking at the trees only as enemies, as 'intruders' who occupy the soil one needs" (*ET*, 42, 43). Looking ahead to Judge Temple in Cooper's *The Pioneers* (1823), one of the characters in *Voyages in Upper Pennsylvania and New York State* (1801) predicts that "the second generation will regret bitterly that the first destroyed so many trees" (*ET*, 43). And, although he admits the necessity, "even more than one thinks, . . . to strip from the surface of the soil those giants at the foot of which man seems so weak, to clear the land and burn everything that encumbers it, to dry up the swamps, to plant and enclose fruit trees, to open up roads, to build houses and barns," he is also aware of "feelings of disgust" at such massive alterations (*ET*, 42-43). Even worse, he notes, the commitment to cultivation often prevents the farmer from properly "venerating these gigantic pines, which no amount of human skill and cultivation can ever replace" (*ET*, 43).

Finally, what characterizes Crevecoeur's writings is not "the anomaly" of "a curious inconsistency of beginning in hope, ending in equivocation," as Russel Nye suggests,[52] but the purposeful and steady creation of an attitude and vocabulary of ambivalence, inevitably engendered by the terrible contradictions he had exposed. The optimism of Farmer James's early vision of a fraternal pastoral America was, ironically, based on "the bright idea of property, of exclusive right, of independence." Freneau has James ask himself, "Precious soil, I say to myself, by what singular custom of law is it that thou wast made to constitute the riches of the freeholder? What should we American farmers be without the distinct possession of that soil?" (*LAF*, II, 24). Unhindered possession, of course, appeared possible because the eighteenth century could still believe that "many ages will not see the shores of our great lakes replenished with inland nations, nor the unknown bounds of North America entirely peopled" (*LAF*, III, 41). And yet what that "distinct possession" also conferred—and foretold—was the right to master and alter "this mighty continent" (*LAF*, III, 41) and, finally, the encouragement to seek ever more exclusive rights to its possession. Even "the American Belisarius" suffers the pain of having neighbors and brothers-in-law turn against him, contriving "the means of S. K.'s destruction, which was to ensure them the possession of his fine estate" (*SEA*, 237). Moreover, that "great lap of fecundity" (*SEA*, 87), which had made possession so attractive in the first place, also nurtured the archetypal and asocial "only sons" of the wild frontiers and the indolent indulgences of "a people enjoying all that life affords . . . without labour, without fatigue, hardly subjected to the trouble of wishing" (*LAF*, IX, 160-61), while the evils of slavery flourished in the "favoured climates" (*LAF*, IX, 170) of the South.

Unwittingly perhaps, Crevecoeur had, through his various contradictions and ambivalences, exposed the more perilous sides of the pastoral impulse. Southern gentry and "mongrel" frontiersman alike demonstrated its dangerously regressive tendencies, while the desire for increased mastery and control of the "precious soil' resulted only in greedy wranglings over possession. Once the "broad lap of our great *Alma Mater*" becomes an object of possession, Crevecoeur warns, the desired return becomes exploitive, and intimacy turns quickly to violation. But what now, with hindsight, appear to us as mutually exclusive attitudes—the rights of personal possession and the dream of communal brotherhood—are never explicitly recognized as such by Crevecoeur; rather, they stand side by side, in unresolved and unstated tension, the author unwilling to abandon either, and repeatedly asserting the simultaneous possibility of both. Like Jefferson and Freneau, Crevecoeur also gave only grudging acceptance to commerce and manufacture, declaring to the last, "we are a people of cultivators" (*LAF*, III, 40). On this, his increasingly fragile dream of a pastoral reality in America depended, and it was on the reassertion of that dream that he chose to end his *Letters from an American Farmer*. If the literal intimacy of husbandman and soil had been interrupted in the cultivated landscape, Farmer James would seek it once again in the woods, fully "intend[ing] my children . . . for the cultivation of the land" (*LAF*, XII, 228). The "perfect harmony" he seeks may then be realized when *they* have become "expert scholars in husbandry" (*LAF*, XII, 229, 228).

By ending the *Letters* this way, Crevecoeur charted what was to become the central, mythic movement of American history and literature; when the first paradise is stained with blood, one brother asserting his power over another, the American response is to move ever westward, constantly pursuing realms where

. . . God and nature reign;
Their works unsullied by the hands of men.—

The distressed frontiersman's closing plea that "we may be restored to our ancient tranquillity" (*LAF*, XII, 231) confirms the desperate illusion behind Columbus's hope of finding "another isle . . . [where] we may fortune find without a crime." Sharing with Freneau both the attitude of ambivalence that was to characterize most nineteenth-century writing about the landscape and the stylized sequences of recurrent movements westward once the initial idyll had been disrupted, Crevecoeur went beyond his contemporary in removing the extraneous trappings of an archaic diction. In so doing, he exposed once and for all the central metaphor of American pastoral and allowed the archetypal longing for a place where "nature opens her broad lap to receive the . . . new comers" (*LAF*, I, 11) to inform and structure Farmer James's narrative. That the longing would not be fulfilled, grasped—if at all—during a moment of stasis, a moment between initial settlement and ensuing destruction, Crevecoeur also understood. For Mrs. B., it was a three years' idyll in the Wyoming Valley; for Farmer James, a succession of paragraphs in some letters to Europe.

Laying Waste Her Fields of Plenty

Transitions

> *The Kaatsberg, or Catskill Mountains, . . . were ruled by an old squaw spirit, said to be their mother. She dwelt on the highest peak of the Catskills, and had charge of the doors of day and night.*
>
> —WASHINGTON IRVING, *"Rip Van Winkle"*

In spite of occasional doubts and warnings, most American theorists at the turn of the century remained committed to the politics of Jeffersonian democracy and assumed "that in an ideal state everyone had some right to the soil."[53] The opening of new territories seemed only to confirm the optimism with which Crevecoeur's Farmer James had initially looked "forward to the anticipated fields of future cultivation and improvement, to the future extent of those generations which are to replenish and embellish this boundless continent" (*LAF*, I, 12). Consequently, it was not long before the pastoral impulse found itself dangerously confused with the myth of progress.

But then the ideal of contentment never was the sole defining characteristic of American pastoral, as Hallett Smith has persuasively argued it was for Elizabethan England.[54] Implicit in the metaphor of the land-as-woman was both the regressive pull of maternal containment *and* the seductive invitation to sexual assertion: if the Mother demands passivity, and threatens regression, the Virgin apparently invites sexual assertion and awaits impregnation. Hence the conflicting colonial responses of Thomas Morton and John Hammond, the one urging his fellow New Englanders to impregnate the "faire virgin" in order to master and make use of her potentially "fruitfull wombe," the other horrified at the spectre of incestuous violation with which Mary-land had "been deflowred by her own Inhabitants, stript, shorne and made deformed."[55] To his credit, and in spite "of her unnatural disturbances," Hammond vowed "never [to] totally forsake or be beaten off from her," predicting the tenacity with which later settlers would "cross the prairies as of old / The pilgrims crossed the sea," certain that "the blessing of our Mother-land / Is on us as we go." At the opening of each new territory, in fact, the maternal and the sexual were invoked together; in Wisconsin it was said, "the land foams with creamy milk, and the hollow trees trickle with wild honey."[56] It is therefore imperative that we recognize at least some part of our urge to progress, and our historical commitment to conquer, master, and alter the continent as another side of the pastoral impulse. What is so disturbing about that admission, obviously, is the unavoidable confusion it suggests; for, both as Mother and as Virgin, the continent seeks to embrace. To finding an effective response to the power of that invitation, with all its awkward psychological implications, the nineteenth century dedicated not only its artistic energies, but, in the South, its political energies as well.

Properly, the story begins not with the turn of the century, when Charles Brockden Brown bade his characters desert the American garden altogether, in *Wieland*,[57] but in 1819, with the publication of *The Sketch Book*. What Washington Irving succeeded in creating, when he imported "Rip Van Winkle" and "The Legend of Sleepy Hollow" to American shores, was the first coherent fictional outline by which almost all American pastoral literature to follow would be shaped. In escaping the traumas of history and progress, Rip Van Winkle and Brom Bones demonstrated the alternative commitment to a psychological adolescence through which, only, the ambience of the Mother might be maintained. While Rip capitulated wholly to a sleep-inducing, unconscious containment, avoiding thereby both the personal and political responsibilities of adulthood, Brom Bones protected an entire community's pastoral drowsiness by banishing from it the emblem of intellective development and greed that, in combination, must necessarily awaken any Sleepy Hollow.

The endless appeal of Rip resides in his mythic quality as *puer aeternas*, a comic innocent who manages to escape the rest of America's growing pains by sleeping for twenty years in a womb-like "hollow, like a small amphitheatre." The postscript to the tale gives away the pastoral yearning behind its composition by identifying the "Catskill Mountains" as a "region full of fable," reputed by the Indians to be "ruled over by an old squaw spirit, said to be their mother."

In "The Legend of Sleepy Hollow," Ichabod Crane becomes an emblem for everything that threatens to violate the pastoral stasis. Characterized as "a native of Connecticutt, a state which supplies the Union with pioneers for the mind as well as for the forest, and sends forth yearly legions of frontier woodsmen and country schoolmasters," he threatens to intrude conscious thought and the feeble beginnings of art and learning into the drowsing unconsciousness of maternal containment; as a potential "frontier woodsman," dreaming of taking wife and possessions off to "Kentucky, Tennessee, or the Lord knows where," he numbers among those who first clear the forests and submit the virgin landscape to the mastery of men; as "the genius of famine," he threatens to devour what had been so freely offered by this "lap of land," "embosomed in the great State of New York." What "his devouring mind's eye" threatens, in short, is the introduction of the conscious activities of intellective assertion into a drowsing pastoral paradise, whose "dominant spirit . . . is the apparition of a figure on horseback without a head." Katrina, the object of Ichabod's somewhat ambiguous cravings, is merely the human symbol of the opulent abundance to which she is heir: "plump as a partridge; ripe and melting and rosy cheeked as one of her father's peaches." And for her, Ichabod competes with Brom Bones, a true son of Sleepy Hollow—good humored, irresponsible, the "madcap" adolescent par excellence. In winning Katrina, Brom himself takes on "the dominant spirit" of the place and undergoes a kind of symbolic castration in the removal and throwing away of the pumpkin-head. In vanquishing this particular opponent, moreover, Brom has not only abandoned the possibility of his own intellectual development and ego individuation, but also protected both for himself and for the community the continuing regressive, preadolescent impulses suitable to "the drowsy shades of Sleepy Hollow." The "too conscious" and insatiably hungry pedagogue, forever expelled from the womb of "tranquil solitudes," in contrast, discovers the necessity to act and succeed in the urban world of business and politics. As the postscript tells us, "for a country schoolmaster to be refused the hand of a Dutch heiress, is a certain step to high preferment in the state." But Ichabod's rumored success appears, in the tale, as less than satisfactory; his rise from schoolmaster to lawyer to politician has finally brought him only the petty triumphs of "the Ten Pound Court."

With just these two tales, Irving succeeded in preserving, intact, the maternal image of American pastoral at a time when the aggressive, sexually assertive aspect of the impulse was coming more and more to dominate. In the face of this shift, Irving had consigned the maternally oriented pastoral "retreat, whither [one] might steal from the world and its distractions, and dream quietly away the remnant of a troubled life," to the landscape of the imagination. The "Legend," then, is not merely the story of "the blooming Katrina's" rejection of a Yankee pedagogue, but, at its deepest level, nineteenth-century America's first wistful look backward at a pastoral configuration it could no longer tolerate in an era more and more given over to "the great torrent of migration and improvement, which is making such incessant changes in . . . this restless country."[58] What, for the eighteenth century, had been translated into the political terminology of Jeffersonian democracy became, in the nineteenth, the subject for a literature of nostalgia and regret. Freneau's escape from the city into the woods through the "Pilgrim" and "Tomo Cheeki," and Crevecoeur's retreat into the woods, through Farmer James's escape to the Indian village, imaginatively predict Thoreau's real-world retreat to Walden Pond and John James Audubon's "regret that there are on record no satisfactory accounts of the state . . . of the country, from the time when our people first settled it. . . . descriptions . . . of the original state of a country that has been so rapidly forced to change her form and attire under the influence of increasing population."

4.

Singing Her Past and Singing Her Praises

The Nineteenth Century

Nature—the Gentlest Mother is,
Impatient of no Child—
—EMILY DICKINSON

A conscious and determined struggle to formulate for themselves the meaning of their landscape characterizes the writing of nineteenth-century Americans. "An absorbing chapter in the history of American sensibility," as Howard Mumford Jones has described it,[1] it is also a chapter in the study of how culture becomes both benefactor and heir to the eternal human dilemmas. For, just as the growing child must confront and mediate between his conflicting drives for individuation and maternal union,[2] so, too, the American literary imagination found itself forced to choose between a landscape that at once promised total gratifications in return for passive and even filial responses and yet, also, apparently tempted, even invited, the more active responses of impregnation, alteration, and possession. As the tide of emigration pushed westward and the continent became better known, the dilemma became even more acute: each new settlement repeated the eighteenth-century's pattern of confused and conflicting responses followed by frustration. Crevecoeur had probably given the problem its most exquisite formulation when, only a few years earlier, he asked his countrymen, "Have you never felt at the returning of spring a glow of general pleasure, an indiscernible something that pervades our whole frame, an inward involuntary admiration of everything which surrounds us? 'Tis then the beauties of Nature, everywhere spread, seem to swell every sentiment as she swells every juice. She dissolves herself in universal love and seems to lead us to the same sentiments" (*SEA*, 54).

That the pleasures he related stemmed from a response to the total female principle of gratification, incorporating mother and sweetheart, he made clear in following paragraphs by compounding the sexuality of "an uncommon ravishment" with the "majesty" of a maternally plentiful and "fecundated earth."[3] What to do with the conflicting responses these two very different aspects of the feminine would generate was the problem the nineteenth-century writer had to face. It was a problem complicated both by the increased technical know-how of Americans, permitting even speedier and more efficient incursions into nature's precincts, and by the urgency of time: for, although the frontier was not officially closed until 1890, the continent had in fact been crossed by mid-century and few could ignore the meaning of what Cooper called, as early as 1827, in *The Prairie*, the "tide of instant emigration."

Different men, of course, reacted in different ways to what they saw. Growing up on his father's land-patent in upper New York State and, later, seeing military service along the newly settled shores of Lake Ontario, young James Fenimore Cooper saw with dismay the gutting of the forests and the increase of the population. As an adult he attempted, however vainly, to correct some of the abuses he had witnessed by creating a fictional Templeton, not unlike his boyhood Cooperstown and ruled perhaps by wiser men, but standing, still, as an inevitable threat to the wilderness around it.[4] If Cooperstown and Templeton were the direction in which America seemed to be moving, there was another direction—tied to the pastoral longings the continent had inspired from the first—that might also be protected, at least in the pages of fiction. In pursuit of that other possibility, that alternate pastoral configuration, Cooper created a man who claimed he was "form'd for the wilderness." At the same time, in the South, William Gilmore Simms portrayed a society that had long ago committed itself to the passivity of filial responses; the maternal configuration of Washington Irving's Sleepy Hollow was similarly the keynote of Simms's beloved southern landscape, with its self-conscious evocation of the maternal embrace stylized in the huge plantations it had spawned. If the talent of southern writing has, in fact, found its subjects in "the history and the soil of the South," as C. Hugh Holman has suggested,[5] then William Gilmore Simms, contemporary of Cooper, must be credited with giving coherent verbal expression to what might otherwise be called unconscious or even symbolically guided activity. After all, by incorporating the experience of and commitment to maternal containment into the artifacts of social institutions, the South at once acknowledged the power of the pastoral impulse and demonstrated how effectively the "potent remnants of infantile and bodily experience" trace themselves upon the external structures of culture.[6]

Obviously, as psychiatrist Joel Kovel points out, "such symbolically guided activity goes on all the time. Our language, our cultural imagery, the whole world is full of symbolic representatives of repressed trends which the ego, in its everlasting need to synthesize, seizes upon for its action."[7] Which is why, in examining what happened to the pastoral impulse in the nineteenth century, we must look not only to the symbolic configurations expressed through art, but, just as important, to the daily experience of those who, however unconsciously, actually pursued the pastoral possibility. Disturbed always by the uncertainty of his mother's identity, tainted even by the hint of illegitimacy, John James Audubon must have responded to the generous maternity of the new continent much as a previous century's literature had invited others to do; that he also responded to its beauties, his paintings give ample evidence. But, when trying to put the meaning of that landscape into words, remembering the years of wandering across yet unmapped prairies and forests, Audubon revealed, as first-person experience, the difficulty of maintaining the distinction between son and lover, and, just as important, the difficulty of maintaining the precarious balance between intimacy and exploitation. For, insofar as the patterns of the male psyche had seized the power and determined the course of history in nineteenth-century America, the pastoral impulse inevitably implied the threat of incest and, with it, the spectre of violation. Hence, the congruence between fiction and fact in nineteenth-century writing, and in consequence, the urgent importance of understanding how the language through which nineteenth-century Americans depicted their landscape affected their movements on that landscape. If, as Benjamin Lee Whorf suggests, "people act about situations in ways which are like the ways they talk about them,"[8] and if, in fact, language (written or spoken) contains verbal cues to underlying psychological patterns, then the same language can also be examined as a repository of internal experience and external expression through which history is made meaningful.

The Country as It Oughtta' Be: John James Audubon

The people take the earth
as a tomb of rest and a cradle of hope.
Who else speaks for the Family of Man?
—CARL SANDBURG, *"The People, Yes"*

Among those who first wandered across the borderlands and frontier communities of the Ohio and Mississippi valleys was the artist-naturalist, John James Audubon. What resulted from those travels were not only the famous illustrations of birds and small mammals, but, just as important, the unique written record of a man whose memory and imagination remained committed to that brief moment when he and others first "arrived on the banks of the broad stream [of the Mississippi], gaze[d] in amazement on the dark, deep woods around them."[9] However self-consciously literary some of that record may strike us, Audubon himself claimed for his memories "the plain garb of truth," insisting that each be read, not as a "tale of fiction, but [as] the relation of an actual occurrence" (*DAS*, 128-29). While in the first of these sketches, "The Ohio," Audubon claims to be relieving his reader of "the tedium" attendant upon "following an author through the mazes of descriptive ornithology" (*DAS*, 1), his consistently nostalgic evocation of a time when "few inhabitants had yet marched toward" the new territories (*DAS*, 23) suggests also that their composition was motivated by the desire to preserve "memories of an earlier, a simpler and, it was believed, a happier state of society," which, as Henry Nash Smith points out, "long survived as a force in American thought and politics."[10]

Originally published as short chapters scattered throughout the first three volumes of the *Ornithological Biography*, the "Episodes" were finally collected and brought together in a single volume, in 1926, under the title, *Delineations of American Scenery and Character*. Though probably composed several years later from notes and from memory, all the chapters center around "the year 1808, at which time," Audubon tells us, "a great portion of the western country . . . were [*sic*] little more than a waste, or to use words better suited to my feeling, remained in their natural state" (*DAS*, 23). As such, most of the sketches are set in a semicultivated landscape, "before population had greatly advanced" (*DAS*, 11), and they reveal a continuing attempt to experience settlers and landscape in harmony, to see Kentucky, for instance, as "the land of abundance, [supplying] a feast for her children" (*DAS*, 242), and to experience his own and his family's presence as nonexploitive and unintrusive.

In spite of this, the very first sketch suggests the inevitably disruptive outcome of human movement into comparatively untouched natural areas that then echoes, like a nervous refrain, through the subsequent fifty-eight chapters. The piece opens with Audubon and his family slowly making their way in a skiff up the Ohio River in search of new specimens to capture and paint. On both sides of the river stretch "extensive plains of the richest, alluvial land" (*DAS*, 2), dotted with trees from which were suspended "long and flowing festoons of different species of vines, many loaded with clustered fruits of varied brilliancy" (*DAS*, 1). The foliage is described as a rainbow of color, "the autumnal tints [having] already decorated the shores of that queen of rivers, the Ohio" (*DAS*, 1), and, in all, the unobtrusive little family group is well provided for by "shores . . . amply supplied with game" (*DAS*, 3). Audubon remarks "the lonely cabin of a squatter" giving "note of commencing civilization" with no more alarm than he remarks the "echoing notes" of birds announcing the break of day. At this point, the human and the natural appear wholly and even intentionally compatible, as if there were some meaningful design behind a deer's passage foretelling the coming snow, or "the hooting of the Great Owl," or "the sound of the boatsman's horn" all of which, Audubon tells us, "were matters of interest" (*DAS*, 3).

But all too quickly the cacophony of civilization invades the "more mellow" harmonies of this pastoral landscape, and the lazy navigation of the river is halted abruptly. "A loud and strange noise," first thought to be "the yells of Indian warfare," impels the family to seek safety on the shore where, instead of "dissatisfied parties of Aborigines," they discover "an enthusiastic set of Methodists, . . . holding one of their annual camp meetings, under the shade of a beech forest" (*DAS*, 3-4). The incident could be dismissed as humorous, but otherwise trivial, were it not for the fact that it introduces a recurrent pattern in these narratives. Each human interruption of a pastoral mood immediately leads Audubon to consider the meaning of "the destruction of the forest, and [the] transplanting [of] civilization into its darkest recesses" (*DAS*, 4). Setting the tone for what is to follow, then, this first chapter ends with a disturbed and disturbing ambivalence, worth quoting in full:

When I think of these times, and call back to my mind the grandeur and beauty of those almost uninhabited shores; when I picture to myself the dense and lofty summits of the forest, that everywhere spread along the hills, and overhung the margins of the stream, unmolested by the axe of the settler; when I know how dearly purchased the safe navigation of that river has been by the blood of many worthy Virginians; when I see that no longer any Aborigines are to be found there, and that the vast herds of elks, deer and buffaloes which once pastured on these hills and in these valleys, making for themselves great roads to the several saltsprings, have ceased to exist; when I reflect that all this grand portion of our Union, instead of being in a state of nature, is now more or less covered with villages, farms, and towns, where the din of hammers and machinery is constantly heard; that the woods are fast disappearing under the axe by day, and the fire by night; that hundreds of steam-boats are gliding to and fro, over the whole length of the majestic river, forcing commerce to take root and to prosper at every spot; when I see the surplus population of Europe coming to assist in the destruction of the forest, and transplanting civilization into its darkest recesses;—when I remember that these extraordinary changes have all taken place in the short period of twenty years, I pause, wonder, and, although I know all to be fact, can scarcely believe its reality. [*DAS*, 4]

Unable either to wholly applaud or condemn the events he lists, Audubon vacillates between the two. At first, settlement implies both the molester with an axe and the sacrifices "of many worthy Virginians"; but its "transplanting" suggests not only the violation of "darkest recesses," but also the "*forcing* [of] commerce to take root." Clearly distressed at what he finds himself relating, Audubon awkwardly alters his identification of those responsible—from "worthy Virginians" to the less appealing "surplus population of Europe"—and then stops to "pause" and "wonder," as though that might distance him from what he is reluctant to accept as "reality." Admitting, finally, that he cannot decide "whether these changes are for the better or for the worse," he harks back to an earlier time, before the country had been "*forced* to change her form and attire under the influence of increasing population" [italics mine], and hopes to see "our Irvings and our Coopers" preserve "the country as it once existed, and . . . as it ought to be, immortal" (*DAS*, 5). The ending to the first sketch, and, in fact, the entire collection to follow, confirm his earlier claim that he "foresaw with great concern the alteration that cultivation would soon produce along those delightful banks" (*DAS*, 2-3).

Sounding almost like a rewrite of sixteenth-century promotional materials, Audubon at first seems genuinely to have believed that those who first entered the land in its "natural state" (*DAS*, 23) enjoyed something akin to "the golden age, which I here found realized" (*DAS*, 9). "The poor woodsman" and his family exhibit the "homely joys" of a nonexploitive relationship with a receptive and giving natural world: "Poor I ought not to call him, for nature and industry bountifully supply all his wants; the woods and river produce his chief dainties, and his toils are his pleasures" (*DAS*, 282). And, not unlike Crevecoeur, Audubon similarly delineated a fraternal community made possible by a "land of abundance" (*DAS*, 242) in which "Nature herself smiled on the joy of her children" (*DAS*, 245). Here *all* men, "from the governor to the guider of the plough, [meet] with light and merry faces" (*DAS*, 241). What seems to have intruded upon these happy visions, however, was his growing awareness of what "cultivation, year after year, extend[ing] over the western wilds" (*DAS*, 142) really meant. For a brief moment in his chapter on "The Squatters of the Mississippi," he stops to explain *why* the family has moved from Virginia: "The land which they and their ancestors have possessed for a hundred years, having been constantly *forced* to produce crops of one kind or another, is now *completely worn out*" (*DAS*, 138 [italics mine]). And, in detailing those who brave the journey from Virginia to Kentucky, he admits—again, just as briefly—that they are, in reality, "*forcing* their way through the pathless woods to the land of abundance" (*DAS*, 58 [italics mine]).

In an effort to limit the scope of such depredations and, perhaps, the scope of his own involvement in the trek westward, Audubon locates most of his sketches in a semipopulated, only partially cultivated, rural landscape, its human inhabitants still in close touch with nature. Even when, as in the chapter entitled "Hospitality in the Woods," it becomes clear to the reader (through the husband's after-dinner monologue), that the young married couple has inherited both land and slaves and is well on its way to increased land-holding and prosperity, Audubon insists that "their means seemed barely sufficient to render them comfortable" (*DAS*, 82) and has the husband refer to the cabin as "this hut" (*DAS*, 84). The emphasis on "the shelter of [a] humble roof, and the refreshment of . . . homely fare" (*DAS*, 79), which introduces this chapter, effectively stylizes Audubon's experiences in such a way that he can ignore the fact that the crude "first cabin" may finally prove a way-station in the consuming "desire so generally experienced in America, of spreading over the uncultivated tracts, and bringing into cultivation lands that have for unknown ages teemed with the wild luxuriance of untamed nature" (*DAS*, 56).

While it was to be Cooper's achievement to both label and define the pastoral substructure underlying movement into and out of "the dark recesses of the woods" (*DAS*, 242), which Audubon details for himself and others in these sketches, it was nevertheless the feckless young naturalist—and not the fictional Natty Bumppo—who first attempted to find a fit habitation for his impulses while acknowledging the fact that he and others were everyday "push[ing] through an unexplored region of dark and tangled forests, guiding themselves by the sun alone, and reposing at night, on the bare ground" (*DAS*, 57). But the very fact of participating in the opening up and penetration of enclosed spaces in a landscape he repeatedly experienced as feminine—most often in its maternal aspect—forced Audubon to attempt at least a tentative circumvention of the sexually violative and even incestuous activity his very choice of language suggested. Trying, therefore, to expunge what was perhaps only a barely conscious experience of masculine aggression into a feminine ambience, Audubon sets up, in each of the settlers' cabins, a compensatory and virtually archetypal balance of masculine and feminine components. In the newlyweds' cabin, for instance, he tells us: "The only bed I saw was of domestic manufacture, and the counterpane proved how expert the young wife was at spinning and weaving. A fine rifle ornamented the chimney-piece. The fire-place was of such dimensions that it looked as if it had been purposely constructed for holding the numerous progeny expected to result from the happy union" (*DAS*, 82). In still another chapter, he describes "the affectionate mother . . . hushing her dear babe to repose, while a group of sturdy children surround their father, who has just returned from the chase, and deposited on the rough flooring of his hut the varied game which he has procured" (*DAS*, 203). Almost without exception these isolated cabins in the woods or fledgling farms recapitulate, by their very simplicity, the opening chapter's reconciliation of human and natural elements, and they do so, primarily, by alternating and harmonizing male and female activities. The feminine is always depicted as both wife and mother, and the planting or hunting activities of the male are experienced not as a violation, but rather as a means of protecting and providing for the feminine. Obviously, this is humankind playing what were, until this century, its most archetypal roles. Rarely are individual personalities depicted in these episodes, but, instead, immediately identifiable gendered polarities, compatible within their cabin and, together, in harmony with the landscape outside.

The only intruder, in fact, is Audubon himself, always grateful to the families who "generously strive to contribute to the comfort of the stranger who has chanced to visit them" (*DAS*, 281). In a chapter devoted to "A Raccoon Hunt in Kentucky," for instance, the author reminisces about an evening when "the sun went down far beyond the 'far west' . . . The woodland choristers have disappeared, the matron has cradled her babe, and betaken herself to the spinning wheel; the woodsman, his sons, and 'the stranger' are chatting before a blazing fire" (*DAS*, 281).

What is revealing about such passages is the frequency with which Audubon refers to himself as the "stranger"—twice in the brief paragraph from which I have just quoted—and thereby betrays, within human precincts, in these archetypally harmonious frontier cabins, the sense of himself as an intruder which dogs his movement even in "the dark recesses of the woods" (*DAS*, 242). The image of his own unobtrusive little family, happily nurtured by an abundant landscape, is never repeated after the opening chapter; subsequently, Audubon sometimes pictures himself accompanied by his son, but more often, he wanders alone in these sketches. The cabins, therefore, seem to provide a refuge where he may experience himself, as it were, as a member of the family. But, as his own vocabulary choices reveal, he finds no permanent or legitimate role in such scenes and remains, inevitably, the "stranger," as much an intruder inside the cabin as he has been in the landscape without, where, violating his intimacy even as he seeks to preserve it, he kills or maims the "beautiful birds" and small mammals that nature had provided for his admiration. Perhaps this explains why these chapters are so consistently silent about his painting activities; never do we get details of how he managed to study the birds so closely, and only rarely is there a mention of paintbox and brushes. What we get, instead, is a growing ambivalence toward what can only be termed an uncertain landscape from which he recurrently seeks shelter. The pattern is one often repeated: incommodious weather, including "the piercing blast" or "drifting snows," drives him to "the blazing fire of some lonely cabin" (*DAS*, 203). But even the harsher combinations of weather and landscape can be perceived as beautiful by Audubon, with "drifted snows," for instance, becoming a mantle "that covered the face of the country" (*DAS*, 203). So, although sometimes "faint with fatigue, and chilled" (*DAS*, 203), Audubon clung to his perceptions of a beautiful and beneficent landscape and remained, for the most part, unwilling to present a natural world that is seriously threatening or destructive.

In fact, of the fifty-nine sketches that make up *The Delineations of American Scenery and Character*, only five focus on events in which nature is either harmful or threatening. (I leave out of this count the chapter entitled "The Lost One," which I will treat as a special case.) Two of these involve the threat of flood along the Mississippi, "A Flood" and "The Force of the Waters," while the other three deal with an earthquake, a hurricane, and a forest fire. The danger of these disasters is mediated, however, since in each case the story is related either about or by those who have survived and now sit in the comfort of a new home, before a hearth that "sends forth a blaze of light over the happy family" (*DAS*, 203).

Similarly, in the four chapters that treat the potential threat of wild animals, the actual discussion of their danger takes barely a paragraph or two, if even that, while the bulk of the sketch concentrates on the human efforts to destroy the animal. In the chapter detailing "The Pitting of the Wolves," for example, our horror is aroused at the senseless torture of the captive animals, while in "The Traveller and the Pole-Cat," we are amused, rather than irritated, at the anecdote of the unwary traveler sprayed by a skunk. In "Scipio and the Bear," Audubon begins the sketch by offering to assist a farmer "in killing some Bears at the moment engaged in destroying his corn" (*DAS*, 107), and ends it thoroughly revolted at the way in which the farmers have used their slaves, their dogs, and smoking fires "to procure as much sport as possible" (*DAS*, 108). Finally, the brutal torture and killing of a mother bear and her "cubs of no great size" (*DAS*, 108) becomes another emblem of masculine aggression against the feminine along the frontiers, with Audubon pointing up the utter senselessness of the entire venture when he concludes that, "before we had left the field, the horses, dogs, and bears, together with the fires, had destroyed more corn within a few hours, then the poor bear and her cubs had, during the whole of their visits" (*DAS*, 110). Our sympathies are manipulated in such a way as to force us, finally, to experience the men as marauders and the animals as victims.

In effect, the real threats to Audubon's pastoral impulse are not, as we might expect, natural disasters such as earthquake or flood, but, instead, the acquisitional strivings of "the man who, with his family, removed to the [new territories], . . . assured that, in that land of exuberant fertility, he could not fail to provide amply for all his wants" (*DAS*, 57). In only one sketch, however, does he openly admit that the pursuit of economic independence may turn into greed. Entitled "The Prairie," this episode opens innocently enough, with the naturalist embraced "all around" by a landscape "as fresh and blooming as if it had just issued from the bosom of nature. . . . My knapsack, my gun, and my dog, were all I had for baggage and company. But, although well moccasined, I moved slowly along, attracted by the brilliancy of the flowers, and the gambols of the fawns around their dams, to all appearance as thoughtless of danger as I felt myself" (*DAS*, 14).

In the second paragraph, darkness overshadows the prairie, "and the distant howling of wolves gave me some hope that I should soon arrive at the skirts of some woodland" (*DAS*, 14). As usual, he is attracted by a firelight that leads him to the door "of a small log cabin." Here he is received by a woman who, in comparison with the femininity of the natural world, is distinctly unattractive and almost unwomanly—"her voice was gruff, and her attire negligently thrown about her"—and her manner is hardly hospitable. Inside, "a finely formed young Indian," nursing a recent hunting wound, responds with looks and gestures to Audubon's addressing him in French. Audubon then describes how the woman, having spotted his gold watch, is fascinated by it and asks that "her curiosity . . . be gratified by an immediate sight of it" (*DAS*, 15). In response, he tells us, "I took off the gold chain that secured it from around my neck, and presented it to her. She was all ecstasy, spoke of its beauty, asked me its value, and put the chain round her brawny neck, saying how happy the possession of such a watch should make her. Thoughtless, and, as I fancied myself, in so retired a spot, secure, I paid little attention to her talk or her movements" (*DAS*, 15-16). That sense of nameless danger hinted at outside is now picked up with the word "thoughtless" and transferred to the world within the cabin; here, "in so retired a spot," we do not at all feel "secure," but, on the contrary, isolated and vulnerable. If anything, we begin to suspect Audubon's determination to *feel* himself "secure." The suspense builds as he describes the Indian's attempts to send "me expressive glances whenever our hostess chanced to have her back towards us" (*DAS*, 16).

Finally, a paragraph later, Audubon begins vaguely to appreciate the Indian's signals, "my senses [having] been awakened to the danger which I now suspected to be about me" (*DAS*, 16). If we wonder why he chooses to stay in the cabin, we need only remember the howling wolves outside. So, pretending to sleep, Audubon makes himself a pallet of skins, calls his "faithful dog to" his side, and "lay[s] down, with my gun close to my body" (*DAS*, 16). The woman's two sons presently enter, inquire about the stranger and the wounded Indian, and quickly eat and drink themselves into a vicious state. (They have, meanwhile, been apprised of the stranger's valuable watch.) After describing "frequent visits of the whisky bottle to [her] ugly mouth," Audubon's language reduces the woman from a beast-like "dam" to an "incarnate fiend," taking "a large carving knife . . . to the grindstone to whet its edge." Demonic now, and denuded of any hint of femininity, she audibly orders her sons to attack the stranger. The narrative voice realizes that "that night might have been my last in this world, had not Providence made preparations for my rescue" (*DAS*, 17). For, as "the infernal hag was advancing slowly," "the door was suddenly opened, and there entered two stout travellers, each with a long rifle on his shoulder" (*DAS*, 17). Audubon jumps up, greets the strangers and quickly relates what is happening. "The tale was told in a minute. The drunken sons were secured, and the woman, in spite of her defence and vociferations, shared the same fate. The Indian fairly danced with joy, and gave us to understand that, as he could not sleep for pain, he would watch over us. You may suppose we slept much less than we talked. The two strangers gave me an account of their once having been themselves in a somewhat similar situation. Day came, fair and rosy, and with it the punishment of our captives" (*DAS*, 18). The new day, "fair and rosy," returns Audubon to the attractive femininity of the opening landscape and simultaneously banishes the threat of a hostile prairie and a domineering, rapacious mother.

The "delinquents" having been punished, and the Indian and white men having taken their separate paths, Audubon himself turns "well pleased, towards the settlements." At this point he stops the sequential narrative and muses, briefly, over the past "twenty-five years, when my wanderings extended to all parts of our country. This," he claims, "was the only time at which my life was in danger from my fellow creatures. . . . Indeed, so little risk do travellers run in the United States, that no one born there ever dreams of any to be encountered on the road; and I can only account for this occurrence by supposing that the inhabitants of the cabin were not Americans" (*DAS*, 18). The declaration is an odd one, not only because it contradicts the two rescuers' statements that they also had experienced "a somewhat similar situation," but because it so wilfully ignores his own chapter on "The Regulators," which emphasizes the problems with law-breakers and human violence on the frontiers. Obviously, he is trying to maintain his pastoral vision of harmonious families and humble cottages, a vision that cannot allow demonic mothers and violent sons on American soil, nor permit acts of greed and assault on the part of Americans.

The concluding paragraph repeats the pattern introduced in the first chapter; any particular human disturbance of pastoral scenes or moods calls to mind the larger progress of civilization itself: "Will you believe, reader, that not many miles from the place where this adventure happened, and where fifteen years ago, no habitation belonging to civilized man was expected, and very few ever seen, large roads are now laid out, cultivation has converted the woods into fertile fields, taverns have been erected, and much of what we Americans call comfort is to be met with. So fast does improvement proceed in our abundant and free country" (*DAS*, 18). That a consideration of "the place where this adventure happened" brings to mind a landscape "converted [from] woods into fertile fields," with the taverns an ominous reminder of the drunken activities of the mother and her sons, suggests that, at some deeper associational level, Audubon is not entirely pleased with the "improvement" he seems to applaud. He is reminded of it, after all, by a tenuous geographical connection and, more important, by an episode of human violence.

More important still is the way in which the incident inverts the pattern of "Scipio and the Bear." Whereas in that sketch a mother and her cubs had been the victims of Audubon and the party of farmers of which he was a part, here, Audubon becomes the intended victim of an angry mother and her sons. The violence of the sons, moreover, is motivated by their greed to capture and possess, in some ways not unlike Audubon's own necessarily violent acts in pursuit of capturing his beloved birds forever in pen and ink. The "infernal hag" within the darkened hovel, threatening violent death, was, in a sense, a human correlative for the darkened "skirts of some woodland," which, we recall, provided no safer sanctuary. Safety from both, in fact, comes in the form of men bearing rifles. If such plottings seem to suggest the dim outlines of archetype and myth, they also suggest that at some barely conscious level, Audubon finally confronted the precariousness of the balance he maintained between son and lover in the natural landscape and, as a result, grappled with the threatening aspect of the feminine matrix in general.

With his reminiscence of "The Lost One," in fact, the unconscious material only barely hinted at in other chapters becomes a pattern both of internal experience and external action. "A live-oaker . . . with his axe on his shoulder," left his cabin one morning in order to ply "his trade of felling and squaring the giant trees that afford the most valuable timber for naval architecture." Losing his way in the "heavy fogs" which "cover the country," he finds himself enclosed by a grass "so tall that a man of ordinary stature cannot see over it" (*DAS*, 124). This situation immediately reminds Audubon "that such an occurrence happened to myself, at a time when I had imprudently ventured to pursue a wounded quadruped, which led me some distance from the track" (*DAS*, 124). Each experience involves a loss of direction, and each is also precipitated by some kind of incursion into natural wholeness: the forester, obviously, must fell trees; and Audubon must sometimes injure or kill the objects of his interest in order to study and draw them accurately. Both point up the difficulty of maintaining that precarious balance between grateful son and economic (or even artistic) exploiter; for a man in this situation, Audubon warns, "it is necessary . . . to proceed with great caution, lest he should unwittingly deviate from the ill-defined trail which he follows." For Audubon, as for the "live-oaker" through whom he now vicariously relives—or even experiences—his own expiation, the landscape "all around him continued as if enveloped with mystery" (*DAS*, 125). What, in other sketches, had been both attractive and protective in its embrace, here appears threateningly and ominously entrapping: "The huge gray trees spread their giant boughs over him, the rank grass extended on all sides, not a living being crossed his path, all was silent and still and the scene was like a dull and dreary dream of the land of oblivion. He wandered like a forgotten ghost that had passed into the land of spirits" (*DAS*, 125).

Whereas Audubon favors a passive response to the predicament, advising that the man lost in the woods would do "well . . . to lie down, and wait until the fog should disperse" (*DAS*, 124), the live-oaker continues "jogging onwards for several hours," only to admit finally, that he is irretrievably lost. In "turn[ing] his back upon the sun," the Lost One has symbolically indicated a movement out of the realm of conscious activity and into that traditionally associated with the infantile—dark, mysterious, confused and, when the Mother is angry, surrounded by "heavy and chilling dews" (*DAS*,

125). As the first night falls, Audubon describes "the Lost One" praying "fervently . . . to his Maker" (*DAS*, 126). On a psychological as well as a spiritual level, it is a particularly appropriate action. The son who has betrayed his intimacy with the Mother—whether by phallic aggression with the axe, or simply in the greed with which he has reaped her bounty—now turns to the Christian father figure as a protection against her anger. The invocation of so powerful a father, of course, simultaneously absolves the son of any incest fantasy.

After the second day, chronological sequence is confused, and, instead of a progression of time, the live-oaker describes the steady disintegration of his mental and physical wholeness. By the end of the second day, "the terror that had been gradually spreading over his mind, together with the nervous debility induced by fatigue, anxiety, and hunger, rendered him almost frantic." It is his faith in the Christian god, alone, that sustains him:

> "I knew my situation," he said to me. "I was fully aware that unless Almighty God came to my assistance, I must perish in those uninhabited woods. . . . I knew that if I should not meet with some stream I must die, for my axe was my only weapon, and although deer and bears now and then started within a few yards or even feet of me, not one of them could I kill; and although I was in the midst of abundance, not a mouthful did I expect to procure, to satisfy the cravings of my empty stomach." [*DAS*, 127]

There is no explanation of *why* the axe is now useless; however, stripped of its power to help him, and with Audubon's comparison of the Lost One to "a *lame* man groping his way in the dark," the son has not only been rendered impotent, but, indeed, has been symbolically castrated. And, insofar as he is a "man groping his way *in the dark out of a dungeon*, of which he knew not where the door stood" (*DAS*, 128 [italics mine]), he is also experiencing the terror of engulfment within the Mother, her womb now turned into the devouring maw.

Anticipating that quality of guilt that Natty Bumppo would express in *The Prairie* (1827), Audubon is here attempting to reconcile the conflicting pastoral impulses that motivate the frontier woodsman, "felling and squaring the giant trees," and the frontier naturalist, trying to preserve his beloved animals in pen and ink, to not only enjoy and accept nature's bounties passively, but to control and use them in such a way as to threaten the conditions under which they were supplied. The felled trees will provide planks for the ships that navigate the rivers and facilitate the advance of settlers onto the frontier; and the naturalist kills the very animals he is attempting to preserve for posterity. The guilt incurred by such violations will not allow either man to experience the maternal embrace, though still in evidence "in the midst of abundance," as permanently receptive. Instead, the validity of masculine and civilizing activity, as incarnate in the Christian deity, must be reasserted in order that that guilt not turn to insanity.

> For several days after, no one can imagine the condition in which he was, for when he related to me this painful adventure, he assured me that he had lost all recollection of what had happened. "God," he continued, "must have taken pity on me one day, for, as I ran wildly through those dreadful pine barrens, I met with a tortoise. I gazed upon it with amazement and delight, and, although I knew that were I to follow it undisturbed, it would lead me to some water, my hunger and thirst would not allow me to refrain from satisfying both, by eating its flesh, and drinking its blood. With one stroke of my axe the beast was cut in two, and in a few moments I dispatched all but the shell. Oh, Sir, how much I thanked God, whose kindness had put the tortoise in my way! I felt greatly renewed. I sat down at the foot of a pine, gazed on the heavens, thought of my poor wife and children, and again, and again thanked my God for my life, for now I felt less distracted in mind, and more assured that before long I must recover my way, and get back to my home." [*DAS*, 127]

What had once been a bountiful embrace is now "dreadful," and, suggestively, barren. Within its grip, the assertive and independent ego has been momentarily stifled in an amnesiac break in consciousness. The first word of the sentence that announces the return to conscious awareness, and with it, the beginning of a return to the civilized world, is "God." At this point two alternatives are presented to the Lost One: he may either follow the tortoise to a source of water, or satisfy his thirst and hunger immediately by killing it. The passivity of the first, a response appropriate to a filial relationship with maternal nature, he rejects. His choice of the second, driven by "hunger and thirst," is then described in language vaguely reminiscent of the holy communion; by eating the flesh and drinking the blood, the Lost One tells us, he "felt greatly renewed"—and our sense of his renewal is not so much physical as spiritual. It is as though this act has brought him into communion with a masculine God and, thereby, put him in touch with the sanctioned activity of a masculine order. For the first time in the narrative he is able to gaze "on the heavens" and renew his ties with the human world, thinking of his "poor wife and children." Undoubtedly the main turning point in the narrative, this paragraph emphasizes the fact that if man is to survive in the wilderness, he has no choice but to *use* the natural world as the means of that self-preservation. Which is precisely the problem that plagues Audubon throughout. If activity inevitably confers the guilt of violation—and, even more threatening, the guilt of an incestuous violation—the desire to experience the natural world passively is similarly self-defeating. For all her promise, her bounty, her seductive beauty, nature must finally be *made* to provide for man; he dare not wait for all to be given. And so, for the Lost One, salvation comes through activity, not passivity. The tortoise is killed so that he may live and return to the world of men.

If the narrative has, on the one hand, followed the archetypal pattern of Christian death and rebirth, it has also narrated a rebirth out of the embracing and potentially annihilating womb of Mother Nature into the world of civilized men. Though brought to his knees before the terrible power of a retributive maternal order, the man who has felled trees for naval architecture is finally saved by a boat "boldly" advancing through the "tangled brush-wood" meant to impede its progress (*DAS*, 128). The inability to maintain the initial harmony with the maternal leads, inevitably, to an acceptance of the masculine power that wields axes and advances its little boats into the innermost recesses of the natural world. If "The Lost One" is Audubon's attempt to explore the guilt, albeit vicariously, of his own participation in destructive acts along the frontier—helping to kill bears, hunt raccoons, or kill the birds he has chosen to draw—it is also an attempt to reconcile his conflicting impulses to experience and appreciate nature passively with the necessity for active aggression. By identifying his own experience with that of the live-oaker, he participates in a punishment his own internal psychological integrity demands; the process ends, however, in an apparent rejection of the filial response and a renewed acceptance of men's impulse to alter, penetrate, and conquer "the dark deep woods around them" (*DAS*, 139). Which means, of course, that however much the early settlers might admire the land for "the richness of its soul, its magnificent forests, its numberless navigable streams, its salt springs and licks, its saltpetre caves, its coal strata, and the vast herds of buffaloes and deer that browsed on its hills and amidst its charming valleys" (*DAS*, 56), they would finally find themselves cutting the timber and shooting the deer; the rivers will be navigated, facilitating even speedier settlement, and the coal and saltpetre mined. This, then, is the tragic contradiction that informs the language of these sketches, making coherent points of view impossible to maintain, and forcing the narrative voice to evoke the "golden age" experience and deny it at the same time. For Audubon, the natural world was not only the Mother offering her bounty, but also, in some way, the seductress, "afford[ing] ample inducements to the new settler" (*DAS*, 156), inviting him to mine her coal, cut her timber, and paint her beauties.

It is the same contradiction Robert Penn Warren touched on in his 1969 group of poems, *Audubon: A Vision*, attesting at once to the undying power of the pastoral impulse and to the fascination that this man, "With hair worn long like a hunter's, eyes shining, /. . . [whistling] the bird-calls of his distant forests," claiming " '. . . in my sleep I continually dream of birds,' " still holds for the American imagination. In "Love and Knowledge," Warren pictures first the "footless dance" of the birds in flight and then Audubon's response:

> *He slew them, at surprising distances, with his gun.*
> *Over a body held in his hand, his head was bowed low,*
> *But not in grief.*
>
> *He put them where they are, and there we see them:*
> *In our imagination.*
>
> *What is love?*
>
> *One name for it is knowledge.*[11]

Audubon knew another name: violence.

There is a sad and peculiar irony in Audubon's collected memories. For, unable to resolve what is still a central concern within the American psyche—the sense of guilt aroused by the conflict between the impulse to see nature as bountiful and the desire to dominate it and make it bountiful—Audubon attempted to stop time altogether, and preserve the static continuity of a soaring bird and a landscape "before population had greatly advanced" (*DAS*, 11). That he felt himself inadequate to the second is made clear by his opening plea to "our Irvings and our Coopers," whom he considered "fully competent for the task." That such an account had not yet been written, he attributed to "the changes [having] succeeded each other with such rapidity, as almost to rival the movements of their pen. However, it is not too late yet" (*DAS*, 5). But, of course, it *was* too late; by the time Audubon died, in 1851, the frontier had been moved as far as the Pacific. And his own writings, whether he realized it or not, confirmed the contradictions that had forced Irving's characters into presexual adolescence, while his lone wanderings, with a rifle in his hand and a dog by his side, predicted those of America's other great isolate, and pastoral figure, Natty Bumppo.

Natty Bumppo as The American Dream: The Leatherstocking Novels of James Fenimore Cooper

> *He understood that . . . imprisoned in the dark womb of our mother, we come to life without having seen her face, that we are given to her arms a stranger, and that, caught in that insoluble prison of being, we escape it never, no matter what arms may clasp us, what mouth may kiss us, what heart may warm us. Never, never, never, never, never.*
>
> —THOMAS WOLFE, Look Homeward, Angel

Quite apart from the political considerations that originally motivated the piece, and the sometimes questionable analyses of Cooper's personality and character, William Gilmore Simms's 1842 review of Cooper's writings stands even today as one of the more insightful critical commentaries on "this favourite author." Especially useful in understanding the Leatherstocking series, Simms's comments grasped what so many since have failed to note, that Cooper was essentially working on the same problem throughout his novels. As such, as Simms noted, the series "multiplies the same forms, characters, images and objects, through different media—now enlarging and now depressing them—now throwing them into greater shadow, and now bringing them out into stronger light," concentrating its energy on "one man, and fling[ing] him upon the wilderness. . . . Out of this one man's nature, his moods and fortunes, he spins his story." And that "story," developed variously in each of the Leatherstocking novels, is the story of how Natty Bumppo can maintain the pastoral embrace that the other whites in these novels are so determined to escape or open to the daylight; in short, how he alone can enjoy the darkened forest recesses without threatening to become either destructive or intrusive. The many current paperback reprints and television shows based on the series attest to the fact that Americans still stand fascinated, as had Simms in 1842, by the relationship of "the vast unbroken ranges of forest, to its one lonely occupant."

To James Fenimore Cooper, then, must go the credit for giving the first major, and successful, literary coherence to the pastoral impulse in America. And even if the novels do not label things for us as engulfment or incest fantasy—a vocabulary not even available to Cooper—we can hardly ignore the narratives' strong suggestions of sexual tension and infantile regression surrounding Natty's response to and spatial movement within the landscape. For, once having admitted, though reluctantly, that a nonexploitive white community, living happily and harmoniously within the embrace of nature, was no longer even a possibility—its demise there, in the first of the Leatherstocking tales, with the settlement of Templeton—Cooper turned to the possibility of a lone frontiersman, Natty Bumppo, living out the pastoral impulse. It was a dream he pursued through five novels and for eighteen years, creating, as he did so, our most enduring "conception of the frontier white man," a conception that Simms astutely applauded "as an artistical conception of great originality and effect."[12]

If the first of the Leatherstocking novels, *The Pioneers*, published in 1823,[13] explores the inevitable conflict between the individual and the community, the impulse to freedom versus the need for social organization, it does so within a context structured by the two conflicting aspects of the pastoral impulse. On the one hand, there is Natty Bumppo, the man who claims himself " 'form'd for the wilderness,' " desperate to leave the settlements and " 'go where my soul craves to be' "—into the woods (*Pi*, 475). And, on the other hand, there are the settlers of Templeton, variously represented by Judge Temple, determined to awaken the land lying " 'in the sleep of nature . . . to supply the wants of man' " (*Pi*, 235); by Billy Kirby, intent upon hacking and burning his way out of every enclosure, opening up "the depths of the woods" to the "daylight" (*Pi*, 191); and by Cousin Richard Jones, whose gadget-oriented technology, in the course of the novel, intrudes upon all of nature's precincts—lake, land, and sky. While Cooper's narrative descriptions carefully distinguish between Natty's almost passive movement within darkened natural enclosures and the assertive, often aggressive, activity of the others in light, open areas, it is Natty himself who first suggests the psychological meaning behind these contrasts. Reminiscing over an intimacy of many years' duration, the old man attempts to explain to the incredulous young Effingham how much he has cherished his solitary position in the wilderness: " 'I had the place to myself, once,' " he recalls, " 'and a cheerful time I had of it. The game was as plenty as heart could wish, and there was none to meddle with the ground' " (*Pi*, 298). In the woods, then, Natty enjoys a relationship based on privacy and abundance. The only spot " 'more to my liking,' " he continues, lies in the Cattskills, embedded between " 'the High-peak and the Round-top, which lay back, like a father and mother among their children' "; it is a spot to which he no longer climbs in his later years, yet one to which his imagination remains committed. Remembering the many times he had stood there, a human child among their other offspring, he tells Effingham he saw " 'Creation! . . . all creation, lad.' " And, in "sweeping one hand around him in a circle" as he speaks (*Pi*, 300), he graphically illustrates, both in word and gesture, the all-embracing familial relationship he has come to know in the wilderness.

To young Oliver Effingham, of course, Natty's words are all but incomprehensible. For, in spite of the novel's attempt to integrate him into the woodcraft and forest ways of Natty and Indian John, Oliver, like all the other whites in the novel, will always regard the uninhabited wilderness as " 'a sight of melancholy pleasure,' " forever wanting " 'without a living soul to speak to, or to thwart your humor' " (*Pi*, 299). If the phrasings of Effingham's protestations are tempered by a kind of civilized politeness, we come to realize, as the novel progresses, that they really represent no very different quality of response from Billy Kirby's somewhat more open admission that, to him, the forests are " 'a sore sight at any time, unless I'm privileged to work my will on them' " (*Pi*, 232). Part of that "privilege" includes the "deep and careless incision" he makes into each "sugar bush," or maple tree (*Pi*, 227)—an ugly and perhaps too obvious phallic thrust. Even the kindly and well-intentioned Judge Marmaduke Temple, for all his fine conservationist sentiments, describes his estate as a receptacle of hidden "treasures," a "mine of comfort and wealth," which is someday to be entered and made use of. When he encourages his servant, Benjamin, to " 'act thy pleasure with the forests, for this night at least' " (*Pi*, 214), we hear an echo of Kirby's language. The judge's house, a fitting emblem for the community as a whole, boasts a roof that remains, in spite of several coats of paint, "the most conspicuous part" (*Pi*, 33), obtruding like an "offensive member"[14] into the surrounding scenery. Little wonder, then, that Cooper chose to preface his first description of Templeton with a poetic excerpt in which man's despoliation of the wilderness is compared to "some sad spoiler of a virgin's fame" (*Pi*, 26).

And little wonder that Elizabeth Temple, returning to her home after an absence of some years, experiences a sense of loss as she rides out of "the loveliness of the mountain view" and "into the open gate of the mansion-house," where "nothing stood before her but the cold, dreary stone walls of the building" (*Pi*, 50). Cooper effectively utilized her journey to point up the organic wholeness of the natural world in contrast to the rude and unattractive beginnings of settlement. The abortive attempt at fusing human and natural elements, which occurs in the novel's opening paragraph, is consistently denied by everything that follows so that, by the end of the second paragraph, "the inhabited parts of the colony of New York" appear to be expanding out into the countryside in almost cancerous proportions. What "the expedients of the pioneers who first broke ground in the settlement of this country" (*Pi*, 2) initially produces, however, is "a people who often laid aside the axe or the scythe to seize the rifle, as the deer glided through the forests they were felling, or the bear entered their rough meadows to scent the air of a clearing, and to scan, with a look of sagacity, the progress of the invader" (*Pi*, 189). Reminding us of those whom Audubon had described "sporting" with a mother bear and her cubs or cruelly taunting pitted wolves, Cooper's fictionalized settlers appear to be a people who grasp only weapons of destruction. The community's will, clearly, is not bent on Crevecoeur's vision of primal fraternity, but, instead, on the annihilation of passively innocent and even likeable victims. Denying as brutally as possible the "Peaceable Kingdom" vision of America, Cooper details, in chapter 22, the often-quoted attack on the flight of migratory pigeons, and, in chapter 23, Richard's scheme for fishing by seine.

In each case the victims are granted human qualities, so that the reader comes to share both Natty's distress that friends are being destroyed and his outrage at the wanton cruelty of the carnage. Pointedly, Cooper shows us each of Templeton's "leading citizens" involved in the slaughter, with Marmaduke Temple bringing "his musket to a poise" (*Pi*, 245) and Natty crying out against " 'Mr. Oliver . . . as bad as the rest of them, firing into the flocks as if he was shooting down nothing but the Mingo warriors' " (*Pi*, 251). Cousin Richard, with the gadget technology of cannon warfare at his command, has the townspeople acting the part of musket-men "drawn up in battle array" (*Pi*, 253), and he himself experiences the entire activity as a pitched battle, at the end of which he claims, " 'Victory! we have driven the enemy from the field' " (*Pi*, 254).

Similarly, the fishing by seine results in a "whole shoal of victims" (*Pi*, 265) and includes every major character, except, of course, Natty and Indian John, with the narrative voice pointing out that "even Elizabeth and Louisa were greatly excited and highly gratified, by seeing two thousand captives thus drawn from the bosom of the lake, and laid prisoners at their feet" (*Pi*, 265). None but Natty and Mohegan, apparently, are spared the communal guilt.

That some expiation must follow we have already learned from Audubon; the pattern is not merely the idiosyncratic experience of an individual. Insofar as the pastoral impulse is shared by the culture at large, it becomes a pattern by which a number of cultural artifacts are shaped. And in Cooper, as with Audubon, the process of punishment begins in enclosed and engulfing spaces, the judge and his party forcing their way through woods that are "not only difficult but dangerous" (*Pi*, 234). The day's outing, to view a scene promised by Richard (but which only disappoints the little party), provides an opportunity for Judge Temple to detail, for his daughter, the history of Templeton's settlement and expansion. The symmetry of chapter 21 is beautiful: the land that, in its pristine state, had struck the judge with the beauty of its "boundless forest" and "surface branches" now turns upon those who had wished to alter it and becomes, instead, an entrapment, a " dreary and dark wood, where the rays of the sun could but rarely penetrate, and where even the daylight was obscured and rendered gloomy by the deep forests that surrounded them" (*Pi*, 243). Riding out, as though to escape impending disaster, the little group finds itself first embraced by "that dead stillness that often precedes a storm" and then nearly crushed "as one of the noblest ruins in the forest fell directly across their path" (*Pi*, 243). " 'Such a fall as this,' " the judge comments afterward, " 'is very rare' " (*Pi*, 245); and its very rarity leaves us feeling that there has been a purpose behind it all, as though the forest that "awoke to supply the needs of man," has been awakened indeed! Finally, the judge's question, " 'But how is one to guard against the danger?' " remains conspicuously unanswered (*Pi*, 244).

The process of retribution ends, of course, with the fire on Mount Vision. The first sign of danger on the mountain, however, is not the fire, but the "fierce front and the glaring eye of a female panther [with her] . . . quarter-grown cub" (*Pi*, 315) that confronts Elizabeth Temple and Louisa Grant as they attempt to scale the mountain. Incorporating both the angry and threatening mother as well as the protective and nurturing aspect of "both dam and cub" (*Pi*, 316), the panther anticipates, symbolically, the blinding and smoky "canopy" of fire with which Elizabeth and young Effingham are about to be embraced. When they are, in fact, "completely encircled by the fire" (*Pi*, 424), the young man tries valiantly to protect his beloved, while the girl appears almost dimly aware of the justice of her situation. " 'This mountain,' " to the foot of which her father had led the cacophony of civilization, she perceives as " 'doomed to be fatal to me!' " (*Pi*, 424). The following chapter, however, tempers the suggestion of an avenging maternal order by providing a human explanation for the fire. As Natty observes, " 'kearless fellows, who thought to catch a practysed hunter in the woods after dark, had thrown . . . lighted pine knots in the brush . . . that . . . would kindle like tow' " (*Pi*, 432).

Two men die as a result of the blaze, one happily abandoning himself to "the womb of futurity" (*Pi*, 427), the other trapped in a tunnel of his own making, having greedily penetrated the earth's core in search of hidden treasure. The second, Jotham Riddle, demonstrates the dangerous potential of the judge's favorite metaphor, while the first, a "child of the forest" (*Pi*, 79), is redeemed as a man. Indian John's last moments are a kind of apotheosis, eradicating the emasculation and humiliation he has suffered in the white men's precincts; his decorated body stands firm and upright before the summoning voice of the storm and, "as if in obedience to a signal for his departure, . . . [he] stretched his wasted arm towards the west. His dark face lighted with a look of joy" (*Pi*, 440). Nature, her fury abated, a favorite child returned to her embrace, at last releases the long-awaited relief and nourishment, bathing the parched landscape in "large drops of rain" (*Pi*, 441).

But the desire to experience at least some kind of punishment, which seems so much a part of the pattern of pastoral experience in America, has proved *just* that—only a *part* of the pattern. Maternal retribution has brought about only a momentary halt in human activity and only a momentary balance of justice. Nowhere does the novel allow us to believe that future settlement will be any different from what has preceded, or that the violation of nature's precincts will not continue. Interestingly, it is the man "form'd for the wilderness" who also shares the pain of that violation, the attempted search of his hut for hidden treasure paralleling the community's search for nature's hidden treasures. The inversion is completed when Natty, too, uses fire to thwart Hiram Dolittle's progress. Returning to the hut, afterward, to view its smoldering remains and confront his would-be captors, Natty makes the analogy explicit. In his impassioned attack upon the sheriff and his officers, he indicts a society that has not only " 'driven God's creatur's from the wilderness' " but has also " 'driven me, that have lived forty long years of my appointed time in this very spot, from my home and the shelter of my head.' " Cooper here is weaving together the various threads of his story. Mourning " 'the ashes under my feet, as a man would weep and mourn for the children of his body,' " Natty parallels the maternal response of nature, mourning for the pigeons shot in flocks, or the fish hauled in by seine, the trees felled by axe and fire—all children of her own encompassing body. And if he feels kinship with the parent, so, too, with her children, wishing now to be " 'kindred and race' " with " 'the beasts of the forest.' " The intimacy of the identification—with all the sadness and hopelessness it implies—rings out in his closing simile, as the old man calls himself " 'a worn-out and dying deer,' " standing alone, " 'one to many.' " His submission is that of the victimized and helpless: " 'work your will on me,' " he tells Dolittle, and in that phrasing completes his identification with the violated landscape (*Pi*, 369–70).

We are forced, therefore, to reassess what Natty's stance as a lone hunter and a reputed dead shot actually implies. His anger at the " 'wasty ways' " (*Pi*, 369) of the settlers clearly suggests that he is not to be regarded as one of those whom Crevecoeur criticized for having taken advantage of "the unlimited freedom of the woods."[15] In fact, though we are constantly reminded of Natty's hunting skills throughout the novels, we rarely see him aim at anything but evil Indians. Instead, it is generally the restraint of his hunting instincts and the frugality of his meals that are emphasized. He never takes " 'more than can be eat,' " and his notion of a hunt is to give the game " 'some chance for . . . life' " (*Pi*, 272). Still, even if his skill as a hunter can be kept within unabusive bounds, the very fact of Natty's being a white man, skilled in tracking and woodlore, and having, as a result, at least *some* ties to advancing settlement, puts him always in danger of somehow aiding that settlement's violating progress into nature's enclosures. It is precisely this dilemma that Cooper attempts to resolve by his choice of phrasing at the end of the novel, placing Natty "foremost" and thereby suggestively apart from "that band of Pioneers, who are opening the way for the march of our nation across the continent" (*Pi*, 477). But it is not an entirely successful resolution, for, in spite of Cooper's narrative insistence on Natty's harmonious relationship with the natural world, the old hunter has nevertheless been responsible for greeting Judge Temple in his first visit to his estate and in aiding young Oliver Effingham in his claims to ownership of the Otsego shore. And—a fact we cannot ignore—by its very definition, civilization in this novel *is* the destruction of the wilderness. The man whose eye looks forward to bridges, canals, mines, and towns, as does Judge Temple's, will never, like Natty, live happily " 'five years at a time without seeing the light of a clearing bigger that a wind-row in the trees' " (*Pi*, 203). It is therefore difficult to imagine Natty willingly participating in any "opening [of] the way for the march of our nation across the continent." Only a few paragraphs earlier he had rejected the Effinghams' offer of maintenance, and, all the young peoples' entreaties notwithstanding, declared, " 'I love the woods, and ye relish the face of man; . . . I'm form'd for the wilderness; if ye love me, let me go where my soul craves to be ag'in!' " (*Pi*, 475).

Clearly, Cooper had attempted at least three impossible tasks, and, in the course of the novel, resolved to abandon two of them. The possibility of a human settlement harmonious with nature is rejected as early as the opening chapter; the possibility that a man could serve both as spokesman for civilization and as a protector of the natural world proved unworkable, and Judge Temple stands as the first and the last character whom Cooper attempted to fit into that role (with young Oliver Effingham predicting little improvement); but the possibility that a single man might be able to live happily and harmoniously within nature's embrace without either losing his human identity or abusing the nurturing ambience he could not abandon. And so, determined to portray at least a fictional portrait of pastoral experience, Cooper spent the next eighteen years in pursuit of the meaning and substance of the man who could live isolate and contented within the darkened spaces of the woods, and move always in the half-light consciousness "towards the setting sun" (*Pi*, 477). The history of that pursuit is the history of the Leatherstocking novels.

With the second of the series, *The Last of the Mohicans* (1826),[16] the embracing forest vocabulary of *The Pioneers* crystallizes into a fairly consistent vocabulary of enclosure, with the different effect it has on Natty, and on those under his care, most clearly detailed in the episode in the cave behind Glenn's Falls. Guided by Natty and the two Indians, the group enters "the bowels of the earth," with Natty's torch laying "bare the much prized secret of the place." The startled young people first view "the scout, holding a blazing knot of pine" "at the further extremity of a narrow, deep, cavern in the rock, whose length appeared much extended by the perspective and the nature of the light by which it was seen" (*LM*, 71). Natty's "sturdy, weather-beaten countenance and forest attire" suggested to them an "air of romantic wildness" (*LM*, 71-72). Nature could hardly ask for more attractive lovers than the middle-aged Natty, "iron-like in the inflexibility of his frame," or the younger, more supple Uncas, "flexible . . . graceful and unrestrained in the attitudes and movements of nature" (*LM*, 72, 73). The likeness of the cave to the female body, with its various orifices, is almost obscenely hinted at in Natty's "laughing" statement, " 'Such old foxes as Chingachgook and myself are not often caught in a burrow with one hole.' " That the cave also invites the unconsciousness of sleep, however, suggests another kind of embrace—the maternal; enclosed, thus, within "the bowels of the earth," the two men are at once phallic and foetal. " 'The cunning of the place,' " as Natty happily points out, is that " 'the rock is black limestone, which everybody knows is soft; it makes no uncomfortable pillow' " (*LM*, 75).

That the cavern behind Glenn's Falls is supposed to be a place of safety is obvious, but there is also a quiet suggestion, in the language of the narrative, that it may be just a bit too embracing, too confining—indeed, almost suffocating for the civilized whites. Heyward, we are told, removes "the thick skreen" of blankets blocking one of the openings and "breathed the fresh and reviving air from the cataract" (*LM*, 84); and, not much later, "the whole party" is said to issue "from their place of confinement" and experience "a grateful renovation of their spirits, by exchanging the pent air of the hiding-place, for the cool and invigorating atmosphere which played around the whirlpools and pitches of the cataract" (*LM*, 87). It appears that the air currents produced by the falls are somehow necessary to the health and even mental wholeness of the whites; for them it is reviving, as the cave is suffocating. Natty, however, compares the rushing waters to a " 'headstrong man,' " describing their activity as perverse and rebellious, both phrasings suggesting energies beyond control and thereby latently dangerous (*LM*, 75, 76).

The human correlative of the water's "headstrong" maleness almost immediately expresses itself in the actions of Duncan Heyward. Like the falls, and unlike Natty and the Indians, the whites cannot stay comfortably contained within nature's "bowels." Discovered in "the dusky light which pervaded the depth of the cavern" by the acute eyes of a hostile Indian, Duncan forgets "everything but the impulses of his hot blood, . . . levelled his pistol and fired." He does not succeed in killing his Indian adversary, but instead, seems only to have wounded the enclosure that had hitherto provided safety and shelter. "The report of the weapon made the cavern bellow like an eruption from a volcano" (*LM*, 125), and its noise is heard "bursting from the bowels of the rock" (*LM*, 126). Thus blasted by "the impulses of . . . hot blood," the enclosure, which had once been so protective, gives up its charges. The image of violation is complete as "the cavern was entered at both its extremities" and its inmates "dragged from their shelter, and borne into the day" (*LM*, 126). The rape has been followed by a forced birth.

But for Natty there are no forced births and no brutal insistence that he be "borne into the day." The darkened shadows through which he moves continue to take on a slumbering, dreamlike quality in which he alone of the whites "held on his way, with the certainty and diligence of a man, who moved in the security of his own knowledge" (*LM*, 194). It is the same half-conscious, darkened world of *The Pioneers* in which he remains passively and protectedly at home.

Finally, however, Natty's passivity cannot be maintained. Chapter 32 opens in a "verdant and undulating" forest, a place, it seemed, "the foot of man had never trodden, so breathing and deep was the silence in which it lay" (*LM*, 483). But the unconscious and slumbering stillness is to be broken—this time, by the tread of men led by Natty, in "vengeful and vindictive battle." Here the reader probably recalls the novel's opening prediction that "there was no recess of the woods so dark, nor any secret place so lovely, that it might claim exemption from the inroads of those who had pledged their blood to satiate their vengeance" (*LM*, 9). And, by virtue of his own participation in that warfare, attaching himself to the English in their battle with the French over the mastery of this virgin territory, Natty, too, inevitably—though perhaps inadvertently—must share the guilt of that assault.

That the guilt implies, psychologically at least, an erosion of the filial response is made clear in Magua's indictment of white civilization as a whole:

"The Spirit that made men, coloured them differently," commenced the subtle Huron. . . . "Some he made with faces paler than the ermine of the forests: and these he ordered to be traders; dogs to their women, and wolves

> to their slaves. He gave this people the nature of the pigeon; wings that never tire; young, more plentiful than the leaves on the trees, and appetites to devour the earth. He gave them tongues like the false call of the wild-cat; hearts like rabbits; the cunning of the hog (but none of the fox), and arms longer than the legs of the moose. With his tongue, he stops the ears of the Indians; his heart teaches him to pay warriors to fight his battles; his cunning tells him how to get together the goods of the earth; and his arms enclose the land from the shores of the salt-water to the islands of the great lake. His gluttony makes him sick. God gave him enough, and yet he wants all. Such are the pale-faces.
>
> "Some the Great Spirit made with skins brighter and redder than yonder sun," continued Magua, pointing impressively upwards to the lurid luminary, which was struggling through the misty atmosphere of the horizon; "and these did he fashion to his own mind. He gave them this island as he had made it, covered with trees, and filled with game. The wind made their clearings; the sun and rains ripened their fruits; and the snows came to tell them to be thankful. What need had they of roads to journey by! They saw through the hills! When the beavers worked, they lay in the shade, and looked on. The winds cooled them in the summer; in winter, skins kept them warm. If they fought among themselves, it was to prove that they were men. They were brave; they were just; they were happy." [*LM*, 446-48]

In spite of the narrative insistence on Magua's treachery and cunning, the Indian commands a certain respect as the novel progresses. He is never guilty of raping or otherwise abusing the sisters he kidnaps, and, at the last, he fights bravely, trying, though in vain, to escape a dishonorable death. His interest for us in this passage, however, is in his evocation of patterns we have met before. The almost cancerous growth of human population and settlement, which had greeted Elizabeth Temple on her first entrance into Templeton, is echoed here by the description of whites as people whose " 'young [are] more plentiful than the leaves on the trees,' " and whose " 'appetites . . . devour the earth.' " " 'His gluttony makes him sick,' " the Indian declares, " 'and yet he wants all.' " The images of boundless, limitless growth and excessive, devouring taking are also interesting for the way in which they reverse and pervert natural processes. If, earlier, Chingachgook could speak of his own people as " 'the blossoms of . . . summers,' " who had, inevitably, " 'fallen, one by one' " (*LM*, 42), Magua now points to the whites as " 'more plentiful than the leaves on the trees,' " refusing to fall and obey natural cycles. If nature is nurturing, the whites are gluttonous, sickening on the very food they so greedily devour. If nature's maternal caring is an all-embracing containment, then the white men will enact their own perversion of that embrace—devouring the earth by mastering and inclosing " 'the land from the shores of the salt-water to the islands of the great lake.' " And, finally, if they will pervert and destroy the feminine in nature, so, too, they are " 'dogs to their women.' "

In contrast to the whites are the Indians. Though their skin seems to give off its own glow, " 'brighter and redder than yonder sun,' " the sun itself, when associated with these children of nature, takes on only the half-light dimness of a rather unappealing "lurid luminary, . . . struggling [to break] through the misty atmosphere." As with Natty, the Indians' world also opens upon a half-light, "misty" ambience. Similarly, in Magua's subtle style, the Indians never seem to touch the natural world at all, but rather appear to live in it passively caressed and wholly appreciative. If the whites " 'get together the goods of the earth' " in intentional and purposive action, the Indians merely accept what is freely given—" 'this island . . . covered with trees, and filled with game.' " The Indians appear to do nothing; the natural world does all for them: " 'The wind made their clearings; the sun and rains ripened their fruits. . . .' " Until the last two sentences of the second paragraph quoted, in fact, the only verbs with Indians as their subject-agents are "saw," "lay" and "looked on," none of them either very active or effecting, let alone destructive. The Indians are even spared the toils of the hunt, since Magua neatly avoids that problem by making the "skins" the subject of a verb that expresses more purpose than action and assumes volition: " 'Skins kept them warm.' " In short, with relation to the natural world, the Indians are never destructive or harmful; they simply do not act. They are, clearly, nature's "children," passively accepting the bounty she offers. In relation to each other, on the other hand, " 'they fought among themselves . . . to prove that they were men.' " This alone is the appropriate sphere for their aggressive energies. There is even a hint in Magua's wording that the whites are somehow less manly than the Indians: after all, the white man " 'pay[s] warriors to fight his battles,' " while the Indians " 'fought among themselves.' "

Cooper's concentrated use of ergative constructions here, implying that the world acts of its own volition, without human agency, proves a useful grammatical tactic for evoking a picture of idyllic and pastoral harmony. This same kind of stylistic effect has also been employed in large, in terms of narrative structure, as a device for maintaining Natty in a primal harmony with nature. If in the first novel Natty actually acts upon the natural world, as a hunter—but a hunter with restraint and feeling for the creatures he kills—by the second novel, though we know him to be a dead shot and expert huntsman, we never actually see him hunt. The passive or accepting stance, then, depends in part on Cooper's ability to both grammatically and dramatically play *down* the need for active aggression in the world, and on his ability to dissociate Natty from the modes of activity that Magua declares characteristic of the whites. It is, once again, an impossible task, since Natty's function in the novel is to act as guide and scout for the advancing British. Openly admitting that he could not wholly accept the implications of Natty's actions, Cooper chooses to sever Natty's relations with the white world and attach him, instead, to the Indian, pairing him at the end with Chingachgook, his initiator into the ways of the forest and, himself, one of nature's children. Natty's sexual potential is thereby also reinforced, since Chingachgook's phallic identity within the natural world has all along been suggested by the English translation of his name, Big Serpent; by contrast, the Indian conceives himself castrated, " 'a blazed pine, in [the] clearing of the pale-faces' " (*LM*, 519). But it was a precarious compromise, in many ways, and, realizing that he could neither accept the guilt of violation nor free Natty of that guilt (by defusing his sexuality entirely or by denying his "white gifts"), Cooper finally did away with his creation in *The Prairie*.

The Prairie (1827),[17] then, is really the end of a dream. Though Natty still insists upon the possibility of experiencing a primal pastoral harmony between man and the natural world, we realize that he himself has abandoned the garden and chosen, instead, to spend his last days on "the naked prairies" (*Pr*, 432). No longer does Cooper even pretend that Natty could willingly take a place "in that band of Pioneers who are opening the way for the march of our nation across the continent." Rather, as though in self-punishment for his former guilt and in a final attempt to escape its repetition, Natty has cut himself off entirely from white civilization—the necessity of which had become painfully obvious by the end of the second novel—and sequestered himself within nature's most uninviting domain. Not only do the prairies' distance from the settlements make the arrival of the axe and the "chopper" highly improbable, but, more important, their very terrain renders that aggression impotent.

The land itself, in its barren and unwelcoming aspect, is its own best protection against what Cooper calls the "tide of instant emigration" (*Pr*, 2). Like the latently dangerous "headstrong" cataract, the "sudden outbreaking of a people" suggests a denial of restraint or control, as the hitherto "unexplored regions [are] . . . laid open" before "the long files" of those "who first penetrated the wilds" (*Pr*, 2-3). That the vocabulary of this movement "deeper into the land, in quest of . . . [a] natural and more congenial atmosphere," suggests a phallic intrusion, I think, is obvious. It involves, again, those who, "led by the phantoms of hope, and ambitious of sudden affluence, sought the mines of the virgin territory," and in contrast to whom we see again the maternal generosity of a land where the "generous, alluvial bottoms of the rivers never fail to bestow on the most desultory industry" a rich return (*Pr*, 3). In grim and succinct summary, then, we have experienced, at the outset of the third novel, the ever-threatening rape of the Mother.

From this threat Natty has fled, hoping to escape forever, in " 'these vast and naked fields,' " all association with the aggressions of the "Long-knives" (*Pr*, 58). But even here he is to hear, once again before his death, " 'the sound of axes, and the crash of falling trees' " (*Pr*, 19), and to know, once and for all, his own inescapable complicity in that violation. Though, as in the second novel, he himself never directly violates nature's precincts—talking of trapping but never actually shown doing so, aiming at a charging buffalo but missing his shot—he does lead the Bush family to a campsite, shares a meal with them, and then watches, "with a melancholy" and discontented gaze, as Ishmael's sons destroy a grove of cottonwoods. Cooper's language here seems intent on emphasizing the sexual implications of their assault, with the eldest son burying his axe in "the soft body," and then bringing his victim "in submission to his prowess." "His companions," who had previously regarded the proceedings with only "indolent curiosity," seem suddenly aroused by the tree's "prostrate" position and, with a vicious cruelty, advance "in a body" "for a general attack" upon the entire grove. "Stripped," as in rape (*Pr*, 13), even these barren precincts feel the thrust of those who " 'scourge the very 'arth with their axes' " (*Pr*, 82-83). And Natty, in ironic self-recognition, admits, " 'I might have know'd it. . . . Often have I seen the same before; and yet *I brought them to the spot myself*' " (*Pr*, 92 [italics mine]).

As in the two earlier novels, Natty simply cannot dissociate himself from complicity in the raping movement of white settlement westward. And yet, Cooper keeps insisting, this is a character who boasts of total dependence on the Book of Nature for wisdom and who delights in his containment within a feminine natural world: " 'I have been a solitary man much of my time,' " he admits, only to qualify it with, " 'if he can be called solitary who has lived for seventy years in the very bosom of natur' ' " (*Pr*, 296). Natty's identification with nature's maternal and nurturing aspect is again suggested, as he remembers, at one point, " 'Many are the cubs, and many are the speckled fawns that I have reared with these old hands' " (*Pr*, 283). No longer is he even a potential threat to such creatures, since, because of his advanced age, he is now unable to wield his rifle very effectively. But if this apparently denies him any possibility of phallic intrusion, the narrative undercuts it by describing his body as long, firm and decidedly phallic: bidding "defiance to all the usual attacks of human infirmities," the aged Natty still stands tall and erect, "his attenuated frame . . . like the shaft of seasoned oak, dry, naked and tempest-riven, but unbending and apparently indurated to the consistency of stone" (*Pr*, 277).

In a similar vein, the narrative carefully attempts to distinguish Natty from those who would abuse pastoral intimacy, while simultaneously insisting on his independent and assertive masculine ego orientation. Natty insists, for instance, that he is " 'a man who follows his reason,' " in contrast to Ishmael Bush who follows " 'the instinct of the beast' " (*Pr*, 67). By thus pointing up Ishmael's connection to the earth in the unconscious manner of a beast of instinct, its intellective qualities either missing or not wholly developed, Cooper emphasizes the fact that dull, brutish, and instinctual taking may be just as abusive of nature's generosity as is conscious goal-oriented, civilized activity. So important is it to Cooper to establish Natty's reasoning or intellective development that he would have us believe that, while standing before a herd of stampeding buffalo, Natty is "sustained by the firmness and steadiness that intellect can only impart" (*Pr*, 235). But it is just this quality of conscious awareness—his intellect or "reason"—that saves Natty from a total, brute-like dependence upon the Mother.

Besides distinguishing him from the brute power of an Ishmael Bush and the intellective depredations of a Dr. Bat, leaving him just enough of each to counteract the negative aspects of the other, Cooper is also at pains to distinguish Natty from the white men he aids, by crediting him with a perhaps impossible "mixture of decision and resignation." While Middleton and Hover are infinitely more credible in their energetic, often precipitous activity, Natty is defined as a "character, in which excessive energy, and the most meek submission to the will of Providence, were oddly enough combined" (*Pr*, 364). Oddly enough, indeed! The narrative wants to have it both ways: Natty as part of the masculine world in his "excessive energy" and ability to think independently, and yet identified with the feminine in his "meek submission to the will of Providence." The tension is one that Cooper never really resolves in this novel. Instead, he attempts another precarious compromise, allowing Natty the external emblems of manhood, in his ever-present rifle and reputation as a dead shot, but keeping him, nevertheless, embowered, embraced, and unassaulting within nature's "dark and secret recesses." It was, however, a compromise he could not easily sustain, and so, in this novel, he has Natty make his final truce with nature, submitting to her completely in death.

The grave is watched over by the Pawnees, who, like Natty, are also "children of nature," and its only white or civilized touch is the stone placed there by Middleton, "in due time." Its inscription, *"May no wanton hand ever disturb his remains"* (*Pr*, 461), seems a fitting final hint that Natty is once again standing in as surrogate for the woman to whom he has now returned. When Cooper wrote, we remember, she was fast being disturbed by the wanton and violating hand of white emigration and settlement. And it was, no doubt, an uncomfortable (if inexpressible) awareness of what that violation entailed that first pushed Cooper into abandoning his pastoral vision and then, thirteen years later, into reviving its possibility. If, after three novels, Natty could not be entirely dissociated from the brutal raping of nature's precincts, he had nevertheless been the first character in American fiction to at least *promise* entry without violation. As mid-century approached, moreover, American writers began to express a kind of urgency on the subject, fearing, as did William Gilmore Simms, for instance, that "the various charms of scenery which our country possesses" might, indeed, go unsung and forgotten in the wake of "progress." Urging "the national mind" to "pause in its career . . . for a survey of its conquests and itself,"[18] Simms was suggesting, if only by inference, what Cooper had hoped Natty might accomplish. But something had all along been missing in Natty's makeup, and this, too, Cooper felt he had to rectify. It must have been with mixed emotions, then, that Cooper returned to Natty in a fourth novel, still attempting to give literary form to the pastoral impulse, but simultaneously committed to portraying the sexuality of a character who, previously, had been passively and contentedly embowered by the forests' embraces.

The Natty Bumppo of *The Pathfinder* (1840),[19] like his earlier incarnations, insists upon his attachment to the dim but embracing enclosures of the forest, and claims that anyone who " 'would lead me out of the shade of the woods, to put me in the sun of the clearin's!' " (*P*, 185), can be no friend to his happiness. But, as a now middle-aged Natty begins to fall in love with Mabel Dunham, we hear him make other, equally fervent protestations of quite a different sort:" 'But I am human a'ter all; yes, I find I'm very human in some of my feelin's' " (*P*, 281). In assertions like these and in Cooper's attempt to convince us that Natty *could* fall in love, we have the author's last ditch attempt to make a psychologically whole man out of the character to whom he had attributed so many of the externals of manhood. Obviously, of course, Cooper never intended us to take seriously the possibility of Pathfinder's marriage, and so he introduced Jasper Western at the very beginning of the story as a more appropriate suitor; what he wanted to do, really, was to give his character a dimension that he felt had been missing from his makeup.

The central focus of the novel then becomes the contest, between the two competing feminines, for Natty's affections. For a time the comforts of the forest virtually disappear as the narrative follows Natty into the environs of the fort. Here there is a psychological, as well as a physical, displacement of the character, most dramatically illustrated by Natty's "wantonly" shooting two birds from the air, an act of which we would not ordinarily have thought him capable, and completely contradicting earlier statements he has made about himself in the novel (*P*, 177). However, as the act is performed during what we might consider a courting scene, Natty's prowess with the rifle, his one objective phallic emblem, becomes not only an appropriate way of impressing Mabel, but also demonstrates, rather graphically, the quality of relationship he hopes to experience with her.

In response, nature has her own attractions to pit against the " 'pleasant looks, and . . . winning ways' " (*P*, 199) of human females. On board the scud, viewing from its deck the passing "outlines of trees . . . and . . . large bays that lay embosomed in woods," Natty realizes that "notwithstanding he found it so grateful to be near

Mabel . . . his soul [did] pine to be wandering beneath the high arches of the maples, oaks, and lindens, where his habits had induced him to fancy lasting and true joys were only to be found" (*P*, 305).

The initial resolution of the tension occurs, not dramatically, but psychoanalytically, as Natty relates a recent dream to Mabel:

> ". . . the very last night we stayed in the garrison, I imagined I had a cabin in a grove of sugar maples, and at the root of every tree was a Mabel Dunham, while the birds that were among the branches sang ballads, instead of notes that natur' gave, and even the deer stopped to listen. I tried to shoot a fa'an, but Killdeer missed fire, and the creatur' laughed in my face, as pleasantly as a young girl laughs in her merriment, and then it bounded away, looking back as if expecting me to follow." [*P*, 291-92]

The dream is not, as David Noble suggests, an evocation of Natty's desire "to exchange physical nature for human companionship,"[20] but rather, a revelation of the two competing feminines between whom Natty finds himself torn. The cabin, which in dreams represents not so much a physical shelter as a symbol of psychological identity, is here particularly placed "in a grove of sugar maples," enclosing it thereby within the embrace of nature; Natty's internal reality, then, is complete only as the two things harmonize—the cabin *within* the grove—and both the human and the natural elements seem equally important. The sugar maple, as we know from *The Pioneers*, is that delightful tree that gives forth the sweetness of its sap, singularly nurturing and appealing. "At the root" of each of these unique trees "was a Mabel Dunham," who, as the maternal feminine, or Earth Mother symbol, gives nurture to the roots of all growing things. In this case, it is particularly sweet and positive nurturance; and the femininity is not that of a discrete person in any real sense, but rather the impersonal but nevertheless positive femininity of the Mother. Mabel, of course,the only woman to whom Natty has ever responded with personal feeling, is thereby an appropriate emblem through which his unconscious may image the archetypal feminine in nature.

Then Natty does something quite odd, for him: he aims at a fawn, without giving it the benefit of the chase, and, more unusual yet, Killdeer misfires. Subsequently, the fawn takes on flirtatious, coquettish qualities, laughs in the dreamer's face, and then bounds away, " 'looking back as if expecting me to follow.' " Why, we wonder, does a fawn laugh at her hunter and beckon her potential destroyer to follow? Because that destroyer has been rendered impotent; she may flirt all she wants and still be safe from his aggressions. Quite different from the maternal-feminine aspect of Mabel, seated at the root of every tree, the fawn is feminine nature's sexual face. Once we understand the psychological significance of the fawn within Natty's unconscious and internal reality, we also understand why, for the first time in any novel, his trusty gun does not go off. His overwhelming attraction for the real-world sexual Mabel has somewhat severed him from his previous and total embracement within the natural world. But the fawn's flirtation encourages him to think that the natural world, too, will permit a sexual intimacy. That the gun misfires proves that dream to be, once more, an illusion. The Mother *will* not be violated—even if, to keep her hold on Natty, she *appears* to promise such total gratification. That Natty himself could not face the incest possibility is made clear by the fact that it is his own unconscious that, in the dream, deflects that potential threat. Now, having been awakened by Mabel to the possibility of his own sexuality, Pathfinder complains that, " 'instead of sleeping as sound as natur' at midnight, as I used to could, I dream nightly of Mabel Dunham' " (*P*, 476).

His previous containment within the unconscious sleep of the maternal has been seriously threatened, and, in order to elaborate upon and emphasize the psychological implications of the dream, Cooper has Natty repeat it to Jasper Western: " 'The young does sport before me; and when I raise Killdeer in order to take a little venison, the animals look back, and it seems as if they all had Mabel's sweet countenance, laughing in my face, and looking as if they said, "Shoot me if you dare!" ' " (*P*, 476). Natty's potentially destructive powers are being defused; the apparently innocent act of taking " 'a little venison' " is now being experienced as aggression against something essentially feminine, beloved, desirable, and vulnerable. As a result, Natty finds he cannot accept the implicit challenge to assert himself: he would not dare to shoot.

This is the only dream recorded in all five of the Leatherstocking novels, and, as such, it is Cooper's first and only attempt to image for us Natty's internal reality. Its fundamental meaning is subsequently reinforced as Cooper, apparently recognizing for the first time the psychological significance of his creation, describes Natty's mind as "almost infantine in its simplicity and nature" (*P*, 294). The regressive aspect of the man whose psychic reality could be imaged within an embrace of nature, the cabin in the maple grove, for instance, has been admitted at last! It is a containment that has never been challenged, and suggests that Natty has been, all along, presexual, his movements those of the son and not the lover. That this late experience with the sexuality of woman has been " 'so painful and so deep' " as " 'to harrow the very soul,' " underscores Natty's unfamiliarity with this aspect of his own masculinity. "Indeed, in this respect," as Cooper tells us, "the Pathfinder was a mere child," and he drives the point home again in comparing him to an "infant" (*P*, 294). Still, Cooper insists, the external details of Natty's life and mien maintain the appearance of masculine identity—"so stern, stoical, masculine, and severe, in all that touched his ordinary pursuits" (*P*, 294). Which is exactly what had us all so confused; even the admiring Simms had noted the contradiction, disturbed by what he saw as Cooper's repeated failure "to hit the true line that divides the simplicity of nature, from the puerility of ignorance or childhood."[21] But now we realize that Natty's apparently masculine outward identity had no real internal or psychological correlative. Cooper had been merely taking it for granted. As the language of the previous narratives had hinted—with their insistence on the enclosure motif in Natty's world—and now, as the incidents of this fourth novel make clear, Natty had all along been a psychological child, still contained within a world that was predominantly maternal. That was the secret of the almost nonviolating harmony, the second-paradisal intimacy, which he alone, of all the Leatherstocking whites, had been able to maintain within the natural world.

The novel's conclusion suggests that if the primal harmony Natty had previously known is now seriously threatened, it is not completely destroyed. Natty cannot assimilate Mabel, as the forest has assimilated him, into a parental embrace, and through her, he remains forever tied to the possibility of his own sexuality; he continues to pay homage to that possibility in the "valuable presents of furs" he sends her "at intervals of years" (*P*, 500). And, in spite of his pain and his inability " 'to march quite as light-hearted as I once used to could, or to sleep as sound for some time to come,' " Natty acknowledges the positive power of conscious light breaking into the unconscious and embracing slumber. " 'How could I be sorry that a ray of the sun came across the gloom,' " he asks, or " 'that light has broken in upon darkness, though it remained so short a time!' " (*P*, 491). But whether that "light" will be fully realized, even without Mabel's presence, or whether it is doomed to remain only "so short a time," is the psychological impetus for the final novel in the series. With the close of *The Pathfinder* we know only that Natty intends to " 'return to the wilderness and my Maker' "

(*P*, 492), and our final view of him is as a man receding from our sight, "lost in the depths of the forest" (*P*, 500).

At the end of January 1841, Cooper informed his publisher that he had begun "a new tale, in which Leatherstocking would appear as a young man." "It struck me," he explained, "that having written so much about this character, a work of this sort was wanting to fill up his history. In the last book he is called the Pathfinder, and *was in love*: in this he is called the Deerslayer, *and is beloved*."[22] Cooper's search for the substance and meaning of his character's identity was coming to an end.

No longer quite so paradisal, in *The Deerslayer* (1841) the "broad belts of the virgin wilderness" seem wilfully to contain something threatening within their embrace—even for Natty—by "affording forest covers to the noiseless moccasin of the native warrior as he trod the secret and bloody warpath" (*D*, 3). While the earlier novels in the series detailed Indian warfare in the forest recesses, none had opened with such emphatic suggestions of wilfully harbored dangers in those enclosures; there is not even a countering image of the forest taking back the dead in revenge for their invasion or absorbing the armies in the slumberous embrace of death—as appeared in *The Last of the Mohicans*. We are left, rather, with a sense of potential violence, lurking and harbored within the forest depths. Into this world steps a youthful Natty, accompanied by Hurry Harry, and, for a moment, things seem again as they might have in paradise. Breaking out of the forest and "into the brilliant light of the sun," Natty observes, from his perch "on a low, gravelly point," the striking view of the lake that is to be the scenic focus of the chapters to follow (*D*, 20–21). Immediately, Cooper has Natty responding "unconsciously" (*D*, 33) to the forest-enclosed water, which "resembled a bed" in its "placid and limpid" quality, "tempting the onlooker to slumber and repose" (*D*, 21).

Taking the lake as a kind of emblem of the womb, in its slumberous, liquid embrace, we may see its relation to the surrounding trees as indicative of analogous human psychological possibilities, with the trees, like the creatures of the wild, also nature's children. Some, by "inclining to the light," move out of that embrace, toward independence. "In many instances," the narrative tells us, "they extend their long limbs and straight trunks some forty or fifty feet beyond the line of the perpendicular." "These cases," however, "allude only to the giants of the forest"—or, we might say, to the natural counterparts of men who face and conquer maternal engulfment—those "pines of a hundred or a hundred and fifty feet in height." Unfortunately, not all of them make it. The others, those that have not succeeded in their inclination toward the light, remain of "smaller growth," and return to the generative and subsequently enclosing womb, inclining "so far as to steep their lower branches in the water" (*D*, 142). The passage is illuminating because it images so clearly, in natural terms, the opposing possibilities of independence from and engulfment within the maternal embrace. The pastoral paradise, in the course of this last novel, is acknowledged as a potential trap.

The story itself has the youthful Natty realizing that, "for the first time in his life he was in the vicinity of enemies" (*D*, 67). As he takes his place at a window, the ark is described as "just passing through the narrowest part of the stream," constricted and enclosed by "the trees . . . interlocked overhead" (*D*, 67), much like a birth canal. And, in spite of the fact that his first confrontation with hostile Indians lurking in the forest depths includes the entire party aboard the scow, there is a concentration on Deerslayer's perceptions and movements that seems to give the episode a special significance for him alone. With the enclosure of the forest itself a source of danger, "the inclination of the [overhanging] tree" admitting "easy passage" to the Indians intending to board the ark, Deerslayer quickly appraises the situation, and urges those aboard to pull harder (*D*, 67, 68). The ark takes advantage of the rushing current and moves out of the enclosure, continuing "to drift ahead until fairly in the open lake." Here it is comparatively safe (though still "near enough to the land to render exposure to a rifle bullet dangerous") (*D*, 69). The movement has apparently provided an escape from one kind of danger, the threat lurking in enclosed places, but has simultaneously propelled Natty out into a realm in which he is perhaps not much more secure.

In broad outline, Deerslayer's initiation into the blood mystery of death follows the pattern described in the ark's escape. Coming on shore to retrieve a canoe, Deerslayer finds himself the target of an Indian who is also intent on taking possession of the little craft. To escape further danger, the Deerslayer "dashed into the woods and sought a cover." But now "the high and gloomy vaults of the forest" provide a shelter for his adversary, too, the Indian's "body being concealed by an oak" (*D*, 108), just as, previously, the forest enclosures had sheltered the hostile band of Iroquois. Finally, Deerslayer wounds, but does not immediately kill, the Indian, and, in the space of time during which he witnesses his enemy's death throes, he accepts a ceremonial changing of his name. Henceforth, because " 'eye sartain—finger lightning—aim, death,' " the Indian decides he is to be called Hawkeye (*D*, 116). Here, the escape from the dangers lurking in enclosures has been followed by a baptism; and it continues, as previously, with a movement back onto the lake, Deerslayer "quitting the shore under long and steady sweeps of the paddle" (*D*, 118). Significantly, it is only after this initiation into his own potential for causing death and destruction, in chapter 7, that Deerslayer is able to articulate another part of his masculinity—his sexuality—in chapter 8. Here, in a passage perhaps too often quoted and oversimplified, he gives explicit recognition to something we have been waiting to hear him say since the end of *The Pathfinder*. Judith Hutter, a magnificent embodiment of human feminine sexuality, confronts Deerslayer with his own relation to that aspect of women:

> "And where, then, is *your* sweetheart, Deerslayer?"
> "She's in the forest, Judith—hanging from the boughs of the trees, in a soft rain—in the dew on the open grass—the clouds that float about in the blue heavens—the birds that sing in the woods—the sweet springs where I slake my thirst—and in all the other glorious gifts that come from God's Providence!" [*D*, 132]

Although the feminine still retains some of its maternal content, in its ability to protect and nurture, the union that Deerslayer describes is certainly sexual, with its soft, caressing evocation of liquid discharges. In no uncertain terms, Cooper is trying to show us the son reborn as lover.[23] We now realize the full significance of his affirmation of Judith's statement, " 'You mean that, as yet you've never loved one of my sex, but love best your haunts' " (*D*, 132).

A few chapters later there is a similar exchange; Cooper seems most determined that we get his message:

> "And *you*, Deerslayer," said Judith . . . "have *you* never felt how pleasant it is to listen to the laugh of a girl you love?"
> "Lord bless you, gal!—why I've never lived enough among my own color to drop into them sort of feelin's—no, never! I dare to say, they are nat'ral and right, but to me there's no music so sweet as the sighing of the wind in the treetops, and the rippling of a stream from a full, sparkling natyve fountain of pure fresh water." [*D*, 152-53]

Again it is the sexual face of nature that calls—like the laughing doe in the dream of the Pathfinder. This time, however, the sexuality is imaged through the appeal of water, the stream especially being emphasized, evoking, thereby, the liquid discharges of sex as well as the slaking of thirst and the union of masculine and feminine elements. These images all indicate a kind of coming together, but not an annihilating engulfment of one thing by another. By thus deliberately and fundamentally changing the imagery through which Natty describes his world, Cooper reveals his intention that we experience Natty's subsequent movements through nature's enclosures as sexual and no longer as the unconscious movement of the son within a maternal embrace. It is Judith, however, barred forever from the garden herself, who confers upon Natty Killdeer, his constant companion and emblem of phallic power. That he immediately proceeds to abuse that power, in order to test the excellence of the rifle, only expresses once again the underlying tragic paradox that Cooper must constantly confront: man, either as son or as lover, is inevitably guilty of abusing nature's bounty. Given the gun, in chapter 25, Natty immediately and wantonly aims at a distant bird, only to guiltily regret his action in the opening of chapter 26. But of course this is their first warpath, which is precisely the point: what Natty and Chingachgook must learn in their initiation into adult male roles is to control and use properly the potentially threatening power of masculine self-assertion.

This, then, is the real loss of innocence—not the fact that Natty kills his first human being in this novel and involves himself in the wranglings of European culture, as more than one critic has suggested.[24] Breaking out of the maternal and turning to nature in a sexually self-assertive and potentially destructive role—with the power, for instance, of a Hurry Harry—and then abusing that potential for destruction is Natty's fall. As he remarks to Judith, " 'What a thing is power! . . . and what a thing it is to have it, and not to know how to use it!' " (*D*, 464). In some sense, of course, that is exactly the problem encountered by the Europeans as they move into, impose their will upon, and gradually destroy the bountiful American continent. From this point on, Natty is drawn back into the realm of the Mother, and back into the infantile presexuality he had known in all the previous novels. Although Cooper realizes the dangers attendant upon such total envelopment by the maternal feminine—thwarted maturity and inevitable isolation from the human community—he seems unable to create a satisfying alternative. Sexuality looms, for him, as a power far too destructive and uncontrollable, carrying with it, always, the threat of violation. Better to remain the son, he seems to be saying, rather than run the risk of violating the Mother.

Understandably, then, the patterns of movement in this novel have resembled *both* a birth and a regression. As in the first adventure aboard the ark, or later, in his first experience of shedding human blood, Natty's spatial and thereby psychological experience has become a movement from enclosure in the woods to quickened movement on water and then out into the open and tranquil lake. It is, on the one hand, an expulsion from the dark and embracing maternal forest—which now has become a medium for hostile as well as benevolent elements—and out into apparent openness and light; on the other hand, it is also a movement from one kind of containment to another, the first small, dark, and actively dangerous, the other open, calm, liquid, and womb-like, inviting slumber and complete repose. Both, however, deny the possibility of fulfilling and asserting independent consciousness and sexual potency. Judith Hutter, in fact, is rejected because Natty does not " 'feel . . . as if I wished to quit father and mother—if father and mother was livin'; which, however, neither is—. . . in order to cleave unto *her*' " (*D*, 568). What he is saying is that he does not yet wish to give up sonhood to attain full manhood. For, of course, his parents are still living, implicit in the feminine natural world and its Christian father-figure progenitor.

At the end of the novel, fifteen years later, only three men revisit the Glimmerglass: Natty, Chingachgook, and the Indian's son, Uncas. Psychologically, we realize, there has been another kind of return. Forest and lake no longer harbor anything as obviously threatening as the hostile Iroquois, and paradise, apparently, has been restored. We, as readers, however, know the heavy price that has been paid for the resurrection of this pastoral vision. The setting sun, like a dimmed or waning consciousness, leaves the three men in the half-light embrace of the beautiful and seductive Mother. The end is a return to beginnings, as in the constant cycles of nature, and what once hastened a new birth, the river rushing "through its bower of trees," now marks a return. The rock that once projected out from amid the trees, marking the meeting place of those who were to be initiated, is now "wasting away" by the slow but determined castration of waters that had once signified new life and the possibility of sexual union. Surrounding the entire scene are the mountains, curving and undulating like a woman's body, "in their native dress, dark, rich, and mysterious," while in their center, in their most hidden precinct, still stands the lake, in its beckoning "solitude, a beautiful gem of the forest" (*D*, 570-71). Its mysterious and seductive quality is overwhelming, inviting again the slumbering repose of unconscious containment. "Accident or tradition," we read, "had rendered it again a spot sacred to nature" (*D*, 572). The potential sexuality of the human feminine, on the other hand, has been banished from the scene. Hetty has been buried, and Judith Hutter has returned to the settlements and "relapsed into her early failing," a human "victim" of masculine sexual exploitation. All that remains to Natty of "the girl [who] had never touched his heart" is the destructive potential of Killdeer, with which she had endowed him, and a bit of ribbon still clinging to the decaying ark that "he tore away . . . and knotted . . . to the stock of Killdeer" (*D*, 572). In that gesture we have perhaps the novels' only real gesture of purely sexual union.

Realizing, in the first novel of the series, that the human social community, in its various forms, could not maintain a pastoral harmony, Cooper turned, instead, to the single individual—Natty Bumppo. But the precarious balance of independent, masculine activity and passive acceptance of nature's bounty proved impossible, and, with *The Prairie*, Cooper has Natty at first acknowledging his own complicity in the violation of nature's recesses and then disburdening himself of his guilt, in death. The fantasy of total gratification led, inevitably, to the spectre of incest, and that, Cooper realized, could not be permitted. It lasted but a few paragraphs in *The Deerslayer* before he pulled Natty back from manhood to sonhood. Only as son can he maintain the nondestructive, nonexploitive harmony he seeks; but the price, as Cooper tacitly acknowledged, is his adult sexuality and with it, much of what we know as civilized norms. Natty can never experience adult human relations within the social community; the pastoral impulse has led him back into the liquid embrace of nature's womb. Just how aware Cooper was of the psychological substratum behind his vocabulary and landscape descriptions is open to debate; what cannot be dismissed, however, is the dramatic change in vocabulary that occurs in *The Deerslayer* and, before that, the psychological accuracy of the dream sequences and the labeling of Natty as "infantine" and "childlike" in *The Pathfinder*. Though initially Cooper was probably largely unaware of his character's scope and implications, he pursued his study of Natty until, gradually, he was able to make of "the pastoral design" in America what Leo Marx has called "a symbolic structure of thought and feeling, a landscape of mind in which the movement in physical space corresponds to a movement in consciousness."[25] For, infantile and presexual as he is, Natty Bumppo remains, in many ways, an embodiment of The American Dream. A pastoral landscape still seems to beckon to us, calling us into state parks and our children to summer camps, urging us to withdraw from the current and go back to an initial moment of perfect peace, absolute harmony, and freedom from want, within a feminine and wholly gratifying natural world.

Every Mother's Son: The Revolutionary War Romances of William Gilmore Simms

> *Sweet is the swamp with its secrets,*
> *Until we meet a snake . . .*
>
> —EMILY DICKINSON

When, in 1856, William Gilmore Simms apologized to a Buffalo, New York, audience for having "spoken warmly" in defense of southern culture, he explained his passion by declaring, "you would not, surely, have me speak coldly in the assertion of a Mother's honour." Some years later he admonished his son, then a Confederate soldier, "to remember that you are to defend your mother country and your natural mother from a hoard of mercenaries and plunderers."[26] In appealing thus to an emotional identification of the human maternal with the "mother country," Simms was employing a vocabulary that had been operative in the South for over two hundred years. The usage dated back to the period when, as Simms described it, "the marvelous seemed every where to be opened upon mankind," and "all the pulses of mortal imagination seemed to have quickened . . . under a like maternal influence."

To nineteenth-century America's fascination with its history and national identity and to Simms's concern that history be made available "for the Purposes of Art," we must attribute the immense success that Simms's novels, especially the loosely connected Revolutionary War romances, enjoyed in their day. Urgently seeking to disengage itself both from European models and from European critical scorn, the American imagination, following the War for Independence, anxiously sought what Simms attempted to provide:

not merely "the bald history [that], by itself, would be of very little importance," but, rather, "the inspiration . . . [to] be found either in the illustration of the national history, or in the development of the national characteristics." If we accept Simms's own ideal of himself as "the artist . . . who is the true historian," the man "who gives shape to the unhewn fact,—who yields relation to the scattered fragments,—who unites the parts in coherent dependency, and endows, with life and action, the otherwise motionless automata of history,"[27] we are encouraged to seek out in his novels underlying symbolic and psychological structures that give meaning to history.

Even as a formal historian, writing what he hoped would be adopted as the standard school text, *The History of South Carolina* (1840), Simms depicted the "war of the Revolution" as a drama of vulnerable femininity assaulted by masculine aggression. With its coming, South Carolina's "peace, her prosperity, her growing opulence, her improved civilization, her refinement" were all but destroyed, and from it, the colony "emerged . . . covered with wounds, and weeds, and ruin! bleeding and impoverished; her fields laid waste; her cultivation at an end."[28] A more explicit recognition of what that vocabulary implies is given voice by his own idealized *persona*, the invented poet, George Dennison, whose verses Simms is fond of sprinkling through the Revolutionary War romances:

"My country is my mistress,
And in her beauties rare,
I read the sweetest hist'ries
That make a loved one dear:

. . . .

The charms that won our sires
Are fresh and sweet to me,

. . . .

My life, my life, dear mistress,
My life is at thy feet!"[29]

Simms's fictional partisan heroes are, in fact, protecting their pastoral impulse, defending a realm that, as both plot and vocabulary suggest, they are experiencing as feminine.

Written between 1835 and 1855[30] as a series of interlocking historical romances, with each narrative complete in itself, the six titles discussed here (except *Woodcraft*) loosely center on various Revolutionary War events related to the exploits of the guerilla patriot, Francis Marion, popularly known as "the Swamp Fox." Their scene is the "Marion District," which, in the companion volume to the

History, The Geography of South Carolina (1843), Simms described as "uniformly level, intersected in all directions by the finest creeks and rivers," their waters abounding in "the shad and herring," as well as "trout, bream, perch, cat &c." The surrounding lands "are very rich," "the climate is mild and agreeable," and "the settlements are considered healthy."[31] It was an area that, even by the time of the *Geography*, remained chiefly agricultural and only sparsely settled.

"Yet was its sacred and sweet repose about to be invaded. War had prepared his weapon and lay waiting in the shade" (*Par*, 372). For the most part, such sentences serve to break a mood and only rarely introduce descriptions of ruined landscapes or pillaged plantations. And even these we are quite clearly to regard as unfortunate but temporary: Simms's fictional eighteenth-century South is essentially a region without change. The geography is neatly landscaped into either wilderness, consisting of forest and swamp, or plantation; small towns, such as Dorchester in *The Partisan* or Orangeburg in *The Forayers*, occasionally appear, as do the Charleston scenes in *Katharine Walton*, but these more populous places are always described in terms of blending off into or being surrounded by more wild areas. Moreover, all these geographic distinctions appear carefully defined, without any suggestion that one might expand or impinge upon another. There is no hint that the city of Dorchester will grow out into the forest land around it; and the plantations all seem to have reached their final size and state of perfection. The only character who seeks to increase his lands (by possessing other people's plantations, not by tracking out previously uncultivated land), is decidedly villainous.*

Typically, Simms's campsite descriptions suggest an almost womb-like ambience, "deeply embowered," "girdled . . . in" by "thick forest walls" or by "woods too impenetrably dense" (*Par*, 415). Nurture is provided, at its worst, in "the bitter . . . acorn," which, we are assured, "soon ceased to offend [the men's] appetites and tastes" (*M*, 356), or, at its best, in "the blue-cat of the Edisto . . . one of the nicest fish that swims, tender as young love, white as maiden purity, delicate as a dream of innocence" (*F*, 275). And, though admittedly "primitive," the campsites are rarely intended to appear unduly comfortless; if "the greensward" provides "the only seats," and "the green boughs of oak and pine . . . the only roofing,"

*The tory, M'Kewn, in *Woodcraft*.

the men are nevertheless seen happily disposing themselves upon "the green bosom of their mother earth" (*F*, 515). Even "the virgin forest" provides a "rude couch among the trees" (*KW*, 188). At moments, the soldiers who "playfully gambolled about among the forest avenues" (*M*, 153) appear to have returned to the ways of childhood, resting "level with the green bosom of their mother earth—at this season covered with a plentiful clothing of verdure" (*F*, 515).

If we follow any of Simms's many partisan "wayfarers" through "the dark and silent recesses of those thickets that seemed impenetrable from without" (*F*, 11), we consistently enter a region whose landscape, both symbolically and geographically, images a return to a passive, infantile orientation. "Well calculated to arm the instincts of the wayfarer with a tremulous sense of danger," the "threatening shadows" (*F*, 11) soon give way to promises of erotic delight as, in *The Scout*, "wild grape vines . . . fling themselves with the wind in which they swing and sport, arching themselves from tree to tree, and interlacing their green tresses until the earth below becomes a stranger to the sun" (*S*, 15-16). But behind the erotic is the face of the Mother, rewarding not with sexuality, but with nurture and protection:

> Their blue clusters droop to the hand, and hang around the brows of the fainting and feeble partisan, returning from the conflict. He forgets the cruelties of his fellow man, in solacing himself with the grateful tributes which are yielded him by the bounteous nature. Their fruits relieve his hunger and quench his thirst—their green leaves refresh his eye—their shadows protect him from the burning sunbeams, and conceal him from the pursuit of the foe. [*S*, 16]

Immediately, Simms's language limits human self-assertion within the scene, his grammar converting the young Clarence Conway, hero of the tale, into the passive recipient of clusters that "droop to the hand" and "fruits [that] relieve his hunger." Similarly, the pattern of the young man's movement images, at first, a sexual response to the erotic aspect and then, inevitably, a capitulation and withdrawal before the maternal. Our first sight of him emphasizes the fact that he is at once "upright in the center of the little vessel," and yet unobtrusive within the landscape: "no dip of oar, no stroke of paddle betrays his efforts, and impairs the solemn silence of the scene. His canoe speeds along . . . noiselessly." It is difficult to ignore the suggestively phallic images here, with the "upright" young man guiding his canoe by means of an "instrument," or paddle, subsequently termed, "his wand of power" (made, we are told, from "an ordinary cane"). Read by itself, the entire description of his entrance into "secret recesses" that "parted, without a murmur, before his prow, at the slightest touch of this simple agent," proves a very effective description of sexual congress. There is, quite appropriately, the yielding "flexibility" of the male organ as it moves through "the sinuous avenues," "pressing along in silence and in shadow." But just at the point of heightened activity, with the little bark "darting freely forward," the enclosing and all but suffocating maternal embrace becomes dominant again, burying the man "in masses of the thicket, so dense and low" that he is finally forced "to sink upon his knees in order to pass beneath the green umbrageous arches" (*S*, 14–15). Clarence Conway assumes, thereby, in this virtually foetal position, the attitude of the child before the powerful Mother. This, then, is the double-edged meaning of the "security and shelter [that] the swamps of Carolina furnished" (*S*, 14).

In *The Forayers*, a highly charged vocabulary of mystery and initiation suggests that Simms was at least dimly aware that his heroes' passages through densely thicketed swamps outlined a regressive birth process. Inviting the reader to experience the process directly, by being included in the intimacy of the pronoun "we," Simms makes clear that, under ordinary circumstances, such adventures would not be possible for us. The secret signs that lead to "the refuge . . . designedly difficult of access," are visible only to "him who has been taught the cipher": "*You* would not see these marks. No one could see them, were they not shown, or decipher their mystic uses, were they not explained" (*F*, 12).

If, at first, our "breaking boldly through a fence of willows," in order to approach the secret refuge suggests sexual entrance, once beyond the barrier, with "no track" by which to retrace our steps, we find ourselves neither elated nor expansive, but, instead, confined "knee-deep in the swamp . . . surrounded by a wood of cypresses." From this comfortable but confining "fortress," "thick and matted," we attempt escape, "press[ing] boldly up against it," and seeking an outlet by following "a faint gleam of light." Breaking the rhythms of the longer sentences that precede and follow it, the brief statement, "we descend, following this gleam," marks the transition between movement into confinement and our immediate reaction to that confinement: an urgent desire to escape. "Following this gleam," a flickering emblem of potential freedom, we find that the "thick and matted" enclosure "opens sufficiently to admit of our passage." We pass through a canal deeply embowered, reminded that still "our way lies through water," and experience the emergence of the foetus cradled and surrounded by uterine fluids. "The difficult process . . . overcome," at last, we find ourselves "emerging suddenly from the thicket and swamp," only to discover another shelter, albeit "high" and "dry." No longer is the "faint gleam" we thought we had been following in evidence; instead, we find ourselves "upon a hammock . . . covered with mighty trees, . . . and sheltered" (*F*, 11-12).

By utilizing a vocabulary of ritual initiation, the progress has underscored what we will see to be the communal experience of the novels as a whole: human beings move and act within a surrounding landscape described and experienced as feminine, the maternal aspect dominant. Important "not only for the development of masculinity and of the man's consciousness of himself, but for the development of culture as a whole," initiation rites originated, we are told, under "matriarchal conditions," as a "natural complement to the supremacy of the matriarchate." In Simms's passage, however, the deciphering of the secret signs has led back into the maternal. The light, so quickly lost, seems now to have been only a trick to draw us on, so that the potential "self-experience of the [male] ego, . . . recognizing . . . its distinction from the feminine matrix,"[32] has been virtually obliterated by a reverse and reversing initiation.

However much Simms attempts to emphasize the positive, protective and nurturing elements "within those wild and dark recesses," he cannot ignore their "threatening shadows" (*S*, 14). " 'You have lived long enough . . . in our southern country,' " Robert Singleton tells a British officer, " 'to know something of the rattlesnake. If you have ever had occasion to walk into our woods of a summer night, and to have suddenly heard the rattle sounded near you, you can very well conceive the terror which such a sound will inspire in the bosom of any man' " (*KW*, 150). For even "the rank exuberance of its vegetable life" (*S*, 14) suggests a landscape just a bit too overwhelming in its nurture, and one that, like the snake, once the symbol of the Great Mother and her generative mysteries, sometimes manifests what Singleton calls " 'a present and a pressing danger' " (*KW*, 150).

Putting its most ancient mythic associations to surprisingly appropriate use, Simms employs the snake, in *The Forayers*, to signal the impossibility of a wilderness pastoral. Gallantly protecting young Bertha Travis and her mother from British troops, a partisan captain suggests they drive their carriage " 'downward for the swamp, . . . into the lower woods,' " and out of " 'sight of the road.' " Here, Captain St. Julien assures the ladies, " 'in these piney woods, . . . you will find a great variety of flowers,' " which he urges them to pick for a bouquet. He then proceeds with a rather extraordinary catalog of the flowers to be found " 'at this very season,' " punctuated, midway through the passage, by the warning, " 'look out for snakes.' " His next sentence—" 'There is a dragon that always watches over Beauty' " (*F*, 484-85)—hits with a kind of archetypal force. That which threatens Bertha, we quickly realize, is simultaneously protecting the flowers. What we have here is an evocation of the two contrasting faces of the Mother: the flowers her positive, beautiful aspect, and the dragon—or snake—her negative, threatening appearance. In terms of the natural world protecting its precincts against the incursions of humans, the snake manifests the mythic power of the Great Mother protecting her own lovely and vulnerable femininity.

If the rattlesnake seems less in evidence in the plantation scenes than in the wild swamp and forest areas, it is due as much to Simms's own imaginative vision as to the significance of the plantation as a symbol within the South from which he came. Perhaps, in fact, remembering the nature of Simms's devotion to Woodlands, we will be hard pressed to distinguish between the two. At the outset we ought to recall Francis P. Gaines's observation that "the supremacy of the great estate in the thinking of the South cannot be successfully challenged, even though such estates were much fewer in number than has been supposed." When comparing the actual historical reality with its presentation in popular literature and art, in chapter 7 of his helpful little book, *The Southern Plantation: A Study in the Development and the Accuracy of a Tradition*, Gaines notes that "the tradition seems to be wholly reliable in one important respect; it presents the plantation ideal, the great plantation ideal, as dominant in Southern life."[33] Certainly Simms makes the eventual return to plantation life both a thematic and a geographic focus of his romances.

In significant ways, the plantation grounds recapitulate patterns already noted in the swamp and forest scenes. Most obvious is the continued experience of moving beyond and then of being enclosed within "impenetrable barriers"; and, however "trim and tidy" the plantation groves may appear, they nevertheless surround and encircle as had "the free forests" (*M*, 63). In *Mellichampe*, the Piney-Grove plantation, approached through "the fine old avenue, long, overgrown, and beautifully winding, which led to the mansion-house of the Berkeley family," is described as characteristic of "all the old country estates of Carolina" (*M*, 62). In *Katharine Walton*, "the shade trees" are described as surrounding the plantation house "on every side," while a "vast extent of woods . . . encompassed the dwelling" (*KW*, 83–84). Every reference to that estate, in fact, emphasizes the "continuous wall of thicket almost encircling the plantation of Colonel Walton" (*KW*, 128). Similarly, in *The Forayers*, all "the approaches to Holly-Dale . . . conducted you through long, dark, silent avenues of the natural forest, to within three hundred yards of the grounds and dwelling-house" (*F*, 274). Here the mansion house sits above the "level of the plantation," on a promontory . . . sloping away till it subsided into the dense swamp," resembling closely the dry, raised hummocks of the wild swamp campsites. And although the surrounding area is "wholly irreclaimable," that which has been cultivated has been converted to a garden in "which white and red roses clambered at pleasure." The garden is still, however, a geography of enclosures, with "fences enclosing . . . the fields" and "neat white paling circumscribing gardens" (*F*, 274–75).

This repeated representation of the plantation as a highly stylized garden in the wilderness maintains the basic configuration of the swamp and forest campsites, but somewhat mitigates their more dangerous aspect. For, by incorporating both the cultivated and the wild in a single harmonious unit, with "the free forests [bent] in subservience to the will of man" (*M*, 63), the plantation grounds integrate both the unrestrained and often erotic face of the Mother with a stylized version of her potentially annihilating embrace. Any incest fantasy is thus effectively coopted, and the threat of engulfment apparently diminished. As a result, the "dark recesses" of long avenues lined with "solemn oaks" (*Par*, 128) now promise to lead inevitably to a place of security, repose and nourishment.

Such configurations, of course, were not original with Simms. Francis Gaines records that the plantation tradition had for some time been "liberally [employing] the beauty of the landscape-garden; the distant approach through the two avenues of trees, the shrubbery of the lawn, the gardens for flowers, the walks, [and] not infrequently the fountains, the terraces, the offices and outbuildings in picturesque design."[34] What is so interesting about Simms's use of these traditional materials is that he reveals, both in his descriptive vocabulary and, often enough, in his characters' musings, their essential psychological underpinnings. Robert Singleton, for instance, declares that he particularly remembers The Oaks from childhood visits there for " 'the dreamy quiet of all things around' " (*Par*, 47). When once again he visits the plantation and "reclined along the roots of the old tree, . . . sheltered by its branches," he is brought, like the partisan soldiers within the swamp enclosures, to a state "of boyish frolic" (*Par*, 128-29). By physically returning to the plantation grounds, he is simultaneously returning to an "unconscious company" (*Par*, 128) of childhood experience: here, he escapes the world of war and bloodshed and recaptures life "as he had once known" it, "in the buoyancy and thoughtlessness of boyhood." What is so alluring about the maternal embrace, we realize, is its promised release from adult striving and adult assertions, providing, as it does, an ambience in which "his heart grew softened amid its many cares" and returning him, if only momentarily, to the time "when nothing of strife was in his fortunes" (*Par*, 129).

Just as fixed as the landscape demarcations—swamp or forest, plantation or town—are the human social alignments. Within the intimate retreats of the swamps, and under the exigencies of warfare, the wealthy and aristocratic Robert Singleton mingles easily with sons of tavern keepers and poor farmers in his regiment; but he is their commander, and the various friendships of military life never alter the well-accepted prerogatives of the wealthy plantation gentry. Though its historical accuracy should be questioned, the picture of a caste system that dates back before the Revolutionary War remains an essential aspect of the stasis Simms is trying to project onto his fictional South. With everything so clearly marked out, the end of the war will herald, not a possibility of new alignments or less rigid stratifications, but, instead, a return to well-established patterns, minus, of course, the evil tories who will have been removed to England or to the West Indies.

The various romantic young couples who appear in each of the novels serve, by their pairing, to reinforce the caste system, and simultaneously provide plot opportunities for maidenly distresses and heroic rescues. The sexuality of their love affairs, however, is either deflected or completely ignored. The women on the plantations, the nubile and marriageable young daughters and their older, aristocratic mothers, generally appear stamped from the same mould as "the stately and the beautiful Katharine Walton—one of those high-souled creatures that awe while they attract; and, even while they invite and captivate, control and discourage" (*Par*, 104). In *The Forayers*, a somewhat less awesome Bertha Travis comes upon Willie Sinclair sleeping under the shade of a tree on her family's plantation; she reclines beside him and soon falls asleep herself. And, although they are described as lying "side by side, her slender arm across his herculean breast," the intimacy of the embrace is permitted only because it is so unconscious, and thereby totally without active sexuality. The partisan scout who awakens them gleefully calls the scene " 'a pictur' of babies in the wood—babies in the wood' " (*F*, 362). Finally, her young suitor's perfunctory apology " 'that I should sleep like a dullard, without once dreaming what a dear companion was at my side' " (*F*, 363), does more to emphasize the unconscious nature of that sleep, rather than convey any real feeling of regret for a lost sexual moment.

Constrained by the psychological matrix of the Mother, as emblematized and stylized by his fictive plantation landscape, Simms does not portray mature sexuality, but, instead, involves his young couples in preadolescent activities only. In *The Forayers*, when Willie says, " 'the appeal is irresistible,' " he refers not to Bertha's charms, but to the " 'ham and eggs, chickens and salad,' " which she has spread before him (*F*, 330). The potential sexual energy that has been thus deflected is now directed, somewhat brutally, "without any delicate hesitation, and scrupulous nicety" to "slash[ing] away at the ham, [and tearing] the chicken asunder" (*F*, 331). Among the plantation gentry who are so much the focus of these novels, Simms boasts, "happy love . . . begets" not sexual congress or offspring, but, "an appetite" (*F*, 331). The very brutality with which Willie Sinclair appeases that "appetite," however, suggests that, for Simms, the impulse that had been sublimated in its favor must have seemed even more dangerous, a "passion, falsely named love which grows out of a warm imagination and wild blood only . . . seldom entirely [under] control" (*M*, 284).

The character who most fully lives out his experience of being embraced within a maternal landscape, however, is Captain Porgy—virtually a caricature of the psychology of his region's pastoral impulse. Analogous to Cooper's Natty Bumppo in this respect, he appears in five of the six novels discussed here and seems to have been a favorite with the reading public.[35] Forever burrowing into some "snug corner of the encampment" (*Par*, 359), and there serving gourmet feasts garnered from swamp and forest, to his fellow partisans, he is always mindful of his ease—his food, his Jamaican rum, his bodily repose—and refuses to leave an appetite unsated; on those rare occasions when food is not immediately available, he claims to have " 'a personal feeling of revenge to gratify' " (*F*, 176). Food is, in a sense, the emblem of his relationship with the landscape, and within the swamp recesses, his virtually incessant appetite is always and easily satisfied by frogs, fish, and alligator terrapin, or, as he describes them, " 'the comely creatures, the dainty delights—our quail and manna of the swamp' " (*Par*, 317). Not surprisingly, "Porgy's Joy" titles a chapter (in *The Partisan*) in which "this excellent epicure" (*KW*, 364) first finds some terrapin.

The regressive aspect of his excessive orality is further reinforced by his infantile, almost foetal, physical appearance. His bulk is concentrated in a distended stomach and a face boyishly fat and round, while his legs, in comparison, are rather spindly (*KW*, 133). In *The Partisan*, he is described as a "great bodied, and great-bellied man," whose "abdomen and brains seemed to work together" (*Par*, 110–11). So "corpulent" is he, through his "eating perpetually" (*Par*, 110), that other characters describe him as " 'a perfect mountain of flesh' " (*Par*, 98), and the narrative voice, as a "portly person of the most formidable dimensions," with an unusual "abdominal development" (*KW*, 133).

A man well into middle age, he has never married; and, even after the war is over, in *Woodcraft*, he only woos the Widow Eveleigh when forced by circumstances, thoroughly relieved to be refused. Whatever impulses in that area have been left him, he now directs toward serenading the edible creatures of the swamp, "in tones and words as tender as made the burden of his serenade, in the days of his youth, to the dark-eyed damsels upon the waters of the Ashley and Savannah" (*Par*, 320). Such brief notes of sexual possibility are, however, largely subsumed in a matrix predominantly maternal—nurturing, protective, and suggestive of almost prenatal unconsciousness. For, even in the midst of revolution, the swamp remains for Porgy a place in which "all nature appeared to revel in the same luxurious repose." There he enjoys "a resting-place and shelter" within a realm of "dreamy indulgence and repose." At moments he seems at one with the swamp's other children, the trees—all resting "like so many infant shrubs, depending, without root or base, upon its swollen bosom" (*Par*, 484, 485).

Again like Leatherstocking, Porgy is the only character in the series to relate a dream. Asleep, in *The Partisan*, he reenacts the habitual activity of his waking hours, foraging for food, recalling "the scene in which he became the successful captor of the prey." "His dreams, all night," we are told, "had been a mixed vision of *terrapin*."

> There, jutting out from the bank, was the fallen tree; and snug, and safe, and sweet in the imperfect light, there were the grouped victims, utterly unconscious, and drowsing to their doom, even as his eyes had seen them, some six or eight hours before. Nothing could seem more distinct and natural. Then followed his experience in the capture. . . .
>
> But the visions of our fat friend were not confined to the mere taking of his victims. His imagination carried him further; and he was soon busied in the work of dressing them for the table. The very dismembering of the captives—the breaking into their houses, the dragging forth of the precious contents—the spectacle of crowding eggs and generous collops of luxurious swamp-fed meat; all these gave exercise in turn to his epicurean fancies. [*Par*, 344–45]

Conscious and unconscious patterns here *appear* uniquely in harmony. However, by going beyond the previous narrative description of the actual event to "the very dismembering of the captives," the dream not only recapitulates conscious activity, but expresses also the unconscious response to the threatening possibilities implicit in the pastoral impulse itself. For the swamp exacted a heavy price for its generosity: Porgy had been reduced to "the porcine habit," imitating the sounds and movements of a pig in order to approach "the victims" (*Par*, 321). His unconscious response, then, is an understandably brutal retaliation: "the breaking into their houses, the dragging forth of the precious contents." Thus reduced to a pig in one sequence, deprived of sexuality throughout, and overwhelmingly supplied by swamp or forest with sustenance and repose, Porgy at once takes on some of the attributes of that embrace, playing very much a maternal role when providing feasts for his fellows, and, also, exhibits erratic bursts of anger directed at the other " 'dear children of the swamp' " (*Par*, 350). In some ways, like his "victims," Porgy too is trapped within "a clutch from which there was no escaping" (*Par*, 321).

In *The Forayers*, the landscape that had apparently retarded sexual expression bears the brunt of its repressed energy in the most devastating phallic intrusion presented in any of Simms's novels. A frog hunt, led by Porgy, viciously pursues " 'every mother's son of 'em' " (an appellation that always, in these novels, carries derogatory connotations), until "we may reasonably suppose that maternal suffering sent up . . . clamors for the absence of precious young ones" (*F*,

512, 514). And, for all of Simms's heavy-handed parody of Aristophanes, the scene comes off just a bit too bloody, and the attack on the pond just a bit too serious to be really funny. The spectacle of "the long, gaunt backwoodsmen, each with shaft, prong, or trident, striding hither and thither in the bog and lake, striding right and left, poised above their great-eyed enemies, and plunging forward to grapple the wounded and squalling victim before he should sheer off" is hardly a very delightful "picture for the stage" or "an action for the burlesque drama" (*F*, 513). Attempting, unsuccessfully, to scale it down a bit by calling it all "a war of shallow waters," Simms quickly loses the humorous effect of the hyperbole in the larger spectacle of "a massacre!" "Every spearman could count his score or two of slain, . . . [as] emerging from the swamp, each carried his victims aloft, transfixed upon a sharp and slender rod" (*F*, 513).

To appropriately contain this kind of anger, while leaving the maternal matrix undisturbed, another kind of landscape is necessary; and that, of course, is the plantation—which explains why *Woodcraft* (1854), a novel set after the cessation of hostilities, was so essential to a series ostensibly depicting the activities of warfare. The story, in brief, relates the foiling of the evil machinations of the Scotchman, M'Kewn, who, during the war, had secretly collaborated with the British in stealing and shipping slaves to the West Indies; when the British leave, he remains, presenting himself as a loyal patriot, but in reality greedy to take possession of plantation lands he holds under heavy mortgage. Porgy returns to his plantation, now in ruins and heavily mortgaged to M'Kewn, and, determined to restore his property, successfully outwits the villain. Various subplots involve Porgy's wealthy neighbor, the widow Eveleigh, her son, Arthur, and Dory Bostwick, with whom Arthur carries on a mild flirtation; Dory is the daughter of an evil and improvident squatter who has deserted his family to work for M'Kewn. (His family is meanwhile supported by the kindness of the good widow, and, later, by Porgy.) Lance Frampton, a young lieutenant formerly under Porgy's command, marries his sweetheart, Ellen Griffin, after a courtship of several novels, while the girl's mother, the widow Griffin, accepts a proposal of marriage from the widow Eveleigh's overseer, Fordham. The culmination—in terms of story if not in actual time of composition—of the Revolutionary War novels, *Woodcraft* provides Simms the occasion for a fully fleshed-out consideration of the meaning of Porgy's return to a plantation landscape.

The scenery through which he moves, initially, is unfamiliar, one of the rare occasions in these novels where the narrative stops to detail a countryside "stripped wholly of its foliage," dotted with "the ruins of ancient farms and decaying fences" (*W*, 52), and offering to war-weary eyes only the "melancholy" spectacle of a "sterile country . . . reaped by the greedy sickles of the enemy" (*W*, 51). Amid such desolation occurs the single adventure of his homeward journey: significantly, the rescue of a mother and her son. The widow Eveleigh and her son, Arthur, have been waylaid by ruffians employed by M'Kewn and led by Bostwick, who hope to find in her wagon both gold and important documents dangerous to M'Kewn. Even in distress, however, the widow shows a determined bravery, from the first displaying "a noble exhibition of maternal courage, reckless for herself" (*W*, 60), and then, when tied fast with ropes, continuing to maintain a "fruitless indignation . . . fear and ill-suppressed rage," but seeking "no relief even in feminine tears" (*W*, 63). In contrast, the boy appears decidedly the weaker of the two, humiliated before his mother's activity and then, writhing "desperately, but vainly, in his bond," unable, like her, to restrain his tears. "Exhausted with his ineffectual struggles and humbled by the sense of shame and impotence, tears, big and scalding, gushed from his eyes, which he closed, in very mortification, as if to conceal the weakness which he could not control" (*W*, 63). And even though, when loosed from the bonds, he helps Porgy and Fordham rout Bostwick's band, it is the initial impression of a strong mother and weaker son that stays with us and is reinforced by later sequences.

As the novel progresses, we begin to perceive that Porgy has rescued not merely a generous neighbor who will help him put his lands in order, but, indeed, a human correlative of the maternal matrix to which he hopes to return. For the widow Eveleigh, along with Porgy's ancient black *mauma*, Sappho, who bursts in upon the silent and sleeping plantation house one night soon after her "chile's" return, a thin, ghostlike figure, and the loquacious sergeant Millhouse, a soldier who has attached himself to Porgy as friend and overseer, will all prove essential in helping Porgy "to redeem the mortgaged acres of his domain" (*W*, 197). The psychological implications of that return are made clear, once the plantation has been reached, by the sight that first brings tears to Porgy's eyes: his mother's bedroom. "The fragments of an ancient mahogany bedstead lay piled up in one corner," recognized immediately as "the bedstead of his mother," "that on which Porgy had slept when a child." On "the opposite wall" hung a "picture of his mother," not as wife in relationship to a husband, but, instead, as a virginal "fair young woman, . . . when she was yet unmarried." Her presence virtually fills the room, as, "in the active exercise of memory and fancy, [she] seemed still to be looking down upon him" (*W*, 197). With sexuality thus deflected even from the portrait, Porgy proceeds to restore the meaning of that room in the architecture of Glen-Eberly itself.

In doing so, he depends heavily on sergeant Millhouse, the character who carries, in the economic sphere at least, the whole burden of Porgy's self-assertion.[36] In a sense the "real man" in the family, Millhouse directs the rebuilding of fences, slave quarters, and plantation house, oversees the planting and harvesting, and dispatches the slaves to their various tasks. Ironically, his attachment to Porgy began with his own symbolic castration, "his right arm, torn into strips by a brace of bullets," having been "stricken off at his entreaty, by his captain. . . . The wounds healed . . . and he recovered," becoming thereafter "the devoted adherent of a superior, who had the firmness to comply with the stern requisition of the patient, and himself perform the cruel operation, which the sufferer bore without a groan" (*W*, 50). As though in compensation for the lost limb, Millhouse attempts to live out patterns of material acquisition and physical conquest. Urging Porgy to court the widow Eveleigh, for instance, he explains how " 'courtin' is like storming an inimy's batteries. Women expects naterally to be taken by storm.' " The man whose right arm has been severed by his master now insists that that master provide him the vicarious experience of going " 'at it with a rush, sword in hand.' " Describing what virtually amounts to rape, Millhouse demands that Porgy be " 'ready to smite and tear everything to splinters' " (*W*, 298).

Obviously, the overseer holds a very precarious niche in the garden. Porgy himself calls him " 'only a grub, a human grub, with a monstrous instinct for acquisition and saving; no more' " (*W*, 352); and only by careful and constant watching can he succeed in keeping his overseer's propensities under control. Psychologically, Millhouse gives external verbal expression to Porgy's own suppressed sexual energies, and, simultaneously, represents that aspect of necessary economic self-assertion that is denied the master who must himself remain totally passive and unassertive if he is to restore on the plantation the primal landscape of the Mother. " 'But withal,' " as Porgy admits, " 'useful, and to be cherished—at a distance' " (*W*, 352).

In contrast, the widow Eveleigh manifests in both her personal relations and in the surrounding architecture of her domain, patterns that fundamentally express the psychology of matriarchy. She generously supplies Porgy with gifts of food, seed, blankets, and farm equipment, and offers him credit and, when necessary, cash; but when offered, in return, a proposal of marriage, she rejects what she calls " 'the fetters of matrimony' " (*W*, 512), intending to negate thereby " 'a certain imperative mood which,' " she claims, would make Porgy " 'very despotic' " (*W*, 513). Whether her assessment of Porgy is correct or not, her assumption of a basically exploitive or mastering quality in masculine sexual activity leads her, like the landscape, to cater instead to her suitor's orality: in refusing the marriage proposal, she invites Porgy to dinner. "And he stayed" (*W*, 513).

Keeping her son Arthur immature, dependent, and presexual within her generous and affectionate embrace, she effectively curtails his single and misguided attempt at bolting that embrace (by turning to the wicked M'Kewn for companionship), with the ultimatum, " 'I tell you, Arthur Eveleigh, that you must make your choice between this evil genius and your mother.' " At that, "he rushed, with a cry, and threw his arms around her," crying, " 'Forgive me, dear mother, forgive me!' " (*W*, 14). Their harmony had been disrupted by M'Kewn's suggestion to Arthur that his mother was contemplating marriage with Porgy, a possibility that upset and frightened the fifteen-year-old. Once again folding the boy "fondly to her arms," the widow acknowledges that she, too, is dependent upon the mother-son dynamic, preferring to experience all emotional ties and all necessity to love and " 'be beloved' " exclusively in relationship to her son. Only " 'if my own son abandons me,' " she declares, " 'must [I] seek succour elsewhere' " (*W*, 414).

With the house "of ample dimensions" suggesting the slightly plump outline of the widow herself, and the surrounding trees, their growth "extending far beyond all human memory," combining to image the maternal archetype whose power structures these novels, the widow becomes one with "the charm and beauty of her plantation." "Long shadowy avenues, on three sides, conducted to her dwelling which stood among sheltering clumps . . . while the house itself . . . was furnished with all . . . attractions." Even the dangers of regression to infantile unconsciousness seductively beckon beneath "groves, whether of oak or other forest-trees, such as . . . appealed sweetly to the musing fancies" (*W*, 335). An apt emblem for the human female who dominates it, "the plantation of Mrs. Eveleigh

. . . one of the finest and best kept along the Ashepoo" (*W*, 335), appropriately reminds us of all the other plantations depicted in the series.

The only plantation *not* granted a fully detailed set-piece, in fact, is Porgy's Glen-Eberly. But then this plantation is really a symbolic representation of what is finally an internal landscape. As an attempt to tame and restore the ambience of the Mother, with its abundant game and fertile soil happily taken for granted, Porgy's Glen-Eberly binds the economic demands of the culture without and the pastoral impulse of the ego within into a synthetic whole. Its restoration reinforced a whole society's desired experience of containment within maternal bonds, while its grounds embrace the character who most explicitly lived out his filial attachment to the land.

With the plantation garden as "an abstraction of the essential femininity of the terrain," the South had managed to protect its pastoral impulse, actually applying "symbolic vision to the alteration of reality itself."[37] As a psychological phenomenon, the plantation recapitulated infantile gratifications and predicted the inevitability of the South's resistance to abolition; for, even though slavery was fast becoming economically unfeasible, it was nevertheless the very bedrock upon which pastoral ease was supported. Simms's Revolutionary War romances, then, are a kind of verbal index of the dilemma of southern society before the outbreak of the Civil War. In effect, what Simms contributed to his region's literary heritage was not only one of its most endearing "originals," Captain Porgy, but, perhaps more important, patterns of description and narrative action that seemed to declare that the pastoral impulse had become the unchanging reality of an agrarian South.

The novels themselves claim to be returning to some idyllic past, of which war is a horrible but temporary interruption, and, like so much of the architecture and literature of the nineteenth-century South, display a "determination to maintain at whatever cost rigid social patterns inherited from the 18th century."[38] One must not ignore, of course, some of the more obvious progenitors behind his work, including the influence of eighteenth-century English gardening and the often self-conscious attempt to domesticate Scott's historical novel for American purposes; there is also, especially in the later romances, an almost polemic attempt to answer attacks by northern abolitionists. However, by acknowledging the pastoral impulse as a significant, even if unconscious, structuring device, we are better able to understand what particularly in the southern mind made it so responsive to these influences and to appreciate why these influences were adapted in the ways they were. For, behind all the random historical data—the maintenance of an agrarian economy while great cities grew and industry matured in the North, and the lagging population growth,[39] for instance—is the response to a landscape whose maternal embrace, once fixed and stylized on the plantations, was so all-enclosing, and apparently all-sufficing, that it defeated any possibility of progress or alteration, aesthetic or cultural. By giving literary form a society unwilling to break that primal bond, creating young heroes who vehemently insist that " 'true loyalty is to the soil' " (*KW*, 126), Simms became the leading spokesman for southern culture in 1860, hailed by *De Bow's Review* as the man who "reflects . . . the spirit and temper of Southern civilization; announces its opinions, illustrates its ideas, embodies its passions and prejudices, and betrays those delicate shades of thought, feeling and conduct, that go to form the character, the stamp, the individuality of a people."[40] He also continued that habit of southern writing by which plot and narrative structure became the metaphorical utterances of "social and spiritual experience." Commenting on southern writing in general, C. Hugh Holman has noted a tendency to unite "in harmonious accord incongruous or dissimilar things and like a riddle [tell] the truth in hidden ways,"[41] which, in large, applies particularly well to Simms; to unravel that riddle, we need only understand how language and, through it, culture, imposes the archetypal and universal experiences of every man onto the particulars of time and place, creating thereby what we usually label history and art.

The Closed Frontier

> *North America, that sad deep sweet beauteous mystery land of purple forests, and pink rock, and blue water, Indian haunts from Maine to the shore of California, all gutted, shit on, used and blasted . . .*
>
> —NORMAN MAILER, Why Are We in Vietnam?

Eighteenth-century America boasted of its present and looked forward to its future; nineteenth-century America dared only look back. Gone was the political possibility of a democracy based on fraternal community, which Freneau and Crevecoeur had once assumed would follow the European return to a giving and fertile landscape. Gone, even by mid-century, was the initial enthusiasm of those engaged in establishing the various kinds of socialist and communist communities, farming or industrial, into which the hope of reconstituting the fraternal human family had most recently been translated. To European political idealists like Robert Owen and the followers of Fourier, "the United States, with its new social optimism and its enormous unoccupied spaces" appeared to provide the perfect "nursery for these experiments."[42] But, as Hawthorne's *Blithedale Romance* (1851) made clear, even the well-intentioned Brook Farm community could not prosper.

The impulse to reject an old, corrupt, and ungiving "step-dame" and retreat from one Mother to another was finally thwarted by the psychological fact that, insofar as Western civilization involves a patriarchal social organization within which separate male-centered families compete, all movement into unsettled areas inevitably implies conquest and mastery. If Beverley and Byrd and their succeeding generations managed to stylize their containment within, rather than prove their mastery over, the Mother, the rest of the nation had followed in the footsteps of Cooper's Billy Kirby and Richard Jones, busily proving their worth, and their manhood, by overcoming and dominating the natural world. The result, which Audubon could barely admit, let alone accept, was the transforming of nature into wealth.

In effect, the new nation had entered its adolescence, leaving behind (except, perhaps, in the South) the configuration of the Mother and making of the landscape, instead, a field for exercising sexual mastery and assertive independence, its conquering hero captured in the legendary figure of John Henry, the steel-driving man. Graphically performing the rites of this second stage of American pastoral experience, the nineteenth-century miner, "at least half-naked . . . [sat] around on the bench holding with both hands a piece of steel upright between [his] legs, and the steel-drivers, two for each turner, are singing and driving. Now and then the turner does the singing, and the driller adds . . . a grunt as his hammer falls on the steel." If, as Alan Lomax suggests, the traditional John Henry "ballad gives him credit for the noblest lines in American folk-lore," it also credits him with that open and boastful sexuality that left the steel-drivers singing "with a grin on their faces, because of the lusty double meaning of their song":

> *John Henry told his captain,*
> *"Looky yonder what I see–*

Yo' drill's done broke an' yo' hole's done choke,
An' you can't drive steel like me,
Lawd, Lawd, an' you can't drive steel like me."

John Henry was hammerin' on the mountain,
An' his hammer was strikin' fire,
He drove so hard till he broke his pore heart
An' he lied down his hammer an' he died,
Lawd, Lawd, he lied down his hammer an' he died.

Here, then, as Lomax concedes, "is the earthy beginning and the root significance of the John Henry ballad—men at work in the smoky bowels of the earth,"[43] their technology at once the instrument of wealth and the instrument of penetration into nature's darkest and most hidden precincts.

As it gradually became more self-conscious, and as the implications of such a bold exercise of masculine power began dimly to be understood as inextricably connected to the vocabulary of a feminine landscape, the literary attempt to construct an American pastoral vision was inevitably confronted by the same problems that had thwarted its realization in the physical world. Like Spenser and Sidney, three centuries earlier, the pastoral romancer of nineteenth-century America also despaired of imagining "an Arcadia that manages to stay intact."[44] With the pastoral dream of a wholly gratifying return no longer able to make any claims upon the present, writers like Irving, Cooper, and Simms turned to an imaginatively restructured past, and converted the pastoral possibility into the exclusive prerogative of a single male figure, living out a highly eroticized and intimate relationship with a landscape at once suggestively sexual, but overwhelmingly maternal. The very structure of early nineteenth-century pastoral literature, then, from plot to characterization, appears regressive; the novels that gave it expression all betray a guilt-ridden horror, not unlike John Hammond's outcry at the fates of Virginia and Maryland, and their heroes all resort to a compensatory infantilism in order to escape either the guilt of incest or the accusation of rape. Even Audubon, writing of his travels, preferred to ignore the evidence of increasing urbanization in favor of sparsely settled frontier landscapes, and desperately attempted to integrate himself both into the familial comforts of the cabin and into a nonabusive sonhood with nature itself. What Audubon experienced as personal frustration, however, proved a truth that others could not escape, even in fiction. For Cooper, as for Spenser and Sidney, "the harbored places of the world [will inevitably] be ransacked."[45] And the pastoral figure who had attempted to inhabit those spaces remains fixed in our fiction as a perennial outsider, standing both as our society's lost ideal and as its critic.

The concentration on Cooper and Simms in this chapter was purposeful and deliberate. Each was in his time what we might call "popular," his writings giving voice to what were the normative or generally accepted sentiments of the time and exposing its most pressing conflicts. Natty Bumppo and Captain Porgy, therefore, do not exhibit the aberrant or the unusual, but, instead, the commonly shared dilemmas, dreams, and symbols of the society for and out of which they were cast. As Simms himself so aptly put it, "Poetry or romance, illustrative of those national events of which the great body of the people delight to boast, . . . possesses a sort of symbolical influence upon their minds, and seems, indeed, to become a visible form and existence to their eyes."[46] In thus giving "visible form" to the differing patterns of northern and southern pastoral, and, by virtue of their dominating the first forty years of the century's literary scene, Cooper and Simms may also be said to have set the tone or at least suggested directions in which their successors would follow. Moreover, the symbols they created (in their characterizations and in their landscape descriptions)—or, as Simms preferred to call it, to which they gave "visible form,"—eventually, like all symbols, spread out, touched upon, and influenced the developing national self-image. Passing beyond the surface of verbal cognition and out into the field of action, they even helped create history. What constitute the varying emphases in Cooper's and Simms's respective pastoral visions, in fact, mark the differing orientations of North and South that, since the first century of settlement, had foretold the inevitability of the clash of the 1860s; what constitute their similarities point up the vast range of culturally shared experience and, incidentally, suggest the almost identical outcries against technological exploitation with which both regions would try to protect their pastoral heritage in the twentieth century.

In spite of their dissimilar geographies, both Cooper and Simms relegated the maintenance of the pastoral impulse to an isolate and unmarried male figure—each alone in a different way. Porgy, paradoxically, is an integral part of that societal structure that results in, or even demands, his regression. Natty never could be. Read in the order of composition, Cooper's Leatherstocking novels reveal the development of a vision, whereas Simms's Revolutionary War romances repeat essentially the same static and virtually schematic patterns of plot and narrative situation. However unwilling to abandon a communal pastoral possibility Cooper might have been, he nevertheless acknowledged the unstoppable tide of advancing settlement as a negation of that possibility and restricted his lost idyll to the experience of a single character. Simms, on the other hand, reinforced his region's pretensions to rigid social hierarchy and its predilections for highly stylized plantation design, and, in so doing, helped the South create an external environment that manifested a symbolic projection of internal and infantile realities. While most of Cooper's characters assert their independence from the forest's embrace, either gently like Judge Temple, or more brutally, like Billy Kirby, and thereby involve themselves in the dynamics of a masculine and progress-oriented civilization, Simms's characters live out so totally the psychology of the Mother that, within his novels, nothing really changes, neither individuals nor the society of which they are a part. Probably the most significant difference between the two, however, rests on the fact that one needed a settled social organization in which to harbor his pastoral figure, while the other demanded the unlimited and virgin spaces of the frontier. Paradoxically, of course, a frontier that that character helped to explore and destroy. But it was, historically, an accurate picture. Before the end of the century, the frontier was officially declared closed and little room was left for the wanderings of any such as Natty Bumppo; instead, they became part of the nation's legend—as did the meaning of the frontier itself.

For what the vast American West had provided, frontier by frontier, was the repeated invitation to experience pastoral realities, a continuation of the invitations issued to Europeans with the discovery of the New World. In what must be considered one of the most influential pieces of writing about the West produced during the nineteenth century, Frederick Jackson Turner's paper on "The Significance of the Frontier in American History" (read before the American Historical Association in Chicago in 1893), attributed to the West the responsibility for virtually every American virtue or vice. In one of his few later papers on the same subject, he made explicit what had always been the experiential truth of the American continent: the West was a woman, and to it belonged the hope of rebirth and regeneration. To maintain that these are only appropriate to the "categories of myth rather than of economic [or historical] analysis," as some of Turner's critics have asserted,[47] is to ignore all the evidence gathered here that what we label as historical and economic processes are, at least in part, the external projections of internal patterns—be they called psychology or myth. The irrefutable kernel of truth that Turner's vocabulary exposes is that the transition from passively returning to the land as Mother, to exploring it and acting upon it as a repository of wealth, had been repeated from one end of the continent to the other:

European men, institutions, and ideas were lodged in the American wilderness, and this great American West took them to her bosom, taught them a new way of looking upon the destiny of the common man, trained them in adaptation to the conditions of the New World, to the creation of new institutions to meet new needs; and ever as society on her eastern border grew to resemble the Old World in its social forms and its industry, ever, as it began to lose faith in the ideal of democracy, she opened new provinces, and dowered new democracies in her most distant domains with her material treasures . . .[48]

The inevitable confusions and frustrations attendant upon such experience did not end with the closing of the frontier. On the contrary, if each new frontier area repeatedly promised and then denied the gratifications implied by a landscape comprising Mother and, afterward, Mistress, resulting again and again in outcries of disillusionment and frustration, then the closing of the frontier served only to officially acknowledge the fact that there were no more landscapes left upon which to project the pastoral impulse; it was, in short, the final frustration. And, as with all frustrations that cannot be either mediated or resolved, the frustration of the pastoral impulse was finally expressed through anger—anger at the land that had seemed to promise and then defeat men's longings for an ambience of total gratification. It is an anger that, unlike this chapter, did not end with the nineteenth century. What appears today as the single-minded destruction and pollution of the continent is just one of the ways we have continued to express that anger. That we can no longer afford to do so is obvious; our survival may depend on our ability to escape the verbal patterns that have bound us either to fear of being engulfed by our physical environment, or to the opposite attitude of aggression and conquest. Twentieth century pastoral *must* offer us some means of understanding and altering the disastrous attitudes toward the physical setting that we have inherited from our national past.

5.
Making It with Paradise
The Twentieth Century

> *All things considered, it's a gentle and an undemanding*
> *planet, even here. Far gentler*
> *Here than any of a dozen other places. The trouble is*
> *always and only with what we build on top of it.*
> *There's nobody else to blame. . . .*
> —LEW WELCH, "Chicago Poem"

Some Thoughts for Our Bicentennial

What Nick Carraway perceives at the end of F. Scott Fitzgerald's *The Great Gatsby* (1925) is the analogous similarity between Jay Gatsby's fantasy-bred pursuit of Daisy and America's hallowed devotion to an image of the "fresh, green breast of the new world." Both illusions have driven men into "boats against the current, borne back ceaselessly into the past."[1] The cultural psyche of white male America still dreams of that long-ago moment when "the fine old island . . . flowered once for Dutch sailors' eyes," much as Jay Gatsby cherishes one summer night, five years before, when Daisy "blossomed for him like a flower" (*GG*, 182, 112). If, in Nick's eyes, Gatsby appears bent on "recover[ing] something, some idea of himself perhaps, that had gone into loving Daisy," so, too, generations of Americans had attempted to validate themselves and their yearning by seeking to possess that continent that, with its now "vanished trees, . . . had once pandered in whispers to the last and greatest of all human dreams" (*GG*, 111, 182). With Daisy, Gatsby found "he could suck on the pap of life, gulp down the incomparable milk of wonder" (*GG*, 112), not unlike the European immigrants who, three hundred years before, found that they could begin again in the welcoming landscape of a "*Paradise* with all her Virgin Beauties."[2] "The colossal vitality of [Gatsby's] illusion" (*GG*, 97), which had kept his image of Daisy inviolate in his heart for five years, stands, at the end of the novel, as a kind of miniature of American history itself, with its pastoral longings both to return to and to master the beautiful and bountiful femininity of the new continent.

But it was precisely that urge to mastery and possession that the South has blamed for thwarting the pastoral possibility. Angered by the fact that, as Americans "receive the illusion of having power over nature, [they] lose the sense of nature as something mysterious and contingent," several southerners got together in 1930 and issued an agrarian manifesto entitled *I'll Take My Stand*. Noting that, "since 1865 an agrarian Union has been changed into an industrial empire bent on conquest of the earth's goods," they perceived in the difference between what the South had been and what the New South was coming to be, an image of what had happened to the whole of American society. In short, as John Crowe Ransom complained, "the masculine form" had become "hallowed by Americans, . . . under the name of Progress." And what "the concept of Progress" meant to him was the spectre "of man's increasing command, and eventually perfect command, over the forces of nature. . . . Ambitious men fight, first of all, against nature; they propose to put nature under their heel; this is the dream of scientists burrowing in their cells, and then of the industrial men who beg of their secret knowledge and go out to trouble the earth." What this kind of activity threatened, of course, was the matrix that Simms and his contemporaries had taken such great pains to preserve. For the twentieth-century southerner also appreciated the fact that the ambience of the Mother meant that "a sense of family followed our connection with the land,"[3]—and the pleasures inherent in this kind of "connection" are never easily abandoned.

The Southern Agrarians, as they have since been labeled, were perhaps hopelessly naive in arguing, especially in 1930, on the eve of the Great Depression, for an agrarian as opposed to an industrial economy. Nevertheless, compelled by what they felt to be "a filial duty . . . to their own section,"[4] they tried again in 1936, this time in a manifesto entitled *Who Owns America?*[5] C. Hugh Holman points out that "the political-economic doctrines annunciated in these books have had little effect on modern America," and, instead, gained their authors "only the taunting epithet of 'Neo-Confederates.' "[6] Still, the central theme of their protest, insisting upon "so simple a thing as respect for the physical earth and its teeming life,"[7] has continued to be proclaimed in the South, even by those who, like Thomas Wolfe, openly attacked the group. Belonging "to the New South school, which saw in industrial progress the key to a new and better life," Wolfe still acknowledged that the South would always be for him "*the female principle*—the *earth* again . . . a home, fixity."[8] He prophesied for it, however, an emergence from "those decades of defeat and darkness," and an entry into that same industrial progress that characterized the rest of the nation.[9] What Wolfe foresaw when he wrote *The Web and the Rock* in 1939, then, was a South abandoning the maternal matrix and inviting, instead, the aggressions of those who would, as Faulkner described it, force the land to "retreat year by year before the onslaught of axe and saw and log-lines and then dynamite and tractor plows."[10] Faulkner's portrait of Ike McCaslin, the man who, in old age, contemplated the "land which man has deswamped and denuded and derivered in two generations" (*DA*, 733), must therefore be read not merely as a story of the South, but as a comment on the course of an entire nation's pastoral impulse.

As a young boy, going through his initiation into the ways of the woods, in "The Bear," Ike looks upon the natural world around him and recognizes in it his true Mother: "summer, and fall, and snow, and wet and sap-rife spring in their ordered immortal sequence, the deathless and immemorial phases of the mother who had shaped him if any had toward the man he almost was."[11] Looking ahead, anticipating that "he would marry someday," he nevertheless knows that "still the woods would be his mistress and his wife" (*B*, 359). And it is *because* he wants to maintain that intimacy, from boyhood through manhood, that he attempts to reject the means by which others, before him, perhaps even with the same longings, had converted intimacy into violation. He attempts, in short, to repudiate the past, his family's history, and his own inheritance of the land they had possessed and conquered. The dialogue between the young Ike and his elder cousin, McCaslin Edmonds, clearly distinguishes the two modes of pastoral experience. For the older cousin, the course of American history is its own justification, and there is even a kind of "manly" pride expressed in his evocation of a forebear " 'who saw the opportunity and took it, bought the land, took the land, got the land no matter how, held it to bequeath, no matter how, out of the old grant, the first patent, when it was a wilderness of wild beasts and wilder men, and cleared it, translated it into something to bequeath to his children, worthy of bequeathment for his descendants' ease and security and pride, and to perpetuate his name and accomplishments' " (*B*, 290). But for Ike, son and lover of the landscape, it is that very history, and its attendant pride, which must be repudiated. To him, man was put " 'on the earth . . . to hold suzerainty over the earth and the animals on it in His name, not to hold for himself and his descendants inviolable title forever, generation after generation, to the oblongs and squares of the earth, but to hold the earth mutual and intact in the communal anonymity of brotherhood' " (*B*, 291). It is an argument that goes back to the more idealistic statements of the Pilgrim Fathers and that, in effect, revives the eighteenth and early nineteenth centuries' dreams of communal, noncompetitive, primal fraternity. Taking a position that essentially denies the validity of private ownership—at least with regard to the land—Ike answers his cousin by reassessing the meaning of that same history that had been previously used against him:

> "I can't repudiate it. It was never mine to repudiate. It was never Father's and Uncle Buddy's to bequeath to me to repudiate, because it was never Grandfather's to bequeath them to bequeath me to repudiate, because it was never old Ikkemotubbe's to sell Grandfather for bequeathment and repudiation. Because it was never Ikkemotubbe's fathers' fathers' to bequeath Ikkemotubbe to sell to Grandfather or any man because on the instant when Ikkemotubbe discovered, realized, that he could sell it for money, on that instant it ceased ever to have been his forever, father to father to father, and the man who bought it bought nothing." [*B*, 290-91]

I think Cleanth Brooks is somewhat unfair to Faulkner, and to Ike, when he views this as "a kind of logic-chopping." What Faulkner is attempting here, through Ike, is truly monumental: he wants to divest pastoral—its language and its activity—of those destructive and corrupting tendencies that had previously brought men both to pollute and to resent the landscape they had so ardently wished to possess. As Brooks himself makes clear, the flaw in title began when the old Chickasaw Indian chief "first viewed the land as something that could be sold."[12] Metaphorically, Ike is arguing that the illusion of ownership, control, mastery, call it what you will, is the final illusion, and makes him who falls prey to it incapable of knowing the real meaning of the land and man's relation to it.

There is, of course, both a comic and a tragic irony in Ike's gesture of repudiation. As the single white man in *Go Down, Moses* (1942) dedicated to preserving the wilderness, assuming in effect a kind of Christ-figure resonance, Ike becomes a carpenter, using the tools that signify the woods' destruction—just as, earlier, in his initiation into adult manhood, he had had to kill the bear. Moreover, Ike's gesture does nothing to stop the course of history. As an old man in his eighties, he looks upon a "land across which there came now no scream of panther but instead the long hooting of locomotives" (*DA*, 711). As Cleanth Brooks aptly summarizes it, "For Faulkner's Uncle Ike the wilderness has been violated, the dark rich land has been looted. In place of its power and mystery there is now simply the meaningless litter of civilization: neon signs and shining this-year's automobiles and broad plumb-ruled highways and buildings constructed of sheet iron."[13]

In "Delta Autumn," the story that completes Ike's history, Faulkner has his character explicitly acknowledge the end result of American pastoral yearnings: "The woods and fields he ravages and the game he devastates will be the consequence and signature of [man's] crime and guilt, and his punishment" (*DA*, 719). "Then suddenly," the narrative voice tells us, "he knew why he had never wanted to own any of it, arrest at least that much of what people call progress, measure his longevity at least against that much of its ultimate fate. It was because there was just exactly enough of it. He seemed to see the two of them—himself and the wilderness—as coevals" (*DA*, 724). Brooks and others have argued that, "in divesting himself of his legacy—for the best of motives, let us say—[Ike] has thereby reduced his power to act. . . . If Ike's renunciation was a kind of vicarious atonement, an act of sacrifice and expiation, as perhaps in some sense it was, the act can also be viewed as a dodging of responsibility."[14] But then this is precisely Faulkner's point. Always concerned with the difficulties and ambiguities of moral action, Faulkner has here taken the opportunity to point up the hopelessness of pastoral longings by making *any* gesture in their behalf appear ultimately futile. Hence, Ike's repudiation is purposefully made too complex to be fully comprehended even by Ike and too involuted to be believed in, even as an act of faith, by the reader. As soon as the land is experienced as feminine, no masculine activity in relation to it can be both satisfying and nonabusive, and, insofar as we do not wholly control or even understand our responses to that which constitutes the opposite gender, no activity toward it can be wholly "responsible."

The point is made over and over again in "Delta Autumn," most obviously in the story's multileveled analogy between the human feminine and the hunted doe. Early in the story, as Uncle Ike and a new, younger generation ride out toward the woods, some teasing remarks are addressed to Roth Edmonds concerning the hunting of does in one season, while having the same doe to hunt again the next season. The men's guarded and snide references are, of course, to the young girl whom Roth has been meeting in the woods each autumn, and upon whom (unknown to him), he has sired a son. When the girl, with her infant, comes to Uncle Ike's tent one night, Ike discovers not only that she is part black, but, also, that she is related to him by blood, and that that blood carries, once again, an act of miscegenation and incest repeated from out of the family's past. To the old man's entreaties that she leave the South entirely and head north, the girl makes clear that she will make no claim upon the father of her child, nor even reveal to him her true identity. In short, the girl has no intention of seeing Roth Edmonds again. Still, Ike wants to make at least some acknowledgment of familial relationship, and in so doing, he turns the girl's situation into an emblem of the plight of the wilderness itself: he gets the silver hunting horn that General Compson had given him long ago and gives it to her *for her son.* There is no question as to who, in Ike's world, are the hunters. Shortly thereafter, the white men who come every year to the woods to hunt will reveal that this season they have taken not a buck, but a doe. And the story ends on Ike's saddened but tacit acceptance of who, in his world, are inevitably to be the hunted:

> "We got a deer on the ground. . . ."
>
> "Wait," McCaslin said. He moved, suddenly, onto his elbow.
>
> "What was it?" Legate paused for an instant beneath the lifted flap. He did not look back.
>
> "Just a deer, Uncle Ike," he said impatiently. "Nothing extra." . . .
>
> "It was a doe," [Ike] said. [*DA*, 734]

Encapsulated in that last, short line, is an implicit statement of enormous and tragic contradictions. Ike realizes that his earlier warnings have not been heeded: this generation does not understand that to kill does and fawns will reduce the number of bucks in future years. No longer is the annual pilgrimage to the woods an act of initiation into codes of reciprocity and mutual respect between man and the wild; and, in helping to perpetuate that now-meaningless ritual, Uncle Ike incurs the same kind of guilt that burdened Natty Bumppo, responsible for helping to turn intimacy into violation. In short, the end of the story reemphasizes Ike's multifaceted and growing awareness that, before the masculine, the feminine is always both vulnerable and victimized. The closing announcement of the killing of the deer follows immediately upon the girl and her child leaving the old man's tent. And the final irony, again pointing up the difficulty of the masculine acting morally with regard to the feminine, is the fact that the girl has seen Ike's renunciation of his patrimony as indirectly responsible for the spoiling of Roth Edmonds and, in consequence, her own present predicament.

The call for retribution or expiation, with which we have become so familiar by now, interestingly enough follows the girl's visit to the old man's tent. Ruminating on what she has told him, Ike compounds the human feminine with the feminine wilderness as he begins fully to understand *how* the ravaged landscape will prove not only the "signature of [man's] crime and guilt," but also "his punishment" (*DA*, 719). " 'No wonder the ruined woods I used to know don't cry for retribution!' " he thought: " 'The people who have destroyed it will accomplish its revenge' " (*DA*, 734). In other words, in destroying the landscape that had once promised virtually every satisfaction men have sought, men simultaneously destroy something precious, desirable and vulnerable within themselves—the capacity, perhaps, for bringing into being "a nation of people . . . founded in humility and pity and sufferance and pride of one to another" (*B*, 292). To such dreams, the wilderness had once catered. Not that it was all gone—"There was some of it left, although now it was two hundred miles from Jefferson when once it had been thirty." And Ike "had watched it, not being conquered, destroyed, so much as retreating since its purpose was served now and its time an outmoded time" (*DA*, 713). Its purpose, perhaps, had been to awaken man, for one last, "transitory enchanted moment . . . into an aesthetic contemplation he neither understood nor desired, face to face for the last time in history with something commensurate to his capacity for wonder" (*GG*, 182). Or so Nick Carraway had phrased it, in 1925. For Ike McCaslin, twenty years later, the purpose had been served—and then had become sadly, inevitably "outmoded." No code, no renunciation, could maintain both the purity and the quality of intimacy that the young boy had sought with the wilderness. And, not unlike Jay Gatsby's dream, Ike's, too, "must have seemed so close that he could hardly fail to grasp it." But "the orgiastic future that year by year recedes before us" (*GG*, 182), will not and cannot be grasped; the psychological components of pastoral are too volatile—at least in the language through which we have so far attempted to capture it.

If, as Cleanth Brooks suggests, Faulkner acknowledges man's need "to contend with nature," he does not also accept the need "to prey upon it."[15] To the contrary, what Faulkner has attempted to introduce in *Go Down, Moses*, through the voice of Ike McCaslin, is a vocabulary that will at once do away with the notion of the land as something to be either exclusively possessed or preyed upon—like a sexual object—and suggest, instead, an intimacy based on reciprocity and communality: "because it belonged to no man. It belonged to all; they had only to use it well, humbly and with pride" (*DA*, 724). Ike saw "the two of them—himself and the wilderness—as coevals" (*DA*, 724). As such, the land could never be any one man's property, to be passed on from one owner to another; the man and the landscape are simultaneous, interdependent, neither one master of the other. If there is *any* mastery to be acknowledged, it is God's—"He [who] created the earth, made it and looked at it and said it was allright." And it is as God's creation, not as man's possession, that Ike sees mankind holding "suzerainty over the earth and the animals on it" (*B*, 291).

Having completed the psychological process predicted by John Hammond as early as 1656, Faulkner's southerners have, for the most part, endured the agonizing growing pains of Civil War and, still bearing its scars, stand as sexual aggressors before a landscape once revered as Mother. At once hoping to expiate the burden of guilt inherited from the past and simultaneously attempting to forge the possibility of a new and different future, his heroes, his men of honor and self-conscious concern, espouse a doctrine of stewardship—a doctrine only superficially different from Henderson's rediscovery of his familial association with *all* of nature in Saul Bellow's 1959 novel, *Henderson the Rain King*. In taking his greedy, belligerent, and unhappy white American millionaire protagonist back to primitive Africa, Bellow allows him to experience a kind of primal fraternal intimacy with flora and fauna alike. Marking the achievement is his kindness to the young orphan he encounters on the jet plane back to America and the lion cub he carries: "I fondled the animal, which had made a wonderful adjustment to me."[16] "Part clown and part child," as Harold Toliver accurately described him,[17] Henderson seeks redemption through wholehearted and erotic regression, attempting to get back a sense of intimacy he remembers once experiencing: " 'It is very early in life, and I am out in the grass. The sun flames and swells; the heat it emits is its love, too. I hate this selfsame vividness in my heart. There are dandelions. I try to gather up this green. I put my love-swollen cheek to the yellow of the dandelions. I try to enter into the green' " (*HRK*, 250).

The advocates of Berkeley's People's Park, similarly, had tried "to enter into the green" by petitioning university officials for permission to reenter their garden and "water our sod and plant some flowers there." The various "radical" or "illegal" labels attached to their activities notwithstanding, that little community of "sod brothers" was loudly articulating a growing awareness, shared by many Americans, of being exiled from their own landscape, either by fact or contingency. Little wonder, then, that, in giving voice to their anger and frustration, they manipulated the very vocabulary that once pandered to such dreams and, in so doing, demonstrated the full brutality to which that vocabulary, and with it the American pastoral impulse, has been accommodated in recent years:

The University must stop
fucking with our land.
The University must stop
being a motherfucker.[18]

That same year, Berkeley-based journalist Gene Marine recognized in those brutal and brutalizing images the very pattern of our current ecological crises. Claiming that "the rape of America" is still being perpetuated by men who have an "engineering mentality," he severely criticized those who could "build a bridge without looking down into the gully to see whether it might be, in fact, a river teeming with life." That such men follow patterns given only grudging acceptance in our literature—as with Cooper's portrayal of Richard Jones in *The Pioneers*—underscores how thoroughly Americans have abandoned the passive, filial stance appropriate to a maternal pastoral matrix and moved beyond merely sensual appreciation of the Virgin, completing the cycle by making of the landscape The Ravished. As Gene Marine so correctly imaged it, those with an "engineering mentality" are "in every section of every state, ripping, tearing, building, changing," perpetuating, in short, "a rape from which America can never, never recover."[19]

All of which indicates how bound we still are by the vocabulary of a feminine landscape and the psychological patterns of regression and violation that it implies. Fortunately, however, that same language that now appalls us with its implications of regression or willful violation also supplies a framework, open to examination, within which the kinds of symbolic functioning we have examined here get maximum exposure. It gives us, to begin with, at least some indication of *how* those peculiar intersections of human psychology, historical accident, and New World geography combined to create the vocabulary for the experience of the land-as-woman. And it gives us, more importantly, another vantage point from which to understand those unacknowledged but mutually accepted patterns by which Americans have chosen to regulate their lives and interactions for over three hundred years now. Our continuing fascination with the lone male in the wilderness, and our literary heritage of essentially adolescent, presexual pastoral heroes, suggest that we have yet to come up with a satisfying model for mature masculinity on this continent; while the images of abuse that have come to dominate the pastoral vocabulary suggest that we have been no more successful in our response to the feminine qualities of nature than we have to the human feminine. But such speculations are only the beginning: the more we understand how we use language and, conversely, how (in some sense) language uses us, the stronger the possibility becomes that we may actually begin to choose more beneficial patterns for labeling and experiencing that mysterious realm of phenomena outside ourselves and, hopefully, with that, better our chances for survival amid phenomena that, after all, we know only through the intercession of our brain's encodings.

We must begin by acknowledging that the image system of a feminine landscape was for a time both useful and societally adaptive; it brought successive generations of immigrants to strange shores and then propelled them across a vast uncharted terrain. For it is precisely those images through which we have experienced and made meaning out of the discrete data of our five senses (and our cerebral wanderings) that have allowed us to put our human stamp on a world of external phenomena and, thereby, survive in the first place in a strange and forbidding wilderness. And the fact that the symbolizations we chose have now resulted in a vocabulary of destructive aggression and in an active expression of frustration and anger should not make us assume that they may not yet again prove useful to us, or, if not, that we have only to abandon them altogether in order to solve our ecological problems. The habits of language are basically conservative, representing what Benjamin Lee Whorf characterizes as "the mass mind." As he points out, language may indeed be "affected by inventions and innovations, but affected little and slowly."[20] The habits of image-laden language such as we have looked at here, especially, inhibit change because they contain within them an extension, in adult mental processes, of experiential and perceptual configurations inherited from infancy; and, because of the various coincidences through which such configurations got projected out onto the American continent, they have come to reflect not only the integration of universal human dilemmas into cultural patterns, but also the psychic content of the group's shared fantasies —however unacknowledged or unconscious these may have been. Students of language, following Whorf and Edward Sapir, are coming more and more to assert the intimate interaction between language, perception, and action, even going so far, as Whorf does, to argue that once particular "ways of analyzing and reporting experience . . . have become fixed in the language as integrated 'fashions of speaking,' " they tend to influence the ways in "which the personality not only communicates, but also analyzes nature, notices or neglects types of relationship and phenomena, channels . . . reasoning, and builds the house of . . . consciousness."[21] "And once such a system of meanings comes into being, it is never simply abandoned or superseded, as Freud and all other developmental psychologists have repeatedly demonstrated."[22]

Still, if this study has suggested anything, it must be that what we need is a radically new symbolic mode for relating to "the fairest, frutefullest, and pleasauntest [land] of all the worlde";[23] we can no longer afford to keep turning "America the Beautiful" into *America the Raped*. The tantalizing possibility that metaphor, or symbolizing in general, both helps to give coherence to the otherwise inchoate succession of discrete sense data and, also, helps us explore the *possibilities* of experience, suggests that we might, on a highly conscious level, call into play once more our evolutionary adaptive ability to create and re-create our own images of reality. The magic, and even salvation, of man may, after all, lie in his capacity to enter into and exit from the images by which, periodically, he seeks to explore and codify the meaning of his experience. Which suggests that the will to freedom and the will to community, the desire for self-fulfillment, and the attractions of passive acceptance, which were always at the base of the pastoral impulse, might, in some other metaphor, prove finally reconcilable.

A Meditation on Metaphor

> *The world is emblematic. Parts of speech are metaphors, because the whole of nature is a metaphor of the human mind.*
>
> —RALPH WALDO EMERSON, *"Nature"*

It is, of course, absurd to claim that we can account for any complex aspect of human activity by a single factor. Certainly, there are other determinants behind the literary and subliterary works I have examined here under the umbrella of "pastoral," just as there must certainly be other motivations behind some of the historical processes discussed here than the ones I have remarked on. History expresses a complex of intersections, accidents, and motivations; and no symbol is without its layers. Nevertheless, however complexly multidetermined our behavior toward the landscape may be, it is no longer possible to ignore a growing body of evidence that the particular way in which the New World has been symbolized as feminine in American thought and writing bears out a consistent correlation between that set of linguistic images and certain psychological patterns that became codified in our literature and acted out in our history. If the close correlation between what we say and how we act is admitted, then it implies an urgent necessity to understand what it is we really mean—or feel—when we say certain things.

Standard grammar texts that assert that "when metaphors are successful, they 'die'—that is, they become so much a part of our regular language that we cease thinking of them as metaphors at all," grossly oversimplify these unique linguistic phenomena by ignoring the crucial intimacy between language and perception; in other words, we may indeed have long ago ceased to self-consciously or attentively *think about* the feminine in the landscape, but that does not mean that we have ceased to *experience* it or to act in such a way that our behavior apparently manifests such experience at its deepest level of motivation. The implicit assumptions behind statements such as the following are even more dangerous: "Metaphor, simile, and personification are among the most useful communicative devices we have, because by their quick affective power they often make unnecessary the invention of new words for new things or new feelings."[24] Besides the fact that the lumping of these together as though they were merely variations of a single linguistic category is patently absurd (ask any poet!), the statement seems to suggest that these are no more than verbal shorthands for avoiding the naming and/or identifying of new experiences or new phenomena. The possibility that metaphor systems may contain, encapsulated, the group's (be it tribe or nation) most ancient heritages and, in some sense, trace its psychological and historical development, is nowhere suggested; no more than the possibility that new metaphors are themselves new phenomena, at once calling forth, containing, and stylizing our experience. What troubles me most, however, is that such oversimplifications cavalierly assume that when we use metaphor, we do not really *mean* what we say. If nothing else, I hope this study has shown that metaphors do, indeed, mean a great deal and may, in fact, serve as intersecting points for the various components of experience and action.

I expect, however, that any orthodox grammarian will object that I have not been discussing a metaphor at all, since the formal grammatical structure of the phrase, "the land-as-woman," contains the like/as construction usually labeled as simile. My decision to label the pastoral vocabulary, with all its related images, as metaphorical was based on my observation that the American landscape has not been experienced as something similar to, or merely comparable to, but as the female principle of gratification itself, comprising all the qualities that Mother, Mistress, and Virgin traditionally represent for men; perhaps the phrase more properly should have been expressed from the outset as "the land-*is*-woman."

As I am using it, then, the metaphor of "the land-as-woman" implies a varied group of word structures (usually expressed as images), which repeatedly assert the experiential reality of a particular object—in this case, the inherently feminine reality of the vast American landscape. The quality of that experience is variously expressed through an entire range of images, each of which details one of the many elements of that experience, including eroticism, penetration, raping, embrace, enclosure, and nurture, to cite only a few. Together, they make up a mutually interrelating and integrated whole, and it is this whole which the phrase "the land-as-woman" is meant to assert. The grammatical structures of the various images—that is, whether they work by comparison, juxtaposition, or synthesis—are therefore of only limited importance in relation to the effect of the whole system.

The many images of a nurturing maternity or the expressions of a desired return to maternal embraces, among others, suggest that at least part of that system is mythic or archetypal in nature; and this, in turn, raises the possibility that what I have cataloged here may be a universal of human experience, fixed either biologically or psychologically within the human psyche. It is hardly a very novel idea. The search for fixed formal structures built into our gray matter, and hence into our cognitive functions, through the psychological and evolutionary processes to which we are heir, is as much behind Jung's theory of archetypes, as it is behind Levi-Strauss's structuralist analysis of myth, and the linguistics community's assumption of a universal grammar. It is even a commonplace of literary criticism now to cite "the archetypal" as a particular "class of symbols . . . [consisting] of those which carry the same or very similar meanings for a large portion, if not all, of mankind." Philip Wheelwright's explanation of archetypal symbols, with which I largely concur, is characteristic of such discussions:

It is a discoverable fact that certain symbols, such as the sky father and earth mother, light, blood, up-down, the axis of a wheel, and others, recur again and again in cultures so remote from one another in space and time that there is no likelihood of any historical influence and causal connection among them. Why should such unconnected repetitions occur? The reasons are in many cases not at all puzzling. Despite the great diversity among human societies and their ways of thinking and responding, there are certain natural similarities too, both in men's physical and in their basic psychical make-up.[25]

The only fault I find with definitions of this sort is their tendency to imply that these symbol systems, by their very universality, are thereby totally fixed and unavailable to conscious attempts at alteration. Were such the case, this book would never have been written, since it could have done nothing more than foretell the inevitable doom of our continent as a result of the images we have so far used to express its experiential relation to us. The trouble with that kind of thinking is that it confuses that which is, in fact, fixed as part of our chemical or physiological makeup with that which is inherently fluid and adaptive; or, in my terminology, it confuses archetypes with the many and changing symbols through which they are variously imaged. Milton understood this quite well when, in *Paradise Lost*, he compared Satan to all the great heroes of antiquity—Achilles, Aeneas, etc.—and then introduced Christ as a being beyond grammatical comparison or analogy. In Milton's view, Christ introduced into the world a wholly new kind of heroism—different from the physical prowess revered by the ancients—but in some sense sharing in the nobility and inspirational qualities that always characterize the hero archetype in any society. In short, Milton effectively utilized the hero archetype, but changed the means through which it was imaged. With the introduction of Christ into the text, the earlier notions of heroism, ascribed to Satan in Books 1 and 2 through comparison and analogy, are superseded by yet another permutation of the archetype, and Christian heroism becomes identified, not with physical strength and martial aggression, but with such things as love, mercy, charity, and spiritual faith and fortitude.

If we relate this to our study of American pastoral, we are encouraged to explore what, in its symbol system, may be fixed and what available to change. After all, the basic human situation may everywhere be the same, but—as students of human behavior repeatedly observe—"there are infinite ways of dealing with it. Each set of ways is the hallmark of a culture, and follows from the specific conditions of that culture." And insofar as human culture represents a synthesizing process, uniting the demands provoked by a particular environmental, historical, or economic situation with the eternal and unchangeable human needs, we may be better able to see in what unique ways American culture has synthesized "an ever-increasing collection of infantile fantasies, desires and discontents," which, Joel Kovel argues, all cultures must become "heir [to] . . . over historical time." If his contention that "culture must contain, no matter where or when, derivatives of the absolutes of human life . . . for instance, . . . birth and death, sexuality, and hunger," is accurate, then we may also understand how the repeated European response to a New World expressed the kinds of "universal human situations which must find a kind of organized symbolic structure within any culture." In the case of American pastoral, the bedrock of its impulse appears to be what is simultaneously the most universal and most primary of human experiences: infancy, and "the all-encompassing bounds of the mother-infant relationship, [within which] the earliest and most basic states of mental organization develop."[26]

The progress from infancy to adulthood, in fact, may be seen in part as a progress through larger and larger perceptual configurations of "home"—from the maternal embrace to the neighborhood, to a country, a continent, indeed, to whatever we finally believe comprised by that sometimes ambiguous phrase, "the world." When the childhood experience has not been pathogenic, the world visualized as one's home takes on the positive elements of what were previously the parameters of the original home, the maternal embrace (or even, perhaps, the womb). Hence, our need to see the world as rich with pleasure, comfort, gratifications, and easily available means to self-fulfillment. The fact that the details of our childhood experience are not actively remembered does not negate the fact that the images attendant upon that experience remain as preconscious or unconscious structures through which subsequent adult experience is then filtered, or by which it is even measured. Piaget even goes so far as to suggest that the schemas, or organization of perception, elaborated during the period from birth to about seven years, are probably the ones that contribute largely to the structure of dreams and fantasies in the adult.[27]

What the psychiatric community has also shown us, moreover, is that the progress from childhood to adulthood is a difficult one, fraught with conflict and the threat of failure. Though labeled as characteristic of "humankind" in general, the developmental schemas usually outlined in such discussions (or case histories) are those of men; however, as something peculiar to the masculine makeup has so far allowed men to seize the power of history, both in the Old World and the New, and as the pastoral yearnings examined in these pages have been exclusively those of white males, the very limitations of the psychiatric model will prove useful here. For what this classic model details is the painful process by which the male child seeks to emerge from the total helplessness and dependency of infancy and "detach himself from the source upon which he leans." The conflict he faces is that which pits "his active drive for individuation . . . against the current driving him toward maternal union." What Joel Kovel presents as a psychiatric model is particularly illuminating here, because it outlines so neatly the characteristic plot configurations of American pastoral fiction:

> The very hopefulness that a person sustains himself by is at bottom an impossible illusion, nothing less than the wish to return to maternal fusion, and so to negate all that independent and autonomous living has gained. The wish must then be perpetually frustrated, and the frustration must perpetually generate aggression. Hence, from the stage of separation onward . . . the infant becomes ambivalent, hating as well as loving, and will remain so throughout his life.[28]

The dynamic of almost every piece of writing examined here, in fact, appears to repeat a movement back into the realm of the Mother, in order to begin again, and then an attempted (and not always successful) movement out of that containment in order to experience the self as independent, assertive, and sexually active. Where the maternal embrace is not so overwhelming as to thwart that movement, the narrative either erupts with an expression of violence—as the seductive embrace is rejected—or with guilt, as the writer begins to perceive what has resulted from the single-minded cultivation and mastery of the virgin continent. In spite of this, however, and even into our own century, our literature still refuses to give up the myth of harmonious return.

For, as I suggested at the outset, the European discovery of an unblemished and fertile continent allowed the projection upon it of a residue of infantile experience in which all needs—physical, erotic, spiritual and emotional—had been met by an entity imaged as quintessentially female. Emerson must have dimly understood the process, because, in his essay on "Nature," he describes "infancy" as "the perpetual Messiah, which comes into the arms of fallen men, and pleads with them to return to paradise."[29] It is even possible that the repeated thwartings of that yearning for paradise, by poor weather, crop failures, Indian warfare, and disease, only reinforced the projection, since by remaining committed to the real-world possibility of pastoral gratifications in the New World, the earliest settlers managed to mitigate and somehow contain the hardships of pioneer life and the anxiety it produced. As with Crevecoeur's "Mrs. B.," for instance, the ruin of one paradise meant only that the pioneer proceeded further westward in pursuit of another. The initial discovery of the continent, combined with its apparently limitless terrain, provided Americans with a space of almost three hundred years during which to believe that infantile fantasies were about to become adult realities, and, as such, allowed those contents to be "transformed, generalized and put to use in [American] culture"[30] through the metaphorical experience of "the land-as-woman." To sum up, then, what apparently "intersected" to give rise to the fantasy that I have labeled as the American pastoral impulse were at least two accidents of history—the discovery of the new continent, followed, in Europe, by at least two hundred years of the kinds of political oppressions and economic upheavals that drive men to seek more comfortable surroundings—and the reawakening of archetypal patterns derived, finally, from human biology and the human condition. The psychohistorical emphasis of this study, therefore, may be seen as an attempt to grasp the meaning behind historical events by getting at their underlying "fantasy" or psychic structures.[31]

John Woolman's dream of the "Beautiful green Tree" withered by "the Riseing Sun" (and its phallic symbolization, the "Sun Worme"), followed immediately by his waking attack on the mother robin and her brood, effectively expressed how volatile the relations between masculine and feminine orderings could be, and how difficult it was, whether for a nation or for an individual, to shift from experiencing the feminine as all-powerful Mother to experiencing it as something over which the masculine has complete power and control. The congruence of related patterns in both the dream and the attack on the mother robin, underscored by Woolman's own assertion that the dream brought to mind the incident with the robin, also graphically illustrates how closely our waking activities mirror our dream, or fantasy, patterns. In this case, both the dream and the attack on the robin enacted the rejection of comforting and nurturing feminine realms—a rejection that Woolman's biological and psychosocial development demanded—and the ordering of the two in the journal makes it appear that the dream set the stage for the ensuing acting-out.[32] This suggests that our capacity for dreaming and fantasy, and our linguistic ability to convert our dreams and fantasies into coherent, knowable patterns through image and symbol, may be functions of our fundamental biological and physiological makeup, performing basically adaptive and survival-oriented tasks that, previously, only poets and dreamers had guessed at. For, while the Woolman dream might be said to have set the stage for a further or progressive personality development (allowing the maturing male to envision his inevitable separation from and eventual domination of the female), we also know that dreaming is, just as often, regressive, returning us to places and feelings unavailable to us in our waking present, and even allowing us to reconstitute that present. Our shared fantasy of the land-as-woman is a case in point. In this sense, both dreaming and fantasy are (at least in part) a form of remembering—and both seek, often enough, to recapture the totality of gratifications known only once, in the dim past of infancy. It is even possible that the compelling urge to return to that kind of ambience may, on the psychological level, recapitulate the inclination of biological systems toward homeostasis, or equilibrium. Both, obviously, motivate most of the structures we call civilization and, together, they may explain that totality of goals we suppose will be met by culture and social systems.

To understand how the pastoral metaphor was first constituted and then shared as part of the group's communal experience, we need only recall that children, because of their cognitive immaturity, take for granted a whole host of associations and interrelationships that adults find somewhat foreign to their way of thinking. During the first three or four years of life, in fact, thinking, perceiving, and acting are almost indistinguishable, a conjunction usually dismissed as "childish imagination." Whether as a result of physiological developments within the brain, as Piaget's work would seem to suggest,[33] or whether as a result of conventionalization and socialized training of cognition processes in our schools and media, these symbol-making or image-producing propensities of childhood seem to fade with adulthood. Nevertheless, during the period when these symbolizing cognitive processes are operative, they are not only useful, but in the largest sense, adaptive. Peter Castle points to the fact that "for the child symbolic play serves to extend his understanding and comprehension of the world by means of his acting upon it and making it part of him by transforming it in terms of his own wants and needs."[34]

Thus, we see how the mother's body, as the first ambience experienced by the infant, becomes a kind of archetypal primary landscape to which subsequent perceptual configurations of space are related. Hence, perhaps, the young toddler's delight in crawling in, under, and through all sorts of odd places, and the continued attempts to suck milk from the most unexpected objects. For "symbolic play is, of course, a form of thought which takes place in action, involving the child's own body, its motions and those imaginatively transformed physical objects." Simply because, "as we develop, action takes on more and more socialized forms and we no longer make the chair in our living room into a boat afloat on the water, even if we are alone," does not mean either that we have totally lost the ability to perceive the world symbolically, or that our earliest perceptual and conceptual configurations have been wholly superseded or abandoned. On the contrary, these remain in "a kind of storage bin for thoughts and memories," which most psychologists have agreed to call the *preconscious*, available at any moment for conversion "into new symbolic forms." We might say that the American landscape provided the impetus for at least one such "conversion." To accept the psychoanalytic model of a preconscious, then, is to accept the existence of "a psychic agency whose inherent function is the symbolic transformation of thoughts, memories, and perceptions into new discursive and presentational forms, and which in waking life, and to some extent in sleep, is also engaged in regulating the access of these transformed thoughts and memories to motoric expression."[35] It is a model that at once validates this study's contention that American pastoral has always comprised both the elements of private and internal fantasy and the "motoric" expressions of that fantasy in external activity. To put it still another way, American pastoral allowed a landscape of the mind to be projected upon and perceived as an objective and external "real-world" landscape. What we might say occurred, then, was a kind of communal act of imagination, recapitulating in adult activity the symbolic mode characteristic of childhood.

What this suggests, of course, is that the symbolizing function, which Piaget and most other developmental psychologists had relegated to childhood, actually plays a far more vital role in adult activity than we have yet acknowledged. As Peter Castle, a student of his work, has pointed out, while Piaget "is one of the few systematic psychologists who has been able to conceptualize the function and structure of imagination as being both legitimate and coherent in nature, by . . . analyz[ing] it in a developmental context," he has also chosen "to view it either as transitional or 'exceptional' as regards its role in adaptation as a whole."[36] The shared response to the American continent as woman, however, not only suggests how adaptive such functions can be in adult functioning—in this case, helping Europeans accommodate themselves to a virtually unknown terrain and then providing the incentive for them to travel its extent—but also suggests that the ability to perceive the previously unapprehended relations of things is not only the province of poets or children; for, in a sense, Crevecoeur's "nation of cultivators" was also, in Emerson's sense of the word, a nation of poets, making the most of "the wonderful congruity which subsists between man and the world."[37]

The most recent theoretical discussions of adult symbolizing activity, however, seem to see it, for the most part, as exclusive to dreaming, enabling the "potentialities of progress, of going beyond the conventional pattern, and of widening the scope of human life . . . to be released" during and as a result of the sleeping state.[38] One of the most provocative of the recent theoretical approaches appears in *The New Psychology of Dreaming*, where Richard Jones acknowledges the value of dreaming in "making it possible for the ego to gain contact with ideas which are otherwise forbidden," and agrees with other theoreticians that it may thereby "serve adaptive functions." What he adds to that, however, is a biological framework, claiming that "since the D-state [i.e., a particular metabolic state encountered during sleep] is obviously an evolved condition," it is also possible "that dreaming is the augmentative *response* of the *human* psyche to the distinctive neurophysiological conditions of the mammalian D-state." That is, to grossly oversimplify Jones's fine little book, the human psyche latched onto or "augmented" a biological function built into *all* mammals and utilized it for its own purposes; both the augmenting and its result were, Jones argues, evolutionary and adaptive. "In other words," he concludes, "it may be that once Nature committed Man to his point of no return, his capacity to make his own culture—as she committed the tiger to his tooth, the elephant to his trunk, and the baboon to his troop—she then equipped him with the means to make the most of it. This, by making it not merely possible but *necessary* that he dream—every night—about every ninety minutes." His goal, then, is to force the psychoanalytic community to "understand the functions of dreaming from the point of view of species adaptation *and* from the point of view of individual adaptation."[39]

What he does not consider, unfortunately, is the possibility that language often expresses much the same kind of symbolizing activity as that found in dreams—but, necessarily, in a "waking" state. If we see the central metaphor of American pastoral experience, that is, the land-as-woman, as an example in adult thought-processes of the symbolizing activity usually attributed only to childhood or dreams, then we might want to paraphrase Richard Jones's work to suggest the following: The image-making or symbolizing capacity of the human brain is biologically based and universal, and insofar as it continues functioning even into adulthood, it shows the processes of evolutionary adaptation by giving man an additional means of accommodating his many needs and desires to a variety of changing environments. For most of us, the means of utilizing that capacity in the waking state is through language, which, "once acquired, . . . becomes a constant companion to all human behavior."[40] Philip Wheelwright even argues that "thought is not possible to any significant degree without language, nor language without metaphoric activity whether open or concealed."[41]

That the metaphorical experience of the land-as-woman appears now to have only dangerous consequences does not, I hope, mean we have lost our capacity to create adaptive symbols for ourselves, but only that the one we had has now run its course and the time is ripe for still another perceptual configuration for Emerson's "wonderful congruity." The very fact that the archetypal polarities, masculine and feminine, are now undergoing radical alterations in the ways they are imaged and perceived suggests that, insofar as the pastoral metaphor partakes of this polarity, it too may be undergoing changes that will, in the end, prove adaptive and survival-oriented. It is even possible that the choice is already ours. Richard Jones argues, rather persuasively, I think, that "*Homo sapiens* does not suffer the process of natural selection; by virtue of interposing cultures between himself and physical nature, and this by virtue, in turn, of his capacities for generating and transmitting technologies, languages, and social organizations, *Homo sapiens* has emerged as the naturally selective animal."[42] In America, the time has come for us to "adapt" to still another environment—a landscape, in Norman Mailer's words, "all gutted, shit on, used and blasted"[43]—and one, essentially, of our own making. To paraphrase Jones again, it is time to interpose between ourselves and physical nature still another metaphor, with a different experiential configuration; or perhaps only some new images through which to "better" our experience of the land-as-woman. Both are possible, since, in a sense, the wonder of language is that it can be examined and analyzed and, with it, at least some of the underlying experiential configurations that it articulates. Again, the choice is ours: whether to allow our responses to this continent to continue in the service of outmoded and demonstrably dangerous image patterns, or whether to place our biologically- *and* psychologically-based "yearnings for paradise" at the disposal of potentially healthier (that is, survival-oriented) and alternate symbolizing or image systems.

Should we seriously decide to take up this challenge, the questions raised by Norman Mailer at the end of *Armies of the Night* demand our attention:

> . . . America, once a beauty of magnificence unparalleled, now a beauty with a leprous skin. She is heavy with child—no one knows if legitimate—and languishes in a dungeon whose walls are never seen. . . . she will probably give birth, and to what?—the most fearsome totalitarianism the world has ever known? or can she, poor giant, tormented lovely girl, deliver a babe of a new world brave and tender, artful and wild?[44]

It is our old pastoral yearning revived again, its phrasing all too familiar, but its articulation no longer an assertion, only a question. Quoted from a section entitled "The Metaphor Delivered," the passage really gives us no more than a statement of potential and refuses, even, to "deliver" the metaphor it sets up. But the very fact that Mailer, like the advocates of People's Park, chose this particular metaphor in which to pose the question of our future direction illustrates how much it continues to dominate our relations with our continent and, further, promises—what the People's Park usage did not—that the metaphor may itself be a way of exploring and understanding and, if necessary, changing the meaning of those relations. For what Mailer asks us to do here is to take responsibility for the metaphors we choose and, hence, in which we live, and make of them a means to our survival. Such may, in fact, be man's ultimate creative act: to pick and choose among the image systems available to him at any one time and to make of them, periodically, a new reality. In relation to that which is biologically or even physiologically fixed, metaphor (and image-making, in general) may be our way of exploring, again and again, the potent and potential content of our archetypal structures, putting ourselves in touch with their changing contents or even changing those contents at will. Perhaps, to put it another way, we need to "wake up" to our ability to dream the as-yet-unknown and unconventional.

Notes

CHAPTER 1

1. Poem credited to Book Jones, printed in a leaflet issued in Berkeley during the last week of May 1969, by the People's Park Committee (hereafter cited as "People's Park Committee leaflet"). For one of the better detailed accounts of this event, see Sheldon Wolin and John Schaar, "Berkeley: The Battle of People's Park," *New York Review of Books*, 19 June 1969, pp. 24-31. A full collection of pamphlets, leaflets, and newspaper articles about People's Park is available in the Bancroft Library, University of California, Berkeley.

2. A red and black sign printed with the words "sod brother" appeared on shop windows and doors in the south campus area to identify their owners as sympathetic to the demands for a People's Park. The words were also lettered on windows and doors of private homes and became a means of protection from damage by angry and frustrated demonstrators.

3. "People's Park Committee leaflet." While most of the law enforcement groups brought into the area were regarded with hostility both by the student and local communities, the National Guard, which bivouacked on park grounds for two weeks, were more cordially tolerated. Rumors flew that guardsmen were watering the plants behind the fence, and both the underground and establishment local press frequently printed photographs of guardsmen accepting flowers from demonstrators.

4. "People's Park Committee leaflet."

5. Joanna Gewertz, "culturevulture," *Berkeley Monitor*, 31 May 1969, p. 3; "People's Park Committee leaflet."

6. Quoted from leaflet entitled "Ecology and Politics in America," distributed 26-27 May 1969, in Berkeley, by American Federation of Teachers locals 1474 and 1795.

7. The Freudian argument for this approach, with which I only partly concur, but by which my remarks are influenced, is best put forth by Herbert Marcuse, *Eros and Civilization* (1955; reprint ed., New York: Random House, Vintage Books, 1961), pp. 246-47.

8. Robert Johnson, "Nova Britannia: Offering Most Excellent fruites by Planting In Virginia. Exciting all such as be well affected to further the same" (London, 1609), p. 11; Robert Mountgomry, "A Discourse Concerning the design'd Establishment of a New Colony To The South of Carolina In The Most delightful Country of the Universe" (London, 1717), p. 6. Both papers are in *Tracts and Other Papers, Relating Principally to the Origin, Settlement, And Progress of the Colonies in North America, From The Discovery Of The Country To The Year 1776*, comp. Peter Force, 3 vols. (Washington, D.C., 1836-38), vol. 1 (hereafter cited as *Force's Tracts*). All of the papers in *Force's Tracts* are paginated separately.

9. Johnson, "Nova Britannia," p. 11, in *Force's Tracts*, vol. 1.

10. "The First Voyage Made To The Coasts Of America With Two Barks, Wherein Were Captains M. Philip Amadas And M. Arthur Barlowe Who Discovered Part Of The Country Now Called Virginia, Anno 1584. Written By One Of The Said Captains [probably Barlowe, who kept the daily record], And Sent To Sir Walter Raleigh, Knight, At Whose Charge And Direction The Said Voyage Was Set Forth," in *Explorations, Descriptions, and Attempted Settlements of Carolina, 1584-1590*, ed. David Leroy Corbitt (Raleigh: State Department of Archives and History, 1948), pp. 19-20 (hereafter cited as *Explorations of Carolina*); John Smith, "A Description of New England; or, The Observations, and Discoueries of Captain John Smith (Admirall of that Country) in the North of America, in the year of our Lord 1614" (London, 1616), p. 21, in *Force's Tracts*, vol. 2.

11. [M. Arthur Barlowe], "The First Voyage Made to the Coasts of America," in *Explorations of Carolina*, pp. 19, 13; Smith, "A Description of New England," p. 9, in *Force's Tracts*, vol. 2.

12. Paul Shepard, *Man in the Landscape* (New York: Alfred A. Knopf, 1967), pp. 108, 98.

13. Joel Kovel, *White Racism* (New York: Random House, Pantheon Books, 1970), p. 7.

14. Smith, "A Description of New England," title page, in *Force's Tracts*, vol. 2.

15. Richard Hakluyt, "Discourse of Western Planting . . . 1584," in *The Original Writings and Correspondence of the Two Richard Hakluyts*, ed. E. G. R. Taylor, 2d ser. (London: Hakluyt Society, 1935), 77:222 (hereafter cited as *Hakluyt Correspondence*). Hakluyt's note identifies "the work alluded to" as John Ribault's *"The whole and true discouerye of Terra Florida . . .* Prynted at London . . . 1563."

16. Kovel, *White Racism*, p. 99.

17. Most of the original settlers of Jamestown died of either disease or starvation, while only about half of the Pilgrims who landed at Plymouth in December 1620 survived the first winter; of the 900 settlers led by Winthrop to Massachusetts Bay, 200 died during the first year. Howard Mumford Jones has surveyed these materials and pointed out that "it took many years for investors and home officials to learn that you could not found a plantation by dumping a few men on a New World shore. . . . A high percentage of sickness and death accompanied the process of acclimatization" *(O Strange New World* [1952; reprint ed., London: Chatto & Windus, 1965], p. 277).

18. R. D. Laing, *The Politics of Experience* (New York: Random House, Pantheon Books, 1967), pp. 14–15.

19. Thomas Dudley, "Gov. Thomas Dudley's Letter To The Countess of Lincoln, March, 1631," p. 10, in *Force's Tracts*, vol. 2; Francis Higginson, "New-Englands Plantation; or, A Short And Trve Description of The Commodities And Discommodities of that Countrey" (London, 1630), pp. 9, 10, in *Force's Tracts*, vol. 1.

20. John Hammond, "Leah and Rachel; or, The Two Fruitfull Sisters Virginia and Mary-Land," in *Narratives of Early Maryland, 1633-1684*, ed. Clayton Colman Hall (New York: Charles Scribner's Sons, 1910), p. 300; Robert Beverley, *The History and Present State of Virginia*, ed. Louis B. Wright (Chapel Hill: University of North Carolina Press, 1947), p. 319; William Byrd, *William Byrd's Histories of the Dividing Line Betwixt Virginia and North Carolina*, ed. William K. Boyd (Raleigh: North Carolina Historical Commission, 1929), p. 92(*H*). Both the *History* and the *Secret History of the Dividing Line* are printed *en face* in this edition, so that corresponding incidents appear on opposite pages; I have distinguished quotes from the *History* and the *Secret History* by placing a parenthetical *H* after page numbers from the first and *SH* after page numbers from the second. The *Secret History* is printed here for the first time, from the original manuscript probably composed about 1728 or shortly thereafter. According to Boyd's introduction, "As the *History of the Dividing Line* is twice the length of *The Secret History*, it is logical to believe that the latter was the first to be composed and that as the title indicates, it was intended only for a select few, and that the *History of the Dividing Line* was written at a later date for a wider audience. Supporting such a conclusion are letters of Byrd written in 1736 and 1737" (p. xv). We might also note that among other differences, the *Secret History* contains but one unfavorable criticism of the North Carolinians, whereas such criticism is a dominant feature of the *History*. The *History* gives more description of the land and the surveying party's responses to it, while the *Secret History* emphasizes the personal relations between the members of the survey team and includes numerous reflections on women and sex. Both *Histories* emphasize eating and give comparatively few details of the business of surveying.

21. Kovel, *White Racism*, p. 99. For a fuller discussion, see chap. 5, "The Symbolic Matrix," pp. 93-105.

22. Gary Snyder, *Earth House Hold* (New York: New Directions, 1969), p. 119.

23. Charles Hansford, "My Country's Worth," in *The Poems of Charles Hansford*, ed. James A. Servies and Carl R. Dolmetsch (Chapel Hill: University of North Carolina Press, 1961), p. 52. Probably born about 1685, Hansford lived in York County, Virginia, and was by trade a blacksmith; when he died, in 1761, he left in manuscript several poems which he called "A Clumsey Attempt of an Old Man to turn Some of his Serious Thoughts into Verse." The poems are printed here for the first time, with titles supplied by the editors.

24. Byrd, *Histories of the Dividing Line*, pp. 214(*H*), 249(*SH*).

25. Philip Freneau, "To Crispin O'Conner, A Back-Woodsman," in *The Poems of Philip Freneau, Poet of the American Revolution*, ed. Fred Lewis Pattee, 3 vols. (Princeton, N.J.: University Library, 1902-7), 3:74-75. The poem was first published in 1792; the text is from the 1809 edition of Freneau's collected *Poems*. Unless otherwise noted, all quotations from Freneau's poems are from the Pattee edition.

CHAPTER 2

1. [M. Arthur Barlowe], "The First Voyage Made To The Coasts Of America," in *Explorations of Carolina*, pp. 13-20.

2. Ralph Lane, "An Extract Of Master Ralph Lane's Letter To M. Richard Hakluyt, Esquire, And Another Gentleman Of The Middle Temple, From Virginia," in *Explorations of Carolina*, p. 33.

3. Richard Hakluyt, "Discourse of Western Planting," in *Hakluyt Correspondence*, 77:222-23.

4. Christopher Columbus, *Select Documents Illustrating the Four Voyages of Columbus*, trans. and ed. Cecil Jane (London: Hakluyt Society, 1930), 1:12. The Spanish and the English are on facing pages.

5. Quoted from Walter Raleigh's "Discovery of Guiana" (1595), in Howard Mumford Jones, *O Strange New World*, p. 48; Jones's source is Richard Hakluyt, *Principal Navigations* (London, 1598), 10:430. So confused were Europe's ideas of the New World at this time that remarks about any area vaguely in the vicinity of what is now North, South, or Central America were accepted as characteristic of the whole. Jones points out that "by 1607 the New World had stretched to an endless and confusing coastline running from Greenland and Baffin Bay through Gargantuan twistings and turnings to the Strait of Magelland and Tierra del Fuego" (p. 61).

6. Robert Johnson, "Nova Britannia," p. 11, in *Force's Tracts*, vol. 1; John Smith, "A Description of New England," p. 9, in ibid., vol. 2.

7. Robert Mountgomry, "A Discourse Concerning the design'd Establishment of a New Colony," pp. 6, 12, in *Force's Tracts*, vol. 1.; Thomas Morton, "New English Canaan; or, New Canaan, Containing An Abstract of New England . . . Written . . . Upon ten Yeers Knowledge and Experiment of the Country" (London, 1632), p. 10, in *Force's Tracts*, vol. 2.

8. Ibid., pp. 41, 10, 14, 41-42.

9. John Hammond, "Leah and Rachel," in *Narratives of Early Maryland*, ed. Hall, pp. 281-304.

10. George Alsop, "Character of the Province of Maryland," in *Narratives of Early Maryland*, ed. Hall, pp. 343, 344, 348, 344.

11. Robert Beverley, *History of Virginia*, pp. 319, 275, 156, 314.

12. Leo Marx, *The Machine in the Garden* (New York: Oxford University Press, 1964), pp. 86-87.

13. Beverley, *History of Virginia,* pp. 319.

14. Marx, *Machine in the Garden,* pp. 86-87.

15. Mountgomry, "A Discourse Concerning the design'd Establishment Of a New Colony," pp. 11-12, 6, in *Force's Tracts*, vol. 1.

16. John Peter Purry, "A Description Of The Province of South Carolina, Drawn Up At Charles Town, . . . Translated from Mr. Purry's Original Treatise, in French, and published in the Gentleman's Magazine, for August, September, and October, 1732," pp. 5, 10, in *Force's Tracts*, vol. 2.

17. William Byrd, *Histories of the Dividing Line*, pp. 164(*H*), 92(*H*), 304(*H*).

18. William Byrd, "A Journey to the Land of Eden in the Year 1733," in *The Prose Works of William Byrd of Westover*, ed. Louis B. Wright (Cambridge, Mass.: Harvard University Press, 1966), pp. 409, 398. According to the editor's introduction, "Byrd was prompted to write *A Journey* . . . by his experience in surveying lands that he had acquired in the border region. During the survey of the dividing line, he had had an opportunity to observe the quality of the terrain on the border, and the sight had aroused his land-hunger. From the North Carolina

commissioners, who had received frontier land in payment for their services, Byrd bought 20,000 acres at the confluence of the Dan and Irvin Rivers which he christened 'the Land of Eden.' It was to survey this estate that he set out with a party of friends on September 11, 1733" (p. 31).

19. Pat Tailfer, Hugh Anderson, and Da. Douglas, "A True and Historical Narrative Of the Colony of Georgia, In America, From the First Settlement thereof until this present Period" (Charles Town, S.C., 1741), pp. viii, ix, 67 ff., 18, 79, 80, 79, viii, in *Force's Tracts*, vol. 1.

20. "A State Of The Province of Georgia, Attested upon Oath, In The Court of Savannah, November 10, 1740" (London, 1742), containing "Extract of a Letter from the Reverend Mr. Boltzius at Ebenezer, dated the 23rd of July, 1741, to the Reverend Dr. Francke, Professor of Divinity at Hall," p. 19, in *Force's Tracts*, vol. 1.

21. John White, "The Planter's Plea; or, The Grovnds of Plantations Examined, And vsuall Objections answered" (London, 1630), pp. 18, 13, 18, in *Force's Tracts*, vol. 2.

22. Thomas Dudley, "Gov. Thomas Dudley's Letter to the Countess of Lincoln, March, 1631," p. 12, in *Force's Tracts*, vol. 2.

23. Smith, "A Description of New England," pp. 15, 9, 5, 8, 21, in *Force's Tracts*, vol. 2.

24. Johnson, "Nova Britannia," p. 12, in *Force's Tracts*, vol. 1.

25. Jones, *O Strange New World*, p. 180. For an excellent survey of the various types of promotional literature circulated during the sixteenth and seventeenth centuries, see ibid., pp. 179–81.

26. Johnson, "Nova Britannia," pp. 11, 12, in *Force's Tracts*, vol. 1.

27. R. W. B. Lewis, *The American Adam* (1955; reprint ed., Chicago: University of Chicago Press, Phoenix Books, 1966), p. 129. While a number of colonial New England texts echo the fear that the land may not turn out to be as paradisal as hoped, the writings of the divines, especially, attribute any such disappointment to human sinfulness; as a result, man is ultimately responsible for the destruction of the garden because it is his sinfulness that brings down God's wrath, in punishment, upon the landscape. Roger Williams's *A Key into the Language of America*, written in Providence and published in London in 1643, comments on "the raines and fruitfull seasons, the Earth, Trees, Plants &c. filling mans heart with food and gladnesse" in the New World garden, only to castigate "man for his unthankfulnesse and unfruitfullnesse toward his Maker." This, he claims, has been responsible for turning "a paradise in Paradise" into something "now worse / Then *Indian* Wildernesse" (ed. Howard M. Chapin, 5th ed. [Providence: Rhode Island . . . Committee, 1936], pp. 101, 102). Michael Wigglesworth's "God's Controversy with New-England" (1662) also hails a God who turned "an howling wilderness / . . . into a fruitfull paradeis" (ll. 35-36) and blames "riot, & excess" (l. 166) and human "pride & wantonness" (l. 168) for turning "Our fruitful seasons . . . / Of late to barrenness" (ll. 141–42). In his 1693 account of the New England witch trials, "The Wonders of the Invisible World," Cotton Mather sees the present generation as so many "degenerate Plants" as compared to "The first Planters of these Colonies [who] were a chosen Generation of Men," and hence blames the current witchcraft crisis on a people "miserably degenerated from the first Love of our Predecessors"; again, this sermon suggests, human vice threatens the continued prosperity of "this poor Plantation" (quotes from *The Wonders of the Invisible World. Being An Account Of The Tryals of Several Witches Lately Executed in New-England. . . . To Which Is Added A Farther Account Of The Tryals of The New-England Witches, By Increase Mather, D.D., President of Harvard College* [London: John Russel Smith, 1862], pp. 11-13).

28. John Woolman, *The Journal and Essays of John Woolman*, ed. Amelia Mott Gummere (Philadelphia: Friends' Bookstore, 1922), pp. 152-53.

29. Hakluyt, "Discourse of Western Planting," in *Hakluyt Correspondence*, 77:211 ff.

30. Hakluyt, "Notes on Colonisation, By Richard Hakluyt, Lawyer, 1578," in *Hakluyt Correspondence*, 76:120, 121.

31. Hakluyt, "Discourse of Western Planting," in *Hakluyt Correspondence*, 77:224, 225. According to a note, the title *Joyfull Newes* comes from "a translation by Frampton of the

Historia Medicinal . . . de nuestras Indias (1574), of Nicholas Monardes, a learned Spaniard, . . . The English version was published in 1577" (p. 224).

32. Joseph Morgan, *The History of the Kingdom of Basaruah* (1715), ed. Richard Schlatter (Cambridge, Mass.: Harvard University Press, 1946), p. 56. A religious allegory that is simultaneously a commentary on the misuse of worldly and spiritual goods, the *History* suggests the kinds of disappointments experienced and violations committed in the cultivation of the New World garden. The description of meddlesome "digging" (p. 43), is particularly interesting in its assault on a "bank which inclosed the forbidden things"; also, the descriptions of excessive taking and disillusionment: "But the common Produce of the Land is a *multitude of Fruits*, that look very beautiful afar off, but when men come to eat them, they loose their *Taste* before they are well swallowed, and commonly leave a bitter Tang in the stomach" (p. 56).

CHAPTER 3

1. For a theoretical discussion of the psychological processes involved here, see Joel Kovel, *White Racism*, p. 250.

2. Hector St. John de Crevecoeur, *Letters from an American Farmer*, ed. Warren Barton Blake (London: J. M. Dent and Sons; New York: E. P. Dutton, 1912), Letter III, p. 43. All quotations from the *Letters* are from this edition, with the Letter indicated in roman numerals and the page in arabic numerals.

3. Philip Freneau, "On The Fall of General Earl Cornwallis," in *Poems of Philip Freneau*, ed. Pattee, 2:95. The poem was first published in 1781; the text is from the 1786 edition of Freneau's collected *Poems*.

4. Freneau, "To Crispin O'Conner, A Back-Woodsman," ibid., 3:74; Freneau, "On The Fall of General Earl Cornwallis," ibid., 2:95.

5. Harold E. Toliver, *Pastoral Forms and Attitudes* (Berkeley: University of California Press, 1971), p. 42.

6. Henry Nash Smith, *Virgin Land* (1950; reprint ed., New York: Random House, Vintage Books, 1961), p. 144. For an excellent summary of eighteenth-century agrarian theory, see chap. 11, "The Garden of the World and American Agrarianism," pp. 138-50, and chap. 12, "The Yeoman and the Fee-Simple Empire," pp. 151-64.

7. See Leo Marx, *Machine in the Garden*, pp. 126-27. In an otherwise excellent summary of Jeffersonian agrarian theory, Marx suggests that "a fully articulated pastoral ideal of America did not emerge until the end of the eighteenth century," and places that emergence in "1785, when Jefferson issued *Notes on Virginia*, [wherein] the pastoral ideal had been 'removed' from the literary mode to which it traditionally had belonged and applied to reality" (p. 73). We differ fundamentally on this point: I insist that pastoral (as I am defining it) had been applied to the American reality since the sixteenth century and that Jefferson merely continued a long-standing habit of mind, giving it only the addition of political currency.

8. Thomas Jefferson, *Notes on the State of Virginia*, ed. William Peden (Chapel Hill: University of North Carolina Press, 1955), pp. 164-65. The *Notes* are set up as a series of answers to queries, having originally been written in response to a request for information on Virginia from the Marquis de Barbe-Marbois, secretary of the French Legation in Philadelphia. Peden's introduction traces the various publications of the *Notes*, beginning with its first private printing in Paris, 1785; another edition subsequently appeared in London, 1787, and then a pirated American edition was printed in Philadelphia, 1788; the first full authorized American edition came out in Richmond, Virginia, in 1853 (pp. xix-xxvi).

9. See Marx, *Machine in the Garden*, pp. 98 ff.

10. Smith, *Virgin Land*, pp. 141-42.

11. See Kovel, *White Racism*, p. 257.

12. George Washington, "Letter to Wm. Pearce, 1796," quoted in Richard Bridgman, "Jefferson's Farmer before Jefferson," *American Quarterly* 14 (1962): 573. Bridgman footnotes his source as *Writings*, ed. John C. Fitzpatrick (Washington, D.C., 1939), 34:451.

13. Jefferson, *Notes on the State of Virginia*, p. 168.

14. See Kovel, *White Racism*, p. 261.

15. Howard Mumford Jones, *O Strange New World*, p. 352.

16. Jefferson, *Notes on the State of Virginia*, Query IV, p. 19.

17. Quoted in Jones, *O Strange New World*, p. 212. His source is Morgan J. Rhees, *The Good Samaritan: An Oration Delivered on Sunday Evening, May 22d, 1796, in Behalf of the Philadelphia Society for the Information and Assistance of persons Emigrating From Foreign Countries* (Philadelphia, 1796), p. 12.

18. Jefferson, *Notes on the State of Virginia*, p. 34.

19. Jefferson to Archibald Stuart, 25 January 1786, in *The Papers of Thomas Jefferson*, ed. Julian P. Boyd (Princeton, N.J.: Princeton University Press, 1954), 9:218.

20. Mary S. Austin, *Philip Freneau, The Poet of the Revolution*, ed. Helen Kearny Vreeland (New York: A. Wessels Co., 1901), p. 131.

21. Freneau, "America Independent; And Her Everlasting Deliverance from British Tyranny and Oppression," in *Poems of Philip Freneau*, ed. Pattee, 1:282. The poem was first published in Philadelphia, 1778; the text is from the 1809 edition. Henceforth, citations to the three-volume Pattee edition will be made in the text; where Pattee has provided line numbers, I have followed these. When necessary, because of the extreme length of a poem, I have also indicated stanza numbers or section subtitles where they exist.

22. Quoted by Philip M. Marsh, *The Works of Philip Freneau* (Metuchen, N.J.: Scarecrow Press, 1968), p. 99. Marsh notes that Freneau was at this time the editor of the *Jersey Chronicle*, a weekly, in which the poem first appeared on 16 May 1795; it was published again in the 1795 *Poems* (p. 99). Omitted by Pattee.

23. Washington's proclamation of neutrality in 1793 was designed to keep America out of the various European conflicts that followed the French Revolution, spearheaded, on opposing sides, by France and England. Determined to starve France into submission, England systematically interrupted the newly emerging American merchant trade and both confiscated goods and impressed sailors. The Treaty of 1796, negotiated in London by Chief Justice John Jay, committed England to pay indemnities for seized American shipping, but also tacitly accepted the restrictive British definitions of the rights of neutrals in international trade; for these and other reasons, the treaty was not wholly acceptable to some in the United States and, as a result, 1795 saw a storm of controversy over its imminent signing. A brief but clear account appears in Charles Sellers and Henry May, *A Synopsis of American History* (Chicago: Rand McNally, 1963), pp. 86–88.

24. Jones, *O Strange New World*, p. 327, summarizes eighteenth-century "republican culture" as resting upon three central assumptions: "the United States being a republic, it must cherish frugality and simplicity, that the healthiest basis of life was agrarianism, and that the country was as a matter of course the hope of the human race." The last we have yet to outgrow.

25. Quoted by Harry Hayden Clark, in *Poems of Freneau*, ed. Harry Hayden Clark (1929; New York: Hafner Publishing Co. [1960]), p. xvi.

26. The unusual success of Goldsmith's poem in America suggests that it catered to the growing nationalistic pride of the self-consciously "pastoral" nation. James D. Hart, *The Popular Book* (1950; reprint ed., Berkeley: University of California Press, 1963), points out that Goldsmith's poem, first issued in an American edition in 1771, required twelve American editions and many more imports before 1800 (p. 28). After Freneau's, probably the best of the many contemporary "replies" to Goldsmith was Timothy Dwight's "Greenfield Hill," first published in 1794.

27. Quoted by Clark, in *Poems of Freneau*, ed. Clark, p. xvii.

28. These phrases are from stanza 104, omitted from the 1786 edition of the poem, but included in the *Poems of Philip Freneau*, ed. Pattee, 1:252. A full description of textual changes is provided by Pattee, 1:249–53.

29. Ibid., 2:104–7, follows text and title of 1782, when poem was first published as "Plato, The Philosopher, to his Friend Theon"; in the 1795 and 1809 editions of Freneau's collected *Poems*, the title is "To an Old Man."

30. Ibid., 2:91. First published 1781 as "A Moral Thought."

31. Marsh, *Works of Philip Freneau*, pp. 39-41. Marsh also notes that Freneau was managing editor of the *Freeman's Journal* from 1781 through 1789 (p. 39).

32. See Marsh, *Works of Philip Freneau*, pp. 101-5.

33. *Poems of Philip Freneau*, ed. Pattee, 3:176-77. The original title, "The Millennium—To a Ranting Field Orator," was changed, in the 1815 edition of Freneau's *Poems*, to "Ode X, to Santone Samuel" (see Pattee's note, 3:176).

34. Marsh, *Works of Philip Freneau*, p. 106.

35. Ibid., p. 169.

36. Marsh notes that Freneau's 1815 *Collection of Poems, on American Affairs, and a Variety of Other Subjects*, "made almost no impression on the reading public" and suggests that the June 1815 review "in the *Analectic Magazine* may have expressed the general attitude: 'Readers of a very refined taste will not, probably, relish the general style . . . for it is marked with a certain rusticity' " (ibid., p. 171).

37. Ibid., p. 178. Omitted by Pattee.

38. Toliver, *Pastoral Forms and Attitudes*, p. 28.

39. See "The Indian Student," *Poems of Philip Freneau*, ed. Pattee, 2:371-74, and "Stanzas Occasioned by the Ruins of a Country Inn, unroofed and blown down in a storm," ibid., 2:110-11.

40. Letter quoted by Russel B. Nye, "Michel-Guillaume St. Jean de Crevecoeur: *Letters from an American Farmer*," in *Landmarks of American Writing*, ed. Hennig Cohen, Voice of America Forum Lectures (Washington, D.C.: U.S. Information Service, 1970), pp. 36-37.

41. Marx, *Machine in the Garden*, p. 108.

42. Crevecoeur, *Letters from an American Farmer*, Letter III, p. 43.

43. Marx, *Machine in the Garden*, pp. 113-14.

44. Nye, "Michel-Guillaume St. Jean de Crevecoeur," p. 41.

45. Hector St. John de Crevecoeur, *Sketches of Eighteenth-Century America*, ed. Henri L. Bourdin, Ralph H. Gabriel, and Stanley T. Williams (New Haven: Yale University Press, 1925), pp. 228 ff. Most of these sketches were probably composed either during or after he had completed the letters that make up the original *Letters from an American Farmer*; in some cases, they may represent materials excised from that volume. A few were included in the 1787 enlarged French edition of the *Letters*, but the rest remained in manuscript until this 1925 edition. All quotations from the *Sketches* are from this edition.

46. The Pennsylvania Quaker artist Edward Hicks (1780-1849) applied his sign painter's technique to a series of over eighty paintings illustrating the biblical text from Isaiah, "The wolf also shall dwell with the lamb, and the leopard shall lie down with the kid." In each of the many versions of the painting, white men and Indians are seen conferring peaceably together, while children sit happily side by side with both domestic and wild animals, all stylized to portray the contemporary hope that America might in fact prove the world's first "Peaceable Kingdom." For further information, see the *Encyclopedia of World Art* (New York: McGraw-Hill, 1959), 1:290, and Oliver W. Larkin, *Art and Life in America*, rev. and enl. ed. (New York: Holt, Rinehart and Winston, 1966), pp. 220-30.

47. John White, "The Planters Plea, p. 18, in *Force's Tracts*, vol. 2.

48. Nye, "Michel-Guillaume St. Jean de Crevecoeur," p. 44. I also question his assertion, pp. 43-44, that Letters X and XI reflect the book's "hasty preparation for editing and publication." My own view is that they contribute to the overall dramatic structure of the *Letters* by insisting on the discord that informs nature itself (X) and then by attempting, one last time, to assert the pastoral possibility (XI) before it is irrevocably destroyed by James's experience in the final Letter (XII). Although I differ with him on this point, I am nevertheless grateful to Professor Nye for his sensitive and thorough analysis of the *Letters*, and I heartily recommend his article to both the general and the scholarly reader.

49. Dedicated to the French philosopher Raynal, the book was first published in London, in 1782, under the title *Letters From an American Farmer, describing certain Provincial Situations, Manners, and Customs, and Conveying some idea of the state of the People of North America: written*

to a Friend in England, by J. Hector St. John. A French edition appeared in 1784 and again, in expanded form, in 1787. So popular were the *Letters* that the original English version was reprinted five times in the next ten years, the enlarged edition three times, and there were two editions of a German and a Dutch translation. (See Nye, "Michel-Guillaume St. John de Crevecoeur," p. 48n.)

50. Quoted by Albert E. Stone, Jr., in the foreword to J. Hector St. John de Crevecoeur, *Letters from an American Farmer and Sketches of Eighteenth-Century America* (New York: New American Library, Signet Classic, 1963), p. xiii.

51. In 1790 Crevecoeur returned in ill health to France; on his estate near Rouen, he occupied his time by composing a three-volume account of his American travels, first published in Paris in 1801 as *Le Voyage dans la haute Pensylvanie et dans l'etat de New York*. The time of the "voyage" is given as about 1790, during a period when Crevecoeur was actually in France. The first-person narrator is apparently an American, accompanied in his travels by a young German named Herman. Crevecoeur claimed, in a preface, that he was only translating an English manuscript that had been found in Copenhagen after a shipwreck and that he was merely an editor, not the author. All quotations from this work are from *Crevecoeur's Eighteenth-Century Travels in Pennsylvania and New York*, trans. and ed. Percy G. Adams (Lexington: University of Kentucky Press, 1961).

52. Nye, "Michel-Guillaume St. John de Crevecoeur," p. 45.

53. Jones, *O Strange New World*, p. 300.

54. Hallett Smith, *Elizabethan Poetry* (Cambridge, Mass.: Harvard University Press, 1952), pp. 2–8. In what is still one of the most incisive analyses of Elizabethan pastoral materials, Professor Smith notes that "Elizabethan pastoral poetry is essentially a celebration of this ideal of content, of *otium*" (p. 8).

55. Thomas Morton, "New English Canaan," p. 10, in *Force's Tracts*, vol. 2; John Hammond, "Leah and Rachel," in *Narratives of Early Maryland*, ed. Hall, p. 300.

56. Hammond, "Leah and Rachel," in *Narratives of Early Maryland*, ed. Hall, p. 300; "The Kansas Emigrants," popular ballad of the free-staters, early nineteenth century, and Wisconsin promotional literature, both quoted in Dorothy Anne Dondore, *The Prairie and the Making of Middle America* (Cedar Rapids, Ia.: Torch Press, 1926), pp. 263, 206. For a summary of the enthusiasm with which the new territories were depicted, see chap. 4, "The Louisiana Purchase and Non-Imaginative Treatments to 1870," pp. 153-209.

57. Charles Brockden Brown, *Wieland* (1798). In what must be one of the most bitter and disillusioned examinations of American pastoral possibilities, this novel concludes by having Clara and Pleyel, newly married, leave their Philadelphia estates for "the shore of the ancient world," taking up permanent residence abroad. Inhabiting what had once been their New-World garden is Carwin, the bringer of evil in the tale, often referred to as a "snake," now hiding "himself in a remote district of Pennsylvania" (quoted from the Hafner Classics edition, ed. Fred Lewis Pattee [1926; reprint ed., New York: Hafner Publishing Co., 1964], pp. 266, 268).

58. Washington Irving, "The Legend of Sleepy Hollow," and "Rip Van Winkle," in *Selected Prose*, ed. Stanley T. Williams (1950; reprint ed., New York: Holt, Rinehart and Winston, 1964), pp. 90–107 and 162–92.

CHAPTER 4

1. Howard Mumford Jones, *O Strange New World*, p. 353.

2. See Joel Kovel's concise and provocative psychoanalytical framework in *White Racism*, pp. 283–84, 260.

3. Hector St. John de Crevecoeur, *Sketches of Eighteenth-Century America,* pp. 54-55. Collected and published in English for the first time in this edition, these sketches represent "More Letters from an American Farmer" and were probably composed in the late 1780s.

4. Cooper tried to correct the mistaken notion that his picture of Templeton, in *The Pioneers*, was taken directly from his memories of Cooperstown. "In point of fact," as he wrote critic and editor Horatio Hastings Weld, in 1842, "few of the recollections of a new set-

tlement that dictated the Pioneers, were obtained at Cooperstown, at all. This village was commenced several years anterior to my birth, and before my memory would have served for such a purpose, had grown into more comparative note in the State, . . . I was sent to school, too, at six, and did not have an opportunity of seeing much of a frontier, until ordered, at nineteen, on Lake Ontario, on service.—It was *there*, I obtained most of my notions of a new country, as well as several of the characters introduced into the Pioneers. The whole, however, is so blended together, as to make a rigid analysis of the pictures difficult" (*The Letters and Journals of James Fenimore Cooper*, ed. James Franklin Beard [Cambridge, Mass.: Harvard University Press, Belknap Press, 1964], 4:259). For additional memories of Cooper's boyhood in and knowledge of Cooperstown, see ibid., 1:3–4, 6–7, and 3:215–16.

5. C. Hugh Holman, "Literature and Culture: The Fugitive-Agrarians," in *The Roots of Southern Writing* (Athens: University of Georgia Press, 1972), p. 193. The essays collected here, representing some of the best and most provocative writing about the South and its literature, must surely stand as a goldmine of various and fruitful critical approaches to a complex and multifaceted subject.

6. See Kovel's interesting ideas on this subject, *White Racism*, p. 250.

7. Ibid., p. 288.

8. Benjamin Lee Whorf, *Language, Thought and Reality*, ed. John B. Carroll (1956; reprint ed., Cambridge, Mass.: M.I.T. Press, 1969), p. 148.

9. John James Audubon, *Delineations of American Scenery and Character*, ed. Francis Hobart Herrick (New York: G. A. Baker and Co., 1926), p. 139. All quotations from Audubon are from this edition. These sketches were first published as short chapters in the first three volumes of *Ornithological Biography* (Edinburgh, 1831-39). Originally from France and the West Indies, Audubon frequently traveled back and forth between the United States and Europe so that he might personally supervise the engraving and publication of his work in England.

10. Henry Nash Smith, *Virgin Land*, p. 139.

11. Quoted from Robert Penn Warren, "The Sound of That Wind," in *Audubon* (New York: Random House, 1969), pp. 26, 30.

12. William Gilmore Simms, "The Writings of James Fenimore Cooper," originally published as "Cooper, His Genius and Writings," *Magnolia* 1 (1842): 129-39; reprinted in William G. Simms, *Views and Reviews in American Literature, History and Fiction*, ed. C. Hugh Holman (Cambridge, Mass.: Harvard University Press, Belknap Press, 1962), pp. 292, 274, 269. The piece was motivated by Simms's desire to rescue Cooper's literary reputation from "the numerous malicious aspersions" cast upon it as a result of Cooper's political pronouncements; Professor Holman succinctly outlines Cooper's anti-Whig publications (p. 258n.).

13. All quotations from *The Pioneers* (1823) are from *The Works of James Fenimore Cooper*, vol. 4 (New York: G. P. Putnam's Sons, 1893).

14. For editions after 1825, Cooper rephrased this sentence so that "offensive member" became "offensive shingles" (p. 33), thereby obliterating the *double entendre* of the original phrase; all earlier editions, 1823-25, retain the phrase as quoted.

15. Hector St. John de Crevecoeur, *Letters from an American Farmer*, Letter III, p. 52.

16. All quotations from *The Last of the Mohicans* (1826) are from *The Works of James Fenimore Cooper*, vol. 7 (New York: Stringer and Townsend, 1856).

17. All quotations from *The Prairie* (1827) are from *The Works of James Fenimore Cooper*, vol. 5 (New York: G. P. Putnam's Sons, 1893).

18. William Gilmore Simms, "Americanism in Literature," *Southern and Western Magazine* 1 (1845): 1-14; reprinted in Simms, *Views and Reviews*, ed. Holman, p. 22.

19. All quotations from *The Pathfinder* (1840) are from *The Works of James Fenimore Cooper*, vol. 3 (New York: G. P. Putnam's Sons, 1893).

20. David Noble, "Cooper, Leatherstocking and the Death of the American Adam," *American Quarterly* 16 (1964): 424.

21. Simms, "Writings of James Fenimore Cooper," in Simms, *Views and Reviews*, ed. Holman, p. 273.

22. Cooper to Richard Bentley, 31 January 1841, in Cooper, *Letters and Journals*, ed. Beard, 4:111-12. The work alluded to is *The Deerslayer* (1841), all quotations from which are from *The Works of James Fenimore Cooper*, vol. 1 (New York: G. P. Putnam's Sons, 1893).

23. See Erich Neumann's discussion of the mythic and psychological significance of liquid images for emphasizing "the union of son and mother," in *The Great Mother*, trans. Ralph Manheim, 2d ed. (New York: Bollingen Foundation, 1963), p. 198.

24. See, for instance, Noble, "Cooper, Leatherstocking and . . . Adam," p. 421. The problem with this kind of approach is that it reads the novels in the order of Natty's development, from youth to old age, and ignores the *real* development of the character's meaning, which occurs in the author's mind as he proceeds from one novel to the other in the course of composition.

25. Leo Marx, "Pastoral Ideals and City Troubles," *Journal of General Education* 20 (1969): 263.

26. Quoted by J. V. Ridgeley, *William Gilmore Simms* (New York: Twayne Publishers, 1962), p. 122; *The Letters of William Gilmore Simms*, ed. Mary C. Simms Oliphant, Alfred Taylor Odell, and T. C. Duncan Eaves (Columbia, S.C.: University of South Carolina Press, 1952-56), 4:379.

27. William Gilmore Simms, "The Epochs and Events of American History, as Suited to the Purposes of Art in Fiction," originally delivered as lectures to the Historical Society of the State of Georgia (1842), and later revised for publication in the *Southern and Western Magazine* (March and September, 1845); reprinted in Simms, *View and Reviews*, ed. Holman, pp. 77, 35, 36, under the short title, "History for the Purposes of Art."

28. William Gilmore Simms, *The History of South Carolina* (1840), new and rev. ed. (New York: Redfield, 1860), p. 433.

29. William Gilmore Simms, *The Forayers; or, The Raid of the Dog-Days* (1855), new and rev. ed. (Chicago: Donohue, Henneberry & Co., 1890), pp. 234-35.

30. The novels to be discussed here include, in order of original publication: *The Partisan* (1835); *Mellichampe* (1836); *The Kinsman*, later retitled *The Scout* (1841); *Katharine Walton* (1851); *Woodcraft* (1854); and *The Forayers* (1855). In the 1850s the New York publisher J. S. Redfield (and later his successor, W. J. Widdleton) published the only collected edition of Simms's works which contained the author's own selection and revision of his best works. Still considered the standard edition, until supplanted by the Center for Editions of American Authors editions, Redfield's "New and Revised" series reveals only minimal changes from the original texts, but prefaces are generally considerably enlarged and revised. (*The Kinsman* was for the first time retitled *The Scout* in the Redfield edition.) Stereotype plates from the Redfield editions, including the original illustrations by F. O. C. Darley, were used for many nineteenth-century reprintings, including the Donohue, Henneberry & Co. editions (Chicago, 1889-90) from which all quotations are taken.

31. William Gilmore Simms, *The Geography of South Carolina* (Charleston, S.C.: Babcock and Co., 1843), pp. 102-3.

32. Erich Neumann, *The Origins and History of Consciousness*, trans. R. F. C. Hull (1954; reprint ed., Harper & Brothers, Torchbook, 1962), pt. 1, pp. 140-41. Such rites were customarily associated "with light, the sun, the head, and the eye as symbols of consciousness" (pp. 141-42), and were often experienced as "a second birth, [or] a new generation through the masculine spirit, . . . accompanied by the inculcation of secret doctrines" or other previously unknown and "initiatory" knowledge (p. 144).

33. Francis Gaines, *The Southern Plantation* (Gloucester, Mass.: Peter Smith, 1962), pp. 146, 143.

34. Ibid., p. 167.

35. Appearing first in *The Partisan*, Porgy was then introduced into succeeding novels because of his popularity with the reading public. Just before *Mellichampe* appeared, Simms wrote to a friend, "You have no idea how popular Porgy is with a large majority. He is actually the founder of a sect" (*Letters of William Gilmore Simms*, 1:82).

36. Porgy's slave, Tom, from whom he is never separated in any of the novels, also shares

some of this function; however, the complexity of their relationship, and through it, Simms's attempt at vindicating the institution of slavery, are beyond the scope of the present study.

37. Paul Shepard, *Man in the Landscape*, p. 108. Shepard also suggests that "from a psychiatric standpoint, architecture and land forms are a continuum, an interlocked series entangled with the body image" (p. 100); Kovel, *White Racism*, p. 100. My treatment of the plantation as a psychological configuration coincides with Kovel's suggestion that "to a certain extent, the institutions of a civilization are given life because of the symbolic value they fulfill." As such, "all cultural institutions . . . mean more to men than their manifest function suggests" (p. 5).

38. Alan Gowans, *Images of American Living* (Philadelphia and New York: J. P. Lippincott Co., 1964), p. 281.

39. Gowans points out that "in 1790, populations in the North and South were nearly equal, but by 1850 the census showed 13,527,000 North to 9,612,000 South. In the middle of the 19th century the South was still holding practically the same outlook and values as it had in 1800" (ibid.).

40. *De Bow's Review* 29 (1860): 708.

41. Holman, *Roots of Southern Writing*, p. xiii.

42. Edmund Wilson, *To the Finland Station* (1940; reprint ed., Garden City, N.Y.: Doubleday & Co., Anchor Books, 1953), p. 101. In his fascinating overview of these and related movements, Wilson suggests that they "persisted through the early fifties until the agitation for free farms in the West, culminating in the Homestead Act of 1863, diverted the attention of the dissatisfied from labor organization and socialism." Moreover, even admitting the difficulty of arriving "at any precise estimate of the number of these communities," he notes that "there are records of at least a hundred and seventy-eight" (p. 102).

43. Quoted from Louis Chappell's "fascinating study of the John Henry legend," the description of "the scene of John Henry's everyday work" appears in *Folk Song, USA*, ed. John A. Lomax et al. (1947; reprint ed., New York: Duell, Sloan and Pearce, 1960), pp. 247, 261 (stanzas 12 and 13).

44. Harold E. Toliver, *Pastoral Forms and Attitudes*, p. 15.

45. Ibid., p. 16.

46. Simms, "History for the Purposes of Art," in Simms, *Views and Reviews*, ed. Holman, p. 54.

47. See Smith, *Virgin Land*, p. 297. On pp. 291-305, Professor Smith provides a comprehensive survey of the impact of the Turner thesis and the controversy it aroused.

48. Ibid., p. 298. The quotation is from Frederick Jackson Turner's volume of collected papers, *The Frontier in American History* (1920; reprint ed., New York: Henry Holt & Co., 1950), p. 267. The essay from which this quote is excerpted was originally written for the *Atlantic* in 1903.

CHAPTER 5

1. F. Scott Fitzgerald, *The Great Gatsby* (1925; reprint ed., New York: Charles Scribner's Sons, 1953), p. 182. All quotations are from this edition.

2. Robert Mountgomry, "A Discourse Concerning the design'd Establishment of a New Colony," p. 6, in *Force's Tracts*, vol. 1.

3. "Introduction: A Statement of Principles," in *I'll Take My Stand*, by Twelve Southerners (1930; reprint ed., New York: Harper & Row, Torchbook, 1962), p. xxi; in the same volume see also Andrew Nelson Lytle, "The Hind Tit," p. 202; Louis Rubin's excellent introductory essay, p. xiii; John Crowe Ransom, "Reconstructed But Unregenerate," pp. 10, 9; Stark Young, "Not in Memoriam, But in Defense," p. 347.

4. "Introduction: A Statement of Principles," in ibid., p. xxi.

5. Herbert Agar and Allen Tate, eds., *Who Owns America?* (Boston: Houghton Mifflin Co., 1936).

6. C. Hugh Holman, "Literature and Culture: The Fugitive-Agrarians," in *Roots of Southern Writing*, p. 188.

7. Ransom, "Reconstructed But Unregenerate," in *I'll Take My Stand*, p. 9.

8. Holman, "The Dark, Ruined Helen of his Blood: Thomas Wolfe and the South," in *Roots of Southern Writing*, pp. 128, 119. Rather than repeat Professor Holman's thorough discussion of Wolfe's differences with the Southern Agrarians, I refer the reader to his excellent article, pp. 118-33.

9. See Thomas Wolfe, *The Web and The Rock* (New York: Grosset & Dunlap, 1939), pp. 245-46.

10. William Faulkner, "Delta Autumn," in *The Portable Faulkner*, ed. Malcolm Cowley (1946; reprint ed., New York, Viking Press, 1961), p. 724. This story was originally published as part of *Go Down, Moses, and Other Stories* (New York: Random House, 1942). All quotations in the text are from the Viking edition.

11. William Faulkner, "The Bear," in *Portable Faulkner*, ed. Cowley, p. 359. Published first as a short story in 1935, "The Bear" also appears again as part of *Go Down, Moses* (1942). All quotations in the text are from the Viking edition.

12. Cleanth Brooks, *William Faulkner* (1963; reprint ed., New Haven: Yale University Press, 1966), p. 262.

13. Ibid., p. 31.

14. Ibid., p. 273.

15. Ibid., p. 270.

16. Saul Bellow, *Henderson the Rain King* (1959; reprint ed., New York: Popular Library, 1963), p. 289. All quotations in the text are from this edition.

17. Harold E. Toliver, *Pastoral Forms and Attitudes*, p. 327.

18. Poem credited to Book Jones, "People's Park Committee leaflet."

19. Gene Marine, *America the Raped* (New York: Simon and Schuster, 1969), pp. 200-201, 21.

20. Benjamin Lee Whorf, *Language, Thought and Reality*, p. 156.

21. Ibid., pp. 158, 252.

22. Richard M. Jones, *The New Psychology of Dreaming* (New York: Grune and Stratton, 1970), p. 161.

23. Richard Hakluyt, "Discourse of Western Planting . . . 1584," in *Hakluyt Correspondence*, 77:222.

24. See, for example, S. I. Hayakawa, *Language in Thought and Action*, 3d ed. (New York: Harcourt Brace Jovanovich, 1972), pp. 108, 107.

25. Philip Wheelwright, *Metaphor and Reality* (Bloomington: Indiana University Press, 1962), pp. 111-12.

26. Joel Kovel, *White Racism*, pp. 272, 284, 250, 253.

27. See, for example, Jones, *New Psychology of Dreaming*, pp. 153-66. Jones bases his remarks in these pages on an unpublished work by Dr. Peter Castle.

28. See Kovel, *White Racism*, pp. 251, 260, 261.

29. Ralph Waldo Emerson, "Nature" (1836), in *Selections from Ralph Waldo Emerson*, ed. Stephen Whicher (1957; reprint ed., Boston: Houghton Mifflin Co., Riverside Press, 1960), p. 53.

30. Kovel, *White Racism*, p. 250.

31. Ibid., p. 6, for a fuller theoretical framework.

32. John Woolman, *Journal and Essays of John Woolman*, ed. Gummere, pp. 152-53.

33. Throughout much of the discussion that follows, I repeatedly display my indebtedness to Jean Piaget's pioneering investigations of children's cognitive processes, especially in such works as *Play, Dreams and Imitation in Childhood*, trans. C. Gattegno and F. M. Hodgson (New York: W. W. Norton & Co., 1962) and *The Child's Conception of the World*, trans. Joan Tomlinson and Andrew Tomlinson (1929; reprint ed., London: Routledge and Kegan Paul, 1971).

34. Jones, *New Psychology of Dreaming*, p. 166; the section from which this was quoted is credited to an unpublished work by Dr. Peter Castle.

35. Ibid., pp. 165, 126, 130.

36. Ibid., p. 164.

37. Emerson, "Nature," in *Selections from Ralph Waldo Emerson*, ed. Whicher, p. 52.

38. Jones, *New Psychology of Dreaming*, p. 65; quoted from E. G. Schactel, "On Memory and Childhood Amnesia," *Psychiatry* 10 (1947): 17-18.

39. Jones, *New Psychology of Dreaming*, pp. 131-32, 138-39, 189, 188. To support his contention, Jones leans heavily on the experimental work of Drs. F. Snyder and M. Ullman, citing, "Snyder's focus . . . on the vigilance function of *REM sleep* and its adaptive value in *mammalian* evolution," and "Ullman's focus . . . on the vigilance function of *dreaming* and its adaptive value in *human* evolution, in which adaptation by way of social organization is at a premium" (p. 185). A lengthy list of sources for their work appears on pp. 202-4.

40. John Lotz, "Linguistics: Symbols Make Man," in *Psycholinguistics*, ed. Sol Saporta (1961; reprint ed., New York: Holt, Rinehart and Winston, 1966), p. 1.

41. Wheelwright, *Metaphor and Reality*, p. 128.

42. Jones, *New Psychology of Dreaming*, p. 139.

43. Norman Mailer, *Why Are We in Vietnam?* (New York: G. P. Putnam's Sons, 1967), pp. 221-22.

44. Norman Mailer, *The Armies of the Night* (New York: New American Library, Signet, 1968), p. 320.

Bibliography

Primary Sources

Agar, Herbert, and Tate, Allen, eds. *Who Owns America?: A New Declaration of Independence*. Boston: Houghton Mifflin Co., 1936.

Alsop, George. *A Character of the Province of Maryland* (1666). Publications of the Maryland Historical Society, no. 15. Baltimore: Maryland Historical Society, 1880.

American Federation of Teachers, locals 1474 and 1795. "Ecology and Politics in America." Leaflet issued in Berkeley, Calif., 26-27 May 1969.

Audubon, John James. *Delineations of American Scenery and Character*. Edited by Francis Hobart Herrick. New York: G. A. Baker and Co., 1926.

Bellow, Saul. *Henderson the Rain King*.1959. Reprint. New York: Popular Library, 1963.

Beverley, Robert. *The History and Present State of Virginia* (1705). Edited by Louis B. Wright. Chapel Hill: University of North Carolina Press, 1947.

Brown, Charles Brockden. *Wieland; or, The Transformation: An American Tale* (1798). Edited by Fred Lewis Pattee. 1926. Reprint. New York: Hafner Publishing Co., 1964.

Byrd, William. "A Journey to the Land of Eden in the Year 1733." In *The Prose Works of William Byrd of Westover: Narratives of a Colonial Virginian*. Edited by Louis B. Wright. Cambridge, Mass.: Harvard University Press, Belknap Press, 1966.

______. *William Byrd's Histories of the Dividing Line Betwixt Virginia and North Carolina*. Edited by William K. Boyd. Raleigh: North Carolina Historical Commission, 1929.

Columbus, Christopher. *Select Documents Illustrating the Four Voyages of Columbus*. Translated and edited by Cecil Jane. London: Hakluyt Society, 1930.

Cooper, James Fenimore. *The Deerslayer; or, The First Warpath*. *The Works of James Fenimore Cooper*, vol. 1. New York: G. P. Putnam's Sons, 1893.

______. *The Last of the Mohicans; A Narrative of 1757*. *The Works of James Fenimore Cooper*, vol. 7. New York: Stringer and Townsend, 1856.

______. *The Letters and Journals of James Fenimore Cooper*. Vol. 4. Edited by James Franklin Beard. Cambridge, Mass.: Harvard University Press, Belknap Press, 1964.

______. *The Pathfinder; or, The Inland Sea*. *The Works of James Fenimore Cooper*, vol. 3. New York: G. P. Putnam's Sons, 1893.

______. *The Pioneers; or, The Sources of the Susquehanna: A Descriptive Tale*.

The Works of James Fenimore Cooper, vol. 4. New York: G. P. Putnam's Sons, 1893.

———. *The Prairie: A Tale. The Works of James Fenimore Cooper*, vol. 5. New York: G. P. Putnam's Sons, 1893.

Corbitt, David Leroy, ed. *Explorations, Descriptions, and Attempted Settlements of Carolina, 1584-1590.* Raleigh: State Department of Archives and History, 1948.

Crevecoeur, Hector St. John. *Crevecoeur's Eighteenth-Century Travels in Pennsylvania and New York.* Translated and edited by Percy G. Adams. Lexington: University of Kentucky Press, 1961.

———. *Letters from an American Farmer.* Edited by Warren Barton Blake. London: J. M. Dent and Sons; New York: E. P. Dutton, 1912.

———. *Letters from an American Farmer and Sketches of Eighteenth-Century America.* New York: New American Library, Signet Classic, 1963.

———. *Sketches of Eighteenth-Century America: More "Letters from an American Farmer."* Edited by Henri L. Bourdin, Ralph H. Gabriel, and Stanley T. Williams. New Haven: Yale University Press, 1925.

Emerson, Ralph Waldo. *Selections from Ralph Waldo Emerson: An Organic Anthology.* Edited by Stephen Whicher. 1957. Reprint. Boston: Houghton Mifflin Co., Riverside Press, 1960.

Faulkner, William. *Go Down, Moses, and Other Stories.* New York: Random House, 1942.

———. *The Portable Faulkner.* Edited by Malcolm Cowley. 1946. Reprint. New York: Viking Press, 1961.

Fitzgerald, F. Scott. *The Great Gatsby.* 1925. Reprint. New York: Charles Scribner's Sons, 1953.

Force, Peter, comp. *Tracts and Other Papers, Relating Principally to the Origin, Settlement, And Progress of the Colonies in North America, From The Discovery Of The Country To The Year 1776.* Vols. 1 and 2. Washington, D.C.: Peter Force, 1836-38.

Freneau, Philip. *Poems of Philip Freneau.* Edited by Harry Hayden Clark. 1929. Reprint. New York: Hafner Publishing Co. [1960].

———. *The Poems of Philip Freneau, Poet of the American Revolution.* 3 vols. Edited by Fred Lewis Pattee. Princeton: University Library, 1902-7.

Gewertz, Joanna. "culturevulture." *Berkeley Monitor*, 31 May 1969.

Hakluyt, Richard. *The Original Writings and Correspondence of the Two Richard Hakluyts.* 2d ser. vols. 76, 77. Edited by E. G. R. Taylor. London: Hakluyt Society, 1935.

Hall, Clayton Colman, ed. *Narratives of Early Maryland, 1633-1684.* New York: Charles Scribner's Sons, 1910.

Hansford, Charles. *The Poems of Charles Hansford: A Blacksmith of York County, Virginia, 1685-1762.* Edited by James A. Servies and Carl R. Dolmetsch. Chapel Hill: University of North Carolina Press, 1961.

I'll Take My Stand: The South and the Agrarian Tradition, by Twelve Southerners. 1930. Reprint. New York: Harper & Row, Torchbook, 1962.

Irving, Washington. *Selected Prose*. Edited by Stanley T. Williams. 1950. Reprint. New York: Holt, Rinehart and Winston, 1964.
Jefferson, Thomas. *Notes on the State of Virginia*. Edited by William Peden. Chapel Hill: University of North Carolina Press, 1955.
______. *The Papers of Thomas Jefferson*. Vol. 9. Edited by Julian P. Boyd. Princeton: Princeton University Press, 1954.
Mailer, Norman. *The Armies of the Night: History as a Novel, the Novel as History*. New York: New American Library, Signet, 1968.
______. *Why Are We In Vietnam?* New York: G. P. Putnam's Sons, 1967.
Mather, Cotton. *The Wonders of the Invisible World: Being An Account Of The Tryals of Several Witches Lately Executed in New-England*. London: John Russel Smith, 1862.
Morgan, Joseph. *The History of the Kingdom of Basaruah, and Three Unpublished Letters* (1715). Edited by Richard Schlatter. Cambridge, Mass.: Harvard University Press, 1946.
People's Park Committee. Untitled leaflet. Berkeley, Calif., May 1969.
Simms, William Gilmore. *The Forayers; or, The Raid of the Dog-Days*. New and rev. ed. Chicago: Donohue, Henneberry & Co., 1890.
______. *The Geography of South Carolina*. Charleston: Babcock and Co., 1843.
______. *The History of South Carolina*. New and rev. ed. New York: Redfield, 1860.
______. *Katharine Walton; or, The Rebel of Dorchester*. New and rev. ed. Chicago: Donohue, Henneberry & Co., 1890.
______. *The Letters of William Gilmore Simms*. Vol. 4. Edited by Mary C. Simms Oliphant, Alfred Taylor Odell, and T. C. Duncan Eaves. Columbia: University of South Carolina Press, 1952-56.
______. *Mellichampe: A Legend of the Santee*. New and rev. ed. Chicago: Donohue, Henneberry & Co., 1890.
______. *The Partisan: A Romance of the Revolution*. New and rev. ed. Chicago: Donohue, Henneberry & Co., 1890.
______. *The Scout; or, The Black Riders of the Congaree*. New and rev. ed. Chicago: Donohue, Henneberry & Co., 1889.
______. *Views and Reviews in American Literature, History and Fiction*. Edited by C. Hugh Holman. Cambridge, Mass.: Harvard University Press, Belknap Press, 1962.
______. *Woodcraft; or, Hawks About the Dovecote: A Story of the South at the Close of the Revolution*. New and rev. ed. Chicago: Donohue, Henneberry & Co., 1890.
Snyder, Gary. *Earth House Hold*. New York: New Directions, 1969.
Strachey, William. *The Historie of Travell Into Virginia Britania* (1612). Edited by Louis B. Wright and Virginia Freund. London: Hakluyt Society, 1953.
Tryon, Warren S., ed. *A Mirror for Americans: Life and Manners in the United*

States 1790-1870 as Recorded by American Travelers. 3 vols. Chicago: University of Chicago Press, 1952.

Warren, Robert Penn. *Audubon: A Vision*. New York: Random House, 1969.

Williams, Roger. *A Key into the Language of America* (1643). 5th ed. Edited by Howard M. Chapin. Providence: Rhode Island and Providence Plantations Tercentenary Committee, 1936.

Wolfe, Thomas. *The Web and The Rock*. New York: Grosset & Dunlap, 1939.

Woolman, John. *The Journal and Essays of John Woolman*. Edited by Amelia Mott Gummere. Philadelphia: Friends' Bookstore, 1922.

Secondary Sources

Andrews, William L. "Goldsmith and Freneau in 'The American Village.' " *Early American Literature* 5 (1970): 14-23.

Austin, Mary S. *Philip Freneau, The Poet of the Revolution: A History of His Life and Times*. Edited by Helen Kearny Vreeland. New York: A. Wessels Co., 1901.

Bone, Robert A. "Irving's Headless Hessian: Prosperity and the Inner Life." *American Quarterly* 15 (1963): 167-75.

Bridgman, Richard. "Jefferson's Farmer before Jefferson." *American Quarterly* 14 (1962): 567-77.

Brooks, Cleanth. *William Faulkner: The Yoknapatawpha Country*. 1963. Reprint. New Haven: Yale University Press, 1966.

Carpenter, Frederick I. "The American Myth: Paradise (To Be) Regained." *Publications of the Modern Language Association* 74 (1959): 599-606.

Davis, David Brion. "The Deerslayer, A Democratic Knight of the Wilderness: Cooper, 1841." In *Twelve Original Essays on Great American Novels*, edited by Charles Shapiro, pp. 1-22. Detroit: Wayne State University Press, 1958.

Dondore, Dorothy Anne. *The Prairie and the Making of Middle America: Four Centuries of Description*. Cedar Rapids: Torch Press, 1926.

Donovan, Frank. *Mr. Jefferson's Declaration: The Story Behind the Declaration of Independence*. New York: Dodd, Mead & Co., 1968.

Fiedler, Leslie A. "James Fenimore Cooper and the Historical Romance." In *Love and Death in the American Novel*, pp. 149-211. New York: Criterion Books, 1960.

Gaines, Francis P. *The Southern Plantation: A Study in the Development and the Accuracy of a Tradition*. Gloucester, Mass.: Peter Smith, 1962.

Gowans, Alan. *Images of American Living: Four Centuries of Architecture and Furniture as Cultural Expression*. Philadelphia and New York: J. P. Lippincott Co., 1964.

Hart, James D. *The Popular Book: A History of America's Literary Taste*.

New York: Oxford University Press, 1950. Reprint. Berkeley and Los Angeles: University of California Press, 1963.

Heimert, Alan. "Puritanism, The Wilderness and the Frontier." *New England Quarterly* 26 (1953): 361–81.

Holman, C. Hugh. *The Roots of Southern Writing: Essays on the Literature of the American South*. Athens: University of Georgia Press, 1972.

Jones, Howard Mumford. *O Strange New World: American Culture: The Formative Years*. 1952. Reprint. London: Chatto & Windus, 1965.

Jones, Richard M. *The New Psychology of Dreaming*. New York: Grune and Stratton, 1970.

Kovel, Joel. *White Racism: A Psychohistory*. New York: Random House, Pantheon Books, 1970.

Laing, R. D. *The Politics of Experience*. New York: Random House, Pantheon Books, 1967.

Lawrence, D. H. *Studies in Classic American Literature*. 1923. Reprint. New York: Viking Press, 1964.

Leverenz, David. "A Psychoanalysis of American Literature." Ph.D. dissertation, University of California, Berkeley, 1969.

Lewis, R. W. B. *The American Adam: Innocence, Tragedy and Tradition in the Nineteenth Century*. 1955. Reprint. Chicago: University of Chicago Press, Phoenix Books, 1966.

Lomax, John A.; Lomax, Alan; Seeger, Charles; and Seeger, Ruth Crawford, eds. *Folk Song, U.S.A.* 1947. Reprint. New York: Duell, Sloan and Pearce, 1960.

Lotz, John. "Linguistics: Symbols Make Man." In *Psycholinguistics: A Book of Readings*, edited by Sol Saporta, pp. 1-15. 1961. Reprint. New York: Holt, Rinehart and Winston, 1966.

Marcuse, Herbert. *Eros and Civilization: A Philosophical Inquiry into Freud*. 1955. Reprint. New York: Random House, Vintage Books, 1961.

Marine, Gene. *America the Raped: The Engineering Mentality and the Devastation of a Continent*. New York: Simon and Schuster, 1969.

Marsh, Philip M. *The Works of Philip Freneau: A Critical Study*. Metuchen, N.J.: Scarecrow Press, 1968.

Marx, Leo. *The Machine in the Garden: Technology and the Pastoral Ideal in America*. New York: Oxford University Press, 1964.

———. "Pastoral Ideals and City Troubles." *Journal of General Education* 20 (1969): 251-71.

Merton, Thomas. "The Wild Places." *The Center Magazine* 1, no. 5 (1968): 40–44.

Miller, Perry. "The Romantic Dilemma in American Nationalism and the Concept of Nature." *Harvard Theological Review* 48 (1955): 239–53.

Nash, Roderick. *Wilderness and the American Mind*. New Haven: Yale University Press, 1967.

Neumann, Erich. *The Great Mother: An Analysis of the Archetype*. Translated by Ralph Manheim. 2d ed. New York: Bollingen Foundation, 1963.

———. *The Origins and History of Consciousness*. Translated by R. F. C. Hull. Part 1. 1954. Reprint. New York: Harper & Brothers, Torchbook, 1962.

Noble, David W. "Cooper, Leatherstocking and the Death of the American Adam." *American Quarterly* 16 (1964): 419-31.

Nye, Russel B. "Michel-Guillaume St. Jean de Crevecoeur: *Letters from an American Farmer*." In *Landmarks of American Writing*, edited by Hennig Cohen. Voice of America Forum Lectures. Washington, D.C.: U.S. Information Service, 1970.

Ong, Walter S. "Personalism and the Wilderness." *Kenyon Review* 21 (1959): 297-304.

Philbrick, Thomas. "Cooper's *The Pioneers*: Origins and Structure." *Publications of the Modern Language Association* 79 (1964): 579-93.

Ridgeley, J. V. *William Gilmore Simms*. New York: Twayne Publishers, 1962.

Sanford, Charles L. *The Quest for Paradise: Europe and the American Moral Imagination*. Urbana: University of Illinois Press, 1961.

Shepard, Paul. *Man in the Landscape: A Historic View of the Esthetics of Nature*. New York: Alfred A. Knopf, 1967.

Smith, Hallett. *Elizabethan Poetry: A Study in Conventions, Meaning, and Expression*. Cambridge, Mass.: Harvard University Press, 1952.

Smith, Henry Nash. *Virgin Land: The American West as Symbol and Myth*. 1950. Reprint. New York: Random House, Vintage Books, 1961.

Taylor, William R. *Cavalier and Yankee*. 1957. Reprint. Garden City, N.Y.: Doubleday & Co., Anchor Books, 1963.

Toliver, Harold. *Pastoral Forms and Attitudes*. Berkeley: University of California Press, 1971.

Turner, Frederick Jackson. *The Frontier in American History*. 1920. Reprint. New York: Henry Holt & Co., 1950.

Wheelwright, Philip. *The Burning Fountain: A Study in the Language of Symbolism*. Rev. ed. Bloomington: Indiana University Press, 1968.

———. *Metaphor and Reality*. Bloomington: Indiana University Press, 1962.

Whorf, Benjamin Lee. *Language, Thought and Reality*. Edited by John B. Carroll. 1956. Reprint. Cambridge, Mass.: M.I.T. Press, 1969.

Williams, George H. *Wilderness and Paradise in Christian Thought*. New York: Harper & Brothers, 1962.

Wilson, Edmund. *To the Finland Station: A Study in the Writing and Acting of History*. 1940. Reprint. Garden City, N.Y.: Doubleday & Co., Anchor Books, 1953.

Wright, Louis B. *The Colonial Search for a Southern Eden*. University, Ala.: University of Alabama Press, 1953.

———. *The Cultural Life of the American Colonies, 1607-1763*. New York: Harper & Brothers, 1957.

Index